Sea Fever

Sea
Fever

FROM FIRST DATE
TO FIRST MATE

ANGELA MEYER

RANDOM HOUSE
NEW ZEALAND

For the captain and cabin boy, with love,
and to Jan and David, with love and thanks

A RANDOM HOUSE BOOK published by Random House New Zealand
18 Poland Road, Glenfield, Auckland, New Zealand

For more information about our titles go to www.randomhouse.co.nz

A catalogue record for this book is available from the National Library
of New Zealand

Random House New Zealand is part of the Random House Group
New York   London   Sydney   Auckland   Delhi   Johannesburg

First published 2012

© 2012 Angela Meyer

The moral rights of the author have been asserted

ISBN 978 1 86979 917 5

Cover design: Carla Shale
Cover photograph: Jane Ussher
Text design: Carla Sy

This publication is printed on paper pulp sourced from sustainably
grown and managed forests, using Elemental Chlorine Free (EFC)
bleaching, and printed with 100% vegetable based inks.

Printed in New Zealand by Printlink
Also available as an eBook

CONTENTS

AUTHOR'S NOTE

I am the first to admit that I sometimes get exact details wrong. I have been known to embroider the truth and, to be honest, I am not going to change a habit of a lifetime. In my defence, these are my memories of the truth. Everything happened, even the imaginings. I have condensed parts and expanded on others to keep the pace brisk and, I hope, entertaining.

PROLOGUE

'Ange, it's an aeroplane.'

An Andover is circling above us. The VHF crackles into life.

'Are you the vessel experiencing difficulties?' an American voice asks.

I lunge at the handset. 'Yes, yes we are.'

'OK ma'am, what is your situation?'

I am so happy to hear his voice I almost hyperventilate as I relay all of the things that have gone wrong.

'Copy that, ma'am. A chopper will be overhead in zero five minutes.'

'Thank you, sir. Thank you!' I put the VHF down and scoop up Dashkin, my just-turned-two-year-old son and kiss and hug him, hard.

We listen to the pilot as he radioes the US Coast Guard, giving them our exact position.

'Ross, they're on their way . . . Oh my God, we are going to be OK!' I yell out to the cockpit.

I had thought that if we were lucky the Ecuadorian or Colombian Coast Guard might respond, or maybe a passing ship would be diverted. I never, ever imagined the American Coast Guard would turn up.

1
Sailing Fox

— ·— —

'Perhaps you remember me . . .' I put down my suitcase with one hand and hold the beautifully handwritten letter in the other. My heart starts beating faster. I reread the old-fashioned script again slowly.

Dear Angela,

Perhaps you remember me? We shared a wonderful night together but I had to leave unexpectedly. I'm in town for six weeks; please email me if you would like to meet.

Sincerely, Ross

I take a deep breath. Of course I remember him.

He's the sailor who played 'I Was Made for Loving You' by Kiss on the guitar, who pashed me on the wharf and who stood me up, four months earlier.

Shaking my head, I get up and lug the suitcase into my room. I catch a glimpse of myself in the mirror. A Real Hot Bitch smiles back. For the first time in a long time I'm not obsessing about being single. Two weeks drinking cocktails and reading detective novels on the beach in Koh Phi Phi have done wonders. I stare at my peeling shoulder and can't resist picking it. I am ready for a new chapter in the life of Angela Meyer, one that doesn't involve boys masquerading as men, or foolish booze-fuelled antics.

I am thirty-two. It's time to make some changes.

'Bloody men!' I throw the letter on my dressing table and

unzip my case. 'After spending the best part of two thousand bucks on a trip to Thailand to forget him, he contacts me!' I begin unpacking my white towelling frock (so handy on a beach), three bikinis and my newly purchased gold sandals. I flick on my stereo, desperate to hear something other than the high-pitched Asian pop I have been tormented with for the last fourteen days. Pat Benatar is belting out 'I Am The Warrior'. Some would say this is hardly a step up, but my musical tastes were shaped by *Solid Gold Hits Volume 31*. Good on ya, Pat.

I start singing along with her . . . 'Bang, bang . . .' That's what I am: a warrior fighting heartache. No more crying into my pillow over blokes.

As the clock struck midnight on 1 January 2007 I had made a vow. I would date no more. I would focus on my business, The ManBank; my dance troupe, the Real Hot Bitches; and travel. As the final wail of 'I Am The Warrior' dies out I strike a dramatic pose and look at myself in the mirror. 'Sailor boy, you missed your chance.'

There is only so long you can shoot the energy out of your jazz hands, and soon my arms begin aching.

Looking down, I see the letter has a halo of dust around it. In the time I have been away a thin film of filth has settled on the hairclips, half-used lipsticks and flashy earrings.

Picking up the letter again I start musing . . . He obviously uses expensive ballpoints — no one can flourish an 'A' like that with a Bic. Maybe he had a genuine reason for his disappearing act . . .

It was time for some answers.

We had only dated, if you could call it that, once, four months ago.

It was a nasty night in October 2006, and I was on a date

with a guy called Dylan. We both knew it wasn't going to be repeated; in a last-ditch attempt to have 'fun' we stopped in at a little bar, The Pit, for a nightcap. Sitting in the corner table was Ross.

'Hey Ange, this is my friend Ross,' Dylan said. 'I reckon you two would get on well — he plays in a band and you dance.'

There before me in a spectacular brown-checked jacket was a take-your-breath-away total fox.

'So you dance,' he said slowly, sizing me up. One look at my body and it's obvious I'm not on the payroll of a contemporary dance company who do 'movement phrases' in flesh-coloured undies.

'Bitch, actually. I am the Mistress of the Real Hot Bitches comedy dance troupe,' I answered, hoping it made me seem interesting, a bit naughty and explained the figure.

He raised his bushy brows and gave me the first of his twinkly-eye looks. 'A real hot bitch . . .'

I smiled coyly. 'You should come and watch us sometime.'

'I just might do that,' he said, sipping his red wine.

'Make sure you do,' I tried to 'purr' in a sexy, flirty fashion.

I had been speaking to him for approximately two and a half minutes and already I wanted to ditch my date and hook up with his mate! To hell with dating etiquette. Ross was dark and mysterious and newish in town and I was sure I felt a spark . . . a connection . . . . Oh God, maybe even a vibe . . .

My good manners won over, however, and Dylan and I continued making halting conversation over our nightcaps. I positioned myself to spy on Ross. He looked like he was in good shape, with a great head of hair, and an easiness about him. He wasn't fiddling with a mobile phone and earnestly pretending to text; no, this gent was *reading*. Obviously he was intelligent. Good. I couldn't quite make out the title of the book but it was leather, oxblood with gold lettering.

'OK, well, thanks for a nice night,' Dylan said, finishing the last of his drink. It was time to leave — no point in dragging it out for either of us. I stood up, put on my coat on and accidentally-on-purpose caught Ross' eye. I threw him a casual wave.

He smiled and raised his glass.

I have never been any good at being 'cool'. I started grinning and waved excitedly back, as I tripped over my bag and stumbled out the door.

Fingers crossed he didn't clock that and I'd see him again. *Fox!*

2
Second Time Lucky

———

Three weeks later I am
sweating in a stinking,
humid room.

'Look at your own eyes in the mirror', 'Work the synovial fluid in your knees' (this was the first time I had ever heard of synovial fluid), 'Breathe only through your nose', the teacher instructs us as we drip sweat onto the already reeking carpet. 'Resist the temptation to hydrate, breathe . . .' Yep, I am doing hot yoga.

'Relax your body completely, then, when you are ready, slowly get up and leave the room quietly,' she says, soothing her exhausted charges as we lay prostrate on the rank floor. I can't believe I pay to do this. But if it will make me thinner . . .

I love the feeling of smug satisfaction I get every time I finish the ninety minutes — it's almost as satisfying as downing a glass of wine. Almost.

Suddenly my eyes flick open. Wine! I'm meant to be at a fundraising auction! I leap up and in my best quick-slow-yoga-walk I head for the showers. Five minutes later I'm stuffing my wet, grotty clothes into my handbag.

'Great class, Angela, you really extended well in the Dandayamana-Janushirasana,' the teacher calls as I bolt out the door.

'Thanks,' I yell over my shoulder.

I hightail it up the street towards the fundraiser and lurk at the back while I turn from cerise into my usual pinky-beige colour. Quickly I scan the crowd. Mary's over by the drinks table, Roger's sidling up to pretty girls — nothing unusual.

A flash of check. I freeze. He's here. Wearing the same brown-checked jacket. 'OK, don't be a dick,' I tell myself and I wave at him. He smiles and begins moving towards me.

Sweat's still beading on my forehead. Would it be dreadfully uncouth get out my hanky and wipe it off? I decide it would.

He is closing in. Be cool, Ange, be witty and don't gush. He's here.

'Hello again — Angela, isn't it?' This guy's smooth.

'Yes, Ross, isn't it?' Two can play this game.

'You look hot.'

'Well, I am a Real Hot Bitch!' I laugh. 'Sorry, lame joke, but you're right, I am hot.' I almost choke on the terrible line. 'I have just finished a hot yoga class,' I explain, trying to wipe my forehead. 'You know, the ones where the room is heated to thirty-nine degrees. Madonna's a big fan, and see how good she looks for fifty!'

'Sounds crazy to me. I can't see how exercising in that sort of heat can be good for you. Would you like a drink?'

'Sure, I'd love one.' We push our way through the crowd to the drinks table. I surreptitiously sniff my handbag to make sure the sweaty clothes are well wrapped in their plastic bag. Thankfully, all is OK.

We find ourselves a corner and keep chatting, waiting for the auction to start.

'You're not from Wellington, are you?' I ask.

'No, I'm from Christchurch. I used to run a second-hand bookshop there. Sometimes I sail up here and help out at my friend's picture-framers.'

Ah-ha! I knew he looked familiar.

'I don't know if you remember this, but few years ago I asked you to frame some cross-stitch for me.'

His eyes widened. 'Ahhhh yes, it was rather pornographic cross-stitch, if I recall.' He smirks. 'I couldn't do it though, the timeframe was too tight. It was for an exhibition, wasn't it?'

'Yeah.'

'Did it go well?'

'Yes, it was great,' I say, checking out his bone structure. His cheekbones are higher than mine; could be good for breeding with. 'I took it to London and had a show there,' I add, attempting to sound worldly. Bunnies in baskets weren't my thing. I was having fun subverting feminine handicraft and sending up 1970s porn. Admittedly, not everyone was keen on having a cross-stitched hand job hanging over the fireplace.

'When did you get back?'

'About twelve months ago.'

'And are you enjoying it?'

'I didn't really want to come back but I had to because my father got sick, then I got a job here and started the Real Hot Bitches and The ManBank and now I am here, and yeah I am happy . . . I mean Wellington is not London or Toyko but hey . . .' I rabbit on.

Just then the microphone squeals and the auctioneer announces it's time to start the bidding.

We stand facing the stage; I can feel the warmth of his body as his arm brushes mine. It feels good to be standing next to him. I strain my eyes as I try to check out his profile without moving my head.

'You're a sailor?' Despite his elegant clothes, his face has a rugged manliness which comes from, I assume, hours on the high seas.

'Well, I have done a fair bit of sailing, so I suppose that makes me a sailor.'

Umm, I'd say so. 'What kind of boat do you have?

'She's a thirty-three foot kauri strip-planked cutter.'

'Oh, right, a cutter . . . ' I actually have no idea what he's just said as I've never even been near a yacht.

'I'll open the bidding at two hundred dollars for this luxury gas stove,' the auctioneer calls. We turn to watch the proceedings. Finally it's sold for $1550 and we quickly resume our conversation.

'The ManBank — what's that?' he asks.

Ordinarily I evangelically recruit men for the Bank, but this one I want to keep for myself.

'A dating agency,' I begin. 'Men are collateral and deposit themselves into our coffers, while women open accounts and make short-term withdrawals.'

'Sounds like fun,' he says.

'It's a response to the crappy dating culture we have in New Zealand.' I am attempting to sound like a humanitarian, like I'm providing an important social service. 'I mean, the only way anyone gets together is because of the two a.m. scramble, and where is the romance in that?'

'The two a.m. scramble?'

'Yeah, you know, at two a.m. when everyone is really drunk and the guy you have been talking to all night finally says something like "Wanna come to my place?" and then you wake up the next morning with a massive hangover and feel cheap and nasty and have to do the walk of shame home,' I explain.

He laughs. 'I've never had any trouble finding dates.'

'Well, you are in a minority — literally. There is a shortage of eligible men in New Zealand.' I cough. I can't believe I'm using ManBank facts to flirt with him. It isn't a good strategy. I clock the other single women in the room eyeing him up. 'How about another drink?' I say, eager to keep him to myself.

The rest of the fundraiser passes in a fabulous vino-fuelled flirt-fest. I do lots of laughing, throwing my head back and exposing my neck as apparently this is how to attract men. I mirror body language and accidentally-on-purpose touch him as much as I possibly can. He doesn't run for the hills. Things are looking promising. Before long people are packing up and the fluorescent lights are being turned on.

We start walking out into the cold night air. I don't want the evening to end.

'Would you like to come back to my yacht for a drink?' he asks — reading my mind.

'Sure,' I say, slipping my hand into his and thinking at least it is only 11 p.m. and not 2 in the morning!

We start walking down the hill towards the sea. This is romance plus: a sailor, a yacht! Woohoo!

'Angela, I'll be honest with you — I am not interested in having a girlfriend,' he says, suddenly becoming very serious — no mean feat considering how much booze we have poured down our throats. 'I am circumnavigating the South Island soon and I don't want a girlfriend to complicate that.'

'Did I say I wanted a boyfriend?' God, was I that transparent! By this stage I have decided he's the most interesting man I have ever met: perfect boyfriend material, and quite possibly my future husband. 'That's fine, let's just have a drink,' I lie.

We arrive at the wharf.

'I've forgotten my key,' he says, slapping his pockets. 'We're going to have to climb over the gate.' He hauls himself up over the dangerous-looking spikes, the moonlight rippling over his buttocks. Ha! Rippling buttocks in the moonlight! Clearly, I am quite drunk.

Five minutes later, our hands are on fire.

'I guess it's anti-climb paint,' Ross says, rubbing his hand on his jeans. 'This is *Astra*, my yacht.'

I successfully manage to get on board without making a fool of myself. We duck into the cockpit and climb down the companionway into the salon. Inside it's less a tramping hut, more a gentleman's study. There are books jammed into every space, tasteful mushroom-coloured upholstery, a small framed seascape hung next to an old map of the Pacific. On the port side, there is a guitar.

'Drink?' Ross says, pouring wine into crystal glasses once we have washed our hands.

'Why thank you.' This is all very civilised.

'Have a seat.' There are no chairs as such, just strangely shaped couches. We sip the cheap wine and I continue attempting to be charming and eloquent. 'I'll play a song for you.' Picking up the guitar, he starts strumming . . .

Could it be? It is! It's Kiss, 'I Was Made for Loving You'. His version is more of a ballad than a rock anthem but I can't contain myself — I have moves! Real Hot Bitching dance moves, to this very song. This is a dream date! I get up and dance.

By the time 2 a.m. rolls around, we are both lying in the saloon, cradling the crystal. I try to focus on the photo of two teenage girls Ross has pinned up on the bulkhead.

'Who are they?' I ask.

'My daughters, Holly and Nina.'

I sit up. Blinking hard. At the most he looked a couple of years older than me.

'Your daughters? How old *are* you?'

'I'm forty-five.'

'I thought you were thirty-seven at the most, that means . . . you are thirteen years older than me!' I am impressed that I am able to manage any kind of calculation in these circumstances.

'Is that a problem?'

'No, I'm just surprised you have teenage children. You look so . . . young.'

'Technically Holly isn't a teenager, she's twenty.'

'Twenty!'

Good Lord, what had this man been up to? He must have been twenty-five when she was born. Who has kids at twenty-five? What was the deal?

'Are you married?' I ask, getting up.

'No. I was, but I'm not now.'

'That's good, 'cos I have always drawn the line at married men.'

'How honourable,' he laughs.

'OK, well, I am going home.' Since sitting up I realise it's time for bed. My own bed. 'I have to go to work tomorrow and I need to get some sleep. But thank you for a wonderful evening.'

'I'll walk you out — it can be tricky getting off the boat in the dark.'

I begin gathering up my bag and coat.

'Ange, let's have dinner tomorrow. What's your address? I'll pick you up.'

'I'd love that.' We stumble down the pier and, with the key this time, negotiate the gate.

'Until tomorrow,' he whispers, hugging me close. Soon his lips are against mine. He smells of booze and the boat and potential.

'Mmm, you're a good pash,' I whisper back. 'See you tomorrow.'

At home I lie in bed while the room spins. I decide not to focus on the fact that he doesn't want a girlfriend and allow myself to imagine going sailing around the harbour, chinking cocktails on the deck with the handsome older gent. I'm so smitten.

Beep . . . Beep . . . Beep . . . My alarm clock feels like daggers being stabbed into my brain. My hangover is spectacular, complete with banging headache and double vision. Somehow I get myself out of bed and to work. I float through the day, popping Panadol and treating myself to seafood chowder at lunchtime. Sea food . . . the sea . . . Ross . . . my sore brain's making dodgy leaps. My output is dismal. I employ the trick of having a half-finished Word document open on my desktop so I can tap away if anyone walks by. Finally, at 5 p.m., the fug clears and by the time I get home I feel ready to do it all again.

I put on my best casual but classy outfit: fitted jeans, a black top and high-heeled boots. I apply a little make-up — not too much, men don't like that — and wait for him to turn up.

Damn, we didn't specify a time, I think as 6 p.m. comes and goes. Well, that is a bit early for dinner, I reason. 7 p.m. ticks by. Nothing. 8 p.m. . . . . He can't be far away, maybe he got lost. I don't know his number so I can't call him.

Nine p.m. rolls around and there's still no sign of him. *He is not coming.* Oh God, what a fool. He said he wasn't interested in romance. I am a *dick.* Realising the full horror of being stood up in my own home I rip off my boots, wipe off my lipstick, collapse into bed and begin sobbing into my pillow.

What was I thinking? He said he wasn't interested in a girlfriend. I knew he was heading off sailing soon, but we had such fun the night before . . . Did he have to stand me up? That's the last straw.

The last few years I have dated without much success. It seems my Prince Charming has been eaten by a dragon and I am destined to a life of spinsterhood.

My skin isn't tough enough. I decide I need to get out of here. The next day I buy a ticket to Thailand.

That was four months ago and now I am holding the letter from the sailor in my hand.

Maybe I could just meet him for a drink, demand an explanation. That's what an independent, self-assured woman would do . . . isn't it? What harm would there be in that?

Pulling out my computer, I write him an email and invite him over for a drink that night.

Suddenly the phone rings. Unknown caller flashes on the screen. Probably my mum wanting to know how the trip went.

'Hello?'

'Hi Angela, it's Ross,' he says. Hearing his voice, my heart starts racing.

'Oh hi, that was quick.'

'I've just got back from a bike ride and I got your email. I'll pick up some wine and see you in a couple of hours.'

'OK, sounds great,' I stammer before I can think of anything more cool and detached to say.

I put the phone down. And freak out.

Aaarggghhhh! He is actually coming over! I start running around madly, breathing through my mouth (hot yoga, be damned).

Then I hear a voice. It is my inner bitch speaking to me, telling me to 'bitch it out'. Grabbing my leotard and jamming on my wig I pump up Def Leppard's 'Pour Some Sugar on Me' and high-kick my way to settled nerves.

It works. I feel calm enough to slip into my best animal-print dress. It shows off my new tan and makes my boobs look amazing.

I try not to focus on the fact I have thought about this man every day for the last four months. He had better show up.

The gate squeaks. I take a deep breath and walk into my bedroom so I can pretend I was busy doing something when he knocks at the door.

'Hi, come in,' I say, opening the door.

'Hello, you look great,' he says, leaning in to kiss me. All thoughts of demanding explanations and apologies melt away. How could I resist? He is looking ridiculously handsome in a jaunty polka-dot neckerchief and dark jeans, with a twinkle in his eye. I kiss him back.

'Let me pour you a good long drink,' I say, taking the bottle from his hand. I have a feeling it's going to be a fun six weeks.

3

Bitchin'

For as long as I can remember I've wanted to be a dancer. Not just any dancer, but a Solid Gold Dancer.

When I was seven, our family got its first proper stereo. It was a Hitachi with big foamy speakers and a smoked-glass door, and it came with a free record, *Crystal Gayle's Greatest Hits*. She was amazing. Her hair was so long it went past her bum and touched the ground.

'You sit over there and play the drums,' I say, bossing my long-suffering little sister Charlotte. I had given her a wooden spoon and was making her sit behind Mum's fluffy orange make-up stool. To add insult to injury, she could drum as hard as she liked but she would never make a sound.

'I am going to be Crystal Gayle!' I announce, pulling a jersey onto my head and leaving the arms to dangle down my back.

We put the record on. 'Don't it make my brown eyes blue . . .' Crystal croons into her skinny microphone.

I spin around the living room imagining I have really long Crystal-Gayle locks. I leap over the pouf, attempt the splits and, with the window as my mirror and the toys as my audience, I dance, consumed with the impossibility of making my already blue eyes brown.

Meanwhile, Charlotte has got bored with doing the 'drums' and watching her big sister show pony around. Without me noticing she has inched out from behind the stool and is attempting to encroach on *my* dance space.

'No!' I halt mid-move. 'You are on drums.' I push her back behind the stool.

'I don't want to be on drums.'

'Get behind the stool,' I repeat, giving her a good shove this time.

'Owww, Mummmmmmmmmmy!' she whines.

Oh great, now she gets Mum involved. Our mother always comes to her rescue.

'Girls, play nicely please,' Mum says, coming in from the kitchen. 'Angela, let Charlotte have a turn dancing. You can have a turn on the drums now.'

'Noooo, I am Crystal Gayle. Charlotte is my back-up drums!' I cry.

'Angela, cut it out. If you girls can't play nicely I will turn it off.'

I weigh up my options. There's never any getting around my mother, and she always makes good on her threats. I can get Charlotte back later.

'OK, she can be Crystal Gayle, but only for two minutes,' I concede.

Mum puts the needle back on the record and Charlotte begins dancing. She is nowhere near as good as me.

'One Mississippi, two Mississippi, three Mississippi, four Mississippi, five . . .'

I sit behind the stool counting loudly, 'drumming' very half-heartedly and making my way to one hundred and twenty.

Charlotte glares at me. 'What? I'm just counting. It's a free country.' I have heard this new phrase at school and it seems like a good time to pull it out.

'Muuum, Angela's being . . . a *dick*!' She must be really mad because we aren't allowed to say 'dick' in our house. We also not allowed to say 'snot' or 'fart'; we have to say 'blow nose' or 'smelly'.

Mum comes back into the lounge. 'Charlotte, I don't like that language.' Then, turning to me she snaps, 'Angela, what are you doing to your sister?'

I smile sweetly, my eyes wide with innocence.

'Nothing,' I lie firmly.

I'm still counting in my head. 'It's been two minutes, now it is my turn.'

'Muuuuuum!'

'Oh you two, can't you just play nicely for five minutes?' my exasperated mother says.

Now I have my own son I totally understand this tone. But then, I was seven.

'I just want to dance, Mum.'

'So do I!' whines Charlotte.

We look at each other, then we look at Mum, whose face is growing stormy. We know instantly that we are pushing our luck. We're going to have to pull our heads in if we don't want to spend the rest of the afternoon in our bedroom.

'OK, you can dance on *this* side of the lounge,' I say, marking out the border with the cushions from the couch. 'This is *my* side.' Nothing like ensuring you are on the side with access to the stereo.

I wait until Charlotte has got her jersey 'hair' all in place, then in true evil-older-sister fashion pipe up with, 'I've had enough of Crystal Gayle, it's time for *Solid Gold Hits*.'

She glares at me. 'Angela!' she growls, wanting to whack me for changing the record. But then 'Jessie's Girl' belts out of the speakers as the *Solid Gold Hits Volume 31* album cranks. She loves this song.

We spend the rest of the afternoon imagining we are Stray Cats strutting, acting out 'Bad Habits', being 'Devil Women', and playing with the 'Queen of Hearts'. We strip off our matching green and gold tracksuits and put on our togs and dance, get out Mum's strappy high-heels and dance, practise doing turns and high-kicks, all in preparation for when we are old enough to join the Solid Gold Dancers and be on the telly.

But the glittering world of dance didn't want me.

My teenage dance years were a deeply embarrassing series of humiliations. I tried jazz, but I was shockingly bad, so bad I failed my Grade One exam. I had a coughing fit halfway through, and instead of taking pity on me the adjudicators asked me to leave. Even my two-tone leotard failed to impress.

I tried more 'free-form' dance classes with a guy who looked like Leo Sayer and smelt like an old man's wardrobe. Every Thursday afternoon, he arrived for class at the Methodist Community Hall on his ten-speed, wearing a cropped mesh top and grey marl tights. He acted like he had just stepped off the set of *Footloose* but unfortunately he was no Kevin Bacon. He also sported a double camel-toe, achieved by rolling the waistband of his tights over three times, which hiked them up sufficiently to pull them up hard against his knob and butt crack. How he got away with it in late '80s Palmerston North is a mystery to me.

This man didn't walk, he sashayed. He was constantly stretching and 'shaking it out' and he loved nothing better than 'working his feet' on the bare polished boards as he took us through our isolations.

'Right, class . . . eyes forward . . . five, six, seven, eight . . . let's start with the hips . . . to the right . . . to the left . . . *just* your hips . . . *We don't need another hero* . . . now the chest . . . right . . . middle . . . left . . . middle . . . double time . . . right, middle, left, middle . . . *We don't need to find a way home* . . . Nice work, girls . . . *All we want is life beyond the thunderdome* . . . Angela, less lip-synching, more dancing.'

'Stay warm, keep moving,' he instructs us as he jiggles his hips, edging the grey marl tights even higher. Suddenly his spirit fingers shoot up in the air and his legs fly off the floor into the splits. 'We are going to practise our leaps! Everyone in the back corner,' he calls, drag-running to the back of the hall. We hesitate for a moment, giving the trail of musty sweat wafting in his wake time to dissipate.

My fellow dance-mates are tall, willowy creatures with

slender thighs, pert boobs and flicky hair. They are much closer to the Solid Gold Dancers than I will ever be.

'OK girls . . . We are going to drag-run to the middle then I wanna see a leap!' Great! I think, drag-runs! Something I have nailed! I start focusing on the opposite corner and shaking out my arms.

'Angela, you can go first . . . five, six, seven, eight . . .' The music starts and I take off, my back straight, my toes dragging along the floor as I run. My face is the picture of a serene dancer. *I am dance*, I think. Then, as I am readying myself for the leap, I feel my legwarmer catch under my foot. It's too late . . . I've launched myself into the air but without the traction of a spilt-sole jazz shoe I lose my balance. I'm falling. Time stands still. I can hear my Leo-Sayer-lookalike teacher calling to me. 'Annnnnngelaaaaaa . . .'

My arms become windmills; I'm desperately trying to steady myself. Then thwack! I land hard, on my face.

'Ahhhh!' I lift my head up to see him drag-running for all he is worth towards me.

'Angela! Are you OK?' he pants, kneeling down. My face is now level with his crotch.

'Arhhhh,' I groan, slowly pushing myself up. Everything hurts. I feel something wet dripping onto the back of my hand.

'Ewwww, she's bleeding!' cries one of the tall willowys. Round warm drops of blood are bouncing off my hand and hitting the tawny-coloured floor. I can't breathe, my nostrils are full. I put my head back and gag on the sharp metallic taste of blood as it trickles down my throat. I have been vegetarian for two years. Suddenly I feel myself about to vomit. My hands fly to my mouth. Oh dear God *no* . . . how much more embarrassment can a girl take? I can't spew on the dance floor. Miraculously, I manage to keep my mouth shut, but now I have a gob full of blood and spew. I don't want Leo to follow me. I get up dizzily and limp to the toilet.

'I'm fine,' I mumble. So that's what a nose-dive is.

After a couple of weeks off, recovering, it is time to learn the barrel roll. This is the pinnacle of the all the moves I have learnt so far. It involves imagining you are a barrel and flinging yourself over in mid-air. It is pure Solid Gold. Mastering this will take my dance career to a whole new level.

'Stand with your feet shoulder width apart, bend your knees, keep them soft . . . now rock your weight from side to side . . . you are trying to create enough momentum to propel you around. When you feel you are ready . . . commit to the roll!' Leo Sayer is in his element. 'Ba-ba!' he yells as he finishes demonstrating, with a flourish of his hand that is pure musical theatre.

I take a deep breath. 'OK Ange, you can do it . . . soft knees, momentum . . . commit . . .' I whisper to myself. Just as I am rocking myself into the big roll, Leo Sayer calls across the hall, 'What are you doing! You look like a beached whale!'

I blush scarlet. The room starts pulsing. How could I look like a beached whale — I was standing up, not lolling about on the floor! I can feel myself beginning to shake with anger.

'Fuck you and your too-tight tights and squished-up nuts!' I yell at him, as only an enraged fourteen-year-old girl can.

I like a joke but that cut me to the core. I was not going back. Ever.

After my dramatic exit I weigh up my options. Folk dancing is where I excel, but we aren't living in an English village in the Middle Ages so there are limited opportunities to dance around a maypole. Ballet is a write-off, jazz and I are not a good fit and now I have insulted the only 'free-form' dance teacher in Palmerston North.

Reluctantly I realise it is time to put my dreams of dance fame on ice.

4

It Heats Up

For the next fifteen years I danced alone in my lounge, or at pubs around a pile of handbags. Sometimes at parties I would sidle up to a hot guy and pull out a few choice moves. That was it. That was all. No glory days on a pedestal, no bedazzled leotards — just pedestrian moves in non-ticketed venues.

Things reached an all-time low when I was thirty. While my peers were walking down the aisle or being carried over thresholds, I returned home from living in London, broken-hearted. I had no money, no job, no husband, no kids. I was going grey. I couldn't believe my life had come to this. I needed something more than my nightly bottle of booze — I needed something to make me laugh.

Probably due to the fact that I had tormented her for most of her childhood, my sister Charlotte and I hadn't been on speaking terms for the best part of a decade. She, being of much higher moral fibre than I will ever be, extended the olive branch.

'Wanna come round and listen to some records?'

'Yes, please,' I accepted sheepishly.

She had inherited the old family stereo and, as I sat in her lounge feeling sorry for myself, she placed the *Solid Gold Hits* album from our childhood on the turntable.

And we danced, like a wave on the ocean romanced.

After that night things started looking up. I got a job producing theatre in Wellington and I met Rosie Roberts. She loved the Solid Gold Dancers as much as I did. It was a match made in 1980s dance heaven.

One night at 3 a.m., while we are painting Bats Theatre back to black after a production, we uncover an old mix-tape.

'Let's put it on — we need something to help us through this painting,' Rosie says, making her way up to the sound desk. George Michael's voice fills the theatre. We look at each other, our eyes alive with a long-forgotten dream.

'Oh my God . . . remember this song?' Rosie shouts above the music and runs down the stairs to the stage.

'Hell yeah!' I start singing into my paintbrush.

We begin swaying. At first it is nervous side-steps, then the music overcomes us.

It is like we *are* the music, our moves describing the lyrics. It is like acting and dancing at the same time. It is Dracting. It is comedy and dancing at the same time. It is Dramedy!

'Rosie, check this move out!' I call to her as I slap my arse with one hand and the floor with the other.

'That is real hot, what about this!' she yells, spinning on one leg with her arms pumping the sky.

Soon we are beating at our hearts, pointing at our eyes, miming the words. In the instrumental break we find ourselves playing air guitars, really convincingly. Our feet are dancing in a frenzy of not-very-complicated-yet-very-dramatic moves.

At 7 a.m. we are still dancing, like maniacs. We know what we have to do. We need to start a comedy dance troupe.

If we can't join the Solid Gold Dancers, we will create the Real Hot Bitches.

REAL HOT BITCHES
WANTED

More is More! What we lack in technique we make up for in PASSION! We can't fight our nature! Bring back the filth!

That's right, we are calling all REAL HOT BITCHES to join our gang.

This is not for the faint-hearted. It is not for the shy. If you want fame, well fame costs and the bitches aren't paying. 'Cos that's what our fans do. But if the sight of a $2.50 electric blue g-string hanging in the local St Vinnies shop makes your teeth hurt with excitement, then buy that 'tard and drag-run down to the Real Hot Bitches HQ this Saturday afternoon.

STOP. BREAK IT DOWN!

Bitchin' is all about 'tudes and 'tards. It's a verb and a noun. You got that? Damn straight. But you better also meet the following Bitchin' criteria. You must:

- have no dance training. None. Absolutely not.
- have a belief that there is no higher achievement than to become a semi-professional dancer.
- have a belief, nay, conviction, that you're a legend — if only in your own mind.
- carry an 'emergency' mullet wig in your handbag.
- be ready to sign the petition for Patrick Swayze's canonisation as the patron saint of D.A.N.C.E.
- be able to pelvis-thrust. HARD.

- possess an over-inflated/delusional sense of your own dance ability.
- like to warm up with pizza and beer.
- believe that dance, drama and comedy can live together as one and become something much, much more — Dramedy!
- subtlety is not in your vocabulary. Nor in your wardrobe. Or in your make-up purse, for that matter.
- able to use random '80s song lyrics in conversation, e.g. the workplace: 'Oh Trevor, really — you give love a bad name.' In the sack: 'Awwww, push it, push it real good.' At the doctor's: 'How about you hook me up with some of that bad medicine?' When working at a café and an extreme hottie asks for a takeaway flat white and you hand it to him and instead of asking if he would like sugar your subconscious takes over and you stare into his eyes and say, 'You can pour some sugar on me' and when he looks at you awkwardly you don't stop, you start singing 'Come on, fire me up', pull out an incredible arse-slapping move, so powerful he joins in and soon you are both on the counter pouring sugar all over yourselves while the other customers cheer and weep with pent-up emotion.

Other important but not totally critical questions you will need to ask yourself are:

- Were you ever called 'Baby' and put in a corner?
- How many watermelons can you carry?
- Have you daydreamed about being a welder by day and a dancer by night?
- Do you wear sunglasses at night?
- Has anyone described your lips as being like venomous poison?
- Have you ridden the highway to the danger zone?
- Is your tongue firmly in your cheek? And finally, when you go down, IS IT IN A BLAZE OF GLORY?

For a full job description please contact the co-founders, Bitch Mistress Candy le Coque or Dance Bitch Rockit.

Soon Saturdays at the Island Bay Surf Club are full of bitches
desperate for dance. A typical session runs a little something
like this: a Real Hot Bitch choreographs a sensational dance
routine to their favourite song. They then perform it for the
troupe, to mad clapping and whooping, then they teach the
dance-hungry Real Hot Bitches the moves. Once everyone has
sort of 'got it', the troupe divides in half and performs to the
other half, and if they are lucky they can see their reflections
in the window. This stage is extremely important as it enables
everyone to show off. *A lot.*

The moves have names to make them easily recognisable, e.g.

- squashing dwarfs
- Wembley stadium
- tits and teeth
- devil horns
- one-wing dove
- long schlong move
- shake the bottle
- air guitar
- crotch slap
- arse, arse
- New York!
- motorbike hair
- splash the water
- sprinkler
- Douglas Wright move
- pumping dog arms
- pulsing tableau
- dying
- breaking out of the coffin
- hand hip, hand hip hip
- flick your g-string
- freeze
- bitching eyes.

Mrs Blacksmith's Guide to Alter Egos

A Real Hot Bitch also needs an alter ego.

Many a woman has used an alter ego to explore different sides of her personality. I have a particular penchant for them. Unlike a nickname, which is usually something someone else gives you, you get the pleasure of naming your alter ego.

Here are a few of mine:

Candy le Coque. This is my bitchin' name. It's the name I like to use when I squeeze myself into Lycra and dance around possessed by the spirit of a 1980s television backing-dancer. The great thing about this alter ego (and indeed any alter ego) is that I can change my back-story whenever the hell I like. One version goes like this: 'Candy was named after her mother's two favourite foods. Legend has it that little Candy was kidnapped by gypsies, tramps and thieves and forced to dance for her meagre supper. One day Kevin Bacon was walking past and saw her kick-ball change as she danced on a street corner. It was so tight he stopped mid-stride and said, 'Candy, we are both named after food items how about a quick, improvised yet totally awe-inspiring dance?' Candy said yes to Mr Bacon and her life changed *forever*.

Lee Roy Swayze, MaXine HendriX, Shaka Kum, Coco La Chanelle, Jem'appelle Jeff, Pussy Galore, CJ Luvtodanz, Pearl Lusta, Pop Tart, Cyndi Lamas-Arquette, Desaree Knightshade and Rockit are just a few of the wonderful examples of creative bitching alter egos with equally bitching back-stories that are too fluid to pin down.

Ladyboss. I didn't realise it when I created this alter ego, but Jackie Collins has written a book titled *Lady Boss*. I needed a new email address and this one was free and fitting. It is also aspirational, as I would one day like to be a Lady Boss.

Angela Aphrodite Troy. When playing cupid to the dateless, one needs a name that suggests romance — powerful romance, lots of romance. As the CEO of The ManBank (see Chapter Five), I needed a name with gravitas. Who better to name myself after than Helen of Troy, who was so beautiful she had lots of suitors/wannabe daters and Aphrodite, who was a matchmaker to the gods and demi-gods? I figure I might as well aim high and hope for the best.

Two-Ton Tess. She gets the action. The transformation from Angela to Two-Ton Tess involves a fat suit, an orange towelling dress and a curly long black wig. It is a knock-out. When Tess goes to parties or down to the Sunday fruit and veg market, people chat to her, hug her, slap her arse, ask her out, confess their darkest secrets and, wonderfully, offer her fudge. The fake layer of fat melts even the most uptight of city boys.

Mrs Blacksmith. This is not, strictly speaking, an alter ego. It is in fact my married name. Ross made it up a few years ago, using a variation on his mother's maiden name of Smith. It turns out that while it sounds like a common name there are very few people in the world with the family name of Blacksmith. When Dashkin our son was born, we all took it as our name. We invented a family crest and motto of 'Hammer and Tongs' with the byline 'Do it. Make it Happen'.

5

ManBanking

— ◆ —

At the same time as running the Real Hot Bitches, I decided to revolutionise New Zealand's dating culture by opening a dating agency called The ManBank.

'Y ou state here on your collateral assessment form that your dating history could
be described as . . . a dirty, filthy shagger,'
says Jane, pointing to the piece of paper in
front of her.

'Well, I haven't really "dated", as such.
More like got drunk and pulled, if you get my drift,' Josh explains,
taking another large gulp of his beer.

Jane and I smile. Another one.

'Yes, we get your drift,' I say.

We are at one of our twice-weekly 'collateral calls'. As new
business owners, Cleopatra Jane Matahari, my business
partner, and I (as Angela Aphrodite Troy) don't have swanky
offices in which to help overhaul New Zealand's dire dating
culture, so we are conducting these sessions in the back room
of the Matterhorn Bar in Wellington.

'In my capacity as CEO of The ManBank, I would like to
thank you for your honesty. It goes a long way to helping us find
the right date for you,' I say, giving him the once-over.

Josh is tall, early thirties with brown eyes, a great head of
sandy hair and, as they say in the world of dating, a GSOH. He
is *perfect* banking material.

'I have never used a dating agency before, but you girls seem
like fun. I don't really like using the internet sites, but I'm keen

to meet someone outside of my group of mates,' he explains.

'We can certainly help you with that.' Jane smiles encouragingly. 'Like you, there are many good daters suffering internet-dating trawling fatigue,' she says, going back to the form. 'Question five, which song lyric best describes you . . . You have put down "I Wanna Hold You but I Better Not Touch". That's Alice Cooper, isn't it?'

'Yeah, I love that song.'

'Can you talk us through why you choose that lyric?' I ask. I love this bit of the interviews; it's very insightful.

'Well, I really liked this chick at work but she was married, so every day I had that song in my head, you know? I wanted to hold her, but I couldn't.'

I raise my eyebrows. An honourable gent, I think, making a mental note and already imagining who I can set him up with.

'We find the unrequited crush, flirting with the unobtainable and pining after someone who clearly is just not that into you a common trap which many people fall into,' Jane explains.

Suddenly Ross flashes before my eyes. Was I one of those people? Was I falling for the unobtainable? Surely not? Since he came over with the wine we have been inseparable. We have been on long walks, gone biking, made dinner together, gone out drinking, watched movies and I have even met some of his old friends. No, I am not one of *them*. We are having a six-week fling, I tell myself. That is all.

'At The ManBank, we undertake a rigorous screening programme. We meet each of our daters, cross-reference their answers with a reliable referee and once we are sure they are not killers, bigamists or Rohypnol pushers, they are deposited into the bank,' Jane continues.

'Well, that's comforting!' laughs Josh.

'I see you are looking for a woman between twenty-three and thirty-two, with dark hair and no children,' I say, continuing to work my way through his form.

'And she has to be funny, like dogs and be slim,' he says, smiling. 'I can't stand fat people,' he confesses.

I sigh. Another fattist. Since we began running a dating agency we have discovered just how picky people can be.

'We certainly have women/account holders who fit those criteria. How often are you looking to date?'

'Twice a week.'

'Great!'

'How does it work, though — do you call me or what?'

'From here we use our amazing powers of matchmaking to facilitate short-term withdrawals from The ManBank. Fortnightly you will be sent an availability email. Please send your availability back within four days. Depending on the availability of suitable account holders, we will contact you with details of your dates.'

'So you arrange everything?'

'Yes, we take the hassle out of dating. Many people have told us that they don't know where to go on a date and so have been reluctant to ask anyone out.'

'Crazy!'

Jane and I look at each other. We have done this spiel hundreds of times.

'All you have to do is show up on time and be a good date.'

'So how do I know what she looks like? Do you send me a photo?'

'No, we will send you an email and in that we will describe your date, her interests, where to meet her and a code phrase — should you need to use it.'

'A code phrase?'

'Yes, for example she may come up to you are say "Are you here for the beer?" and you would reply "No, I'm here for the bank".'

He laughs, a throaty, masculine laugh. 'OK, sounds good. That'll break the ice.'

'Exactly. Dating should be fun.'

'And it's not an interview for a marriage proposal.'

For all of our daters' bravado and insistence that they are not looking for marriage, we have found that we really have to hammer this home to people.

'Our aim with The ManBank is to inject some humour into the dating world. We try to introduce people to like-minded individuals, but love is a many-splendored thing, so there are no guarantees,' I say using a professional tone, which I hope takes some of the sting out of it.

'OK. So what if I like her and want to see her again?'

'We will send you an interest-rate assessment email the next day. Here you can tell us how your date was, if she behaved in accordance with the code of conduct and signal whether you would like to see her again,' Jane explains.

'This is confidential to The ManBank and will not be passed on to your date,' I add with a smile.

'What if I am late or something?'

'You will be placed in the Crap-Date Class.'

'Which means?'

'We will be reluctant to send you on more dates,' Jane states matter-of-factly. She is far more detached than I am. I'm always too emotionally involved with all the daters, hoping we have made wise choices and that they enjoy their dates. If they don't, I take it personally, as if it is me who has been rejected.

'I am sure you won't be like that, Josh. We just have to cover ourselves,' I add quickly.

'We have a code of conduct we would like you to sign before you leave,' Jane says, sliding the paper across the table and reaching for the pen.

Josh starts reading:

THE MANBANK CODE OF CONDUCT

Dear ManBank Dater,

Welcome to The ManBank. We are thrilled to have your custom.

The ManBank understands that the world of dating can be somewhat daunting, so we have developed a strict Code of Conduct to minimise the trauma. Our Code of Conduct *must be adhered to* on all ManBank dates, by both Collateral and Account Holders. Failure to respect our code will result in closing of your account or placement in our Collateral Crap-Date Class.

- Treat your date with respect.
- Do not show up late. Ten minutes late is rude, not fashionable.
- No delving into the 'ex-files'. You are on a date, not in a therapy session.
- Pay your own way — it saves confusion at the end of the date.
- Make an effort with your presentation.
- Do not expect to receive your date's contact details.
- No unauthorised withdrawals. All second dates must go through The ManBank.
- Txting while on a ManBank date is unacceptable.
- Be charming and eloquent — remember to ask your date about themselves.
- Have fun. It is a date — not the rest of your life.
- Cancellation of dates must be made with The ManBank staff at least twenty-four hours before the date.

I (please print name) _____
agree to adhere to The ManBank Code of Conduct.

Signed: _____

Date: _____

Disclaimer:

i. The ManBank will not be held liable for any crap
dates, acts of God, bad weather, injury sustained, loss of
life, or lack of judgement on behalf of the Dater. (Please
remember to be safe.)

ii. Registration fees are non-refundable. There are no
refunds on packages if you find love or get cold feet.

iii. There is no expiry date on The ManBank dating
packages. The ManBank will endeavour to have you
dating regularly; however, dates are subject to both
parties' availability.

Your delightful divas of dating,
Angela Aphrodite Troy
CEO, The ManBank

Cleopatra Jane Matahari
Country Leader, The ManBank

We need Josh. We are inundated with women in their early thirties — all attractive, educated and independent — but we have a shortage of men for them to date. Josh could easily become our star dater. It is a numbers game and we are, after all, businesswomen.

We hold our breath as Josh picks up the pen and takes another swig of his beer.

Finally he signs the form.

'Welcome to The ManBank!' we both exclaim.

'Now, the last thing we have to do is work out which dating package you would like,' I say. 'We have the Six Pack or the Dater's Dozen. The Dater's Dozen offers great value for money, as you get thirteen dates for the price of twelve.'

'Hell, why not, I'll take a Dater's Dozen,' Josh says, handing over his $120.

We stand up and shake his huge manly hand. 'It is a pleasure doing business with you.'

'We will be in touch soon,' Jane adds.

I look at my watch. It's 8.55 p.m. 'OK Jane, I have to go.'

'Where are you off to?'

'I'm meeting Ross for dinner.'

'Ross? That sailor guy from last year?'

'Yes, he sent me a letter.'

'Smooth.'

'He's in town for six weeks. It turns out he had to leave earlier than expected last year — something about the weather and getting across Cook Strait on the right tide. Anyway, he was going back to Christchurch to help his daughter prepare for her exams.'

'I thought you had sworn off dating?' Jane says, packing up the forms and tucking the night's takings into her purse for safekeeping.

'I know, I know . . . but it is just for six weeks. We are having a great time.'

'Just be careful, Ange — I know how sensitive you are.'

'Mustn't be late and break the code of conduct!' I laugh,

reapplying my lipstick and gathering up my bag.

'I just don't want to see you hurt again,' Jane adds.

'Thanks, Jane,' I say, giving her a hug. 'I promise I will not be crying into my wine in three weeks' time. I am just having some fun while he is here.'

And I hurry out of the bar.

Mrs Blacksmith's Guide to Discovering Your True Dating Identity

A typical example: his name was Rhett, his hair was long, his style naff and frankly my dears, his pick-up lines should have blown away with the wind. 'I want you, I need you baby, and I love a big Jewish nose!' Clearly this man needed help. The first step was to discover his true dating identity and then prescribe a course of rehabilitation.

This incredibly scientific test was developed by Cleopatra Jane Matahari and Angela Aphrodite Troy.

'I'm Here For A Good Time Not A Long Time' Dater. You prefer to date in foreign cities where your behaviour won't haunt you. Sometimes you adopt new identities, e.g. your real name is Louise but tonight you are . . . Pamela.

Detective Dater. For you, dating is a challenge, a chance to employ all the techniques you have learnt from watching cop shows. You google their name, stalk their house and in extreme cases you will call your date pretending to be a librarian and advise them that they have overdue books, all to ascertain just what kind of person they really are.

'It's Not Really A Date, You're Just My Mate' Dater. A Kiwi classic. Here the object of your affections is unaware they are on a date — they think it is just a group of mates getting together enjoying a barbecue. You, however, are analysing their every move, watching the way they put the sauce on the sausage, where the potato salad is placed on the plate, how hard they laugh at Fat Mike's jokes.

Strategic Dater. You know what you want, you know what you like and you will only date people who fall into your predetermined and strictly-adhered-to dating type. Your time is precious and you are not going to waste it dating dickheads. Got it!

'Date Me If You Dare' Dater. You exude an aura of hard-arseness, your body language challenges people to date you . . . you are like a vampire and only those with swan-like necks need apply — if they *dare*.

Devious Dater. You prefer to instigate a date by engineering 'chance' meetings with the object of their desire, e.g. 'Oh, hi! Wow, I had no idea you came to this café every Sunday at 10.25 a.m. for eggs Benedict, a long black and to read the sports section of the paper first before you move onto the property pages! What. A. Surprise! Mind if I join you?'

Canvas Dater. You prefer to ask out as many people as possible for the highest success rate. Sometimes known as the scattergun approach, it can be misinterpreted as you being a bit of a slag. But really, you are a true adventurer, you push boundaries, you take risks, and you get laid often.

Fantasy Dater. You don't actually date, you imagine it. Friday nights are spent sitting at home making small talk with your teddy bear as you order from the handwritten menu you have placed on your own kitchen table — not the most successful approach.

Executive Dater. With you it's all business. Dating you is like being at a job interview. You might say things like, 'Where do you see yourself in five years?' You have your KPIs sorted and targets to meet before the end of the date. If you are a lady, chances are you are wearing a power suit.

Trophy Dater. You would not be seen dead with a minger.

Earnest Dater. You take the dating scene extremely seriously. It is about a lasting connection, even a long-term commitment, probably marriage, kids, a dog . . . maybe even a cat. You don't throw your head back when you laugh and gently caress the stem of the wine glass.

Samaritan Dater. Cannot say no to anybody even if it is against your better judgement.

'Flag The Small Talk, Let's Get Down To Pillow Talk' Dater. You prefer mating to dating.

'Around the World in Eighty Dates' Dater. The world is a big place and you see it through dating. Taurean, Korean, black, Hispanic, Jew; if they've been in (insert name of your town) then they'll have dated you.

Community Service Dater. Sometimes known as the sexual Samaritan of the dating world, you date the broken-hearted, self-conscious, shy, desperately-in-need-of-a-date lost lambs, in the spirit of equal-opportunity dating.

'I Think You're Crash Hot And I Really Want to Spade Ya, Can I Buy You A Jug?' Dater. You use naff pick-up lines while seriously wasted in an attempt to fill the gaping void of loneliness and datelessness.

Schoolyard Dater. You employ your friends to communicate with the object of your desire. You use notes, get your friends to ask leading questions like 'So, Darren, do you want a girlfriend?' and then you spend five hours on the telephone discussing and analysing the answer.

The Not-So-Smooth-Operator Dater. You jump on that empty seat at the bar next to someone who looks vaguely alone and hit on them. Hard.

Total Romantic Dater. It's about movie-style romance for you. You want love notes, flowers, balloon rides, chocolate boxes, expensive dinners and luxury day-spa treatments before you will say yes. It may be time to put the rom-coms back in their DVD cases and enter the real world.

'As If' Dater. You knock back the object of your desire by using rudimentary reverse-psychology techniques like 'As if I would ever go on a date with you!' when really, you actually mean 'I love you so much my hands ache' — again, not the best approach.

'Here's My Jacket' Dater. You see a women shivering and you know that the best way to make her weak at the knees is to drape your jacket over her shoulders. *This works every time.*

'I'm Soooo Crazy, I'm Soooo Wacky, I'm Soooo Wild' Dater. You prefer to employ somewhat peacock-like, loud, show-off techniques in a public forum where the object of your desire has no choice but to say 'yes' when you ask them on a date.

Double Dater. You prefer to date with your best mate in tow.

Creative Dater. You prefer to create home-crafted teaser campaigns, like giving the object of your desire a badge saying 'I think you're great, how 'bout a date' or a serenade of mix-tape classics via phone message, or, in extreme cases, using a sky-writer to tell them you think they're hot while you are casually standing next to them.

Dickhead Dater. 'Fuck, I'm a legend' — actually, you're a myth. You know what chicks want and you know how to pull. You don't need no dating identity chart to help you. Shit no! You sleep with one eye open, holding your pillow tight. Alone.

6
Boyfriend!

———

'I'm not going to marry you,' Ross announces over the octopus balls while we are having dinner at the new yakitori place in town.

'That's a bit of a leap!' I say, spluttering on my sake. 'We have been seeing each other for six weeks.' Where were these big statements coming from?

'I know that women your age want to get married and have kids, and I want to be honest with you, so you know what you are getting into,' he continues.

I sigh. It's becoming boring. 'Look, Ross, I get it. You have no intention of having a serious relationship with me. I haven't asked you for one and I'm not getting into anything because you are not going to be here.'

I know the rules, I am keeping to my part of the deal. This is a fun six-week dating adventure not a long-term, long-distance permanent relationship.

He starts again. 'I'm just saying . . .'

I cut him off. '*All right!* I admit it, at some point in my life I would like to get married and have children. Yes, I think you are great, *but* I have been around the block a few times and I know what this is!'

'OK, Ange,' he says, trying to calm me down. 'In my experience it is good to be really upfront about these things.'

This is our first altercation. I reach for the edamame and begin angrily popping beans into my mouth. We are sitting side by side at the horseshoe-shaped bar. To our left, a lone diner sits hunched over, spilling Kewpie mayonnaise over his trashy paperback as he shovels sushi into his mouth. To our right, actor types are talking loudly about their latest 'fabulous' productions, while in front of us the Japanese chef is fanning the barbecue and sending regular puffs of black smoke our way.

'I suffer from misanthropy. I need long stretches alone at sea to regain my love of my fellow man,' Ross says. Well, he certainly has a healthy self-awareness. I suppose that is encouraging. 'After twenty years in a bookshop serving customers I know that when I start thinking people are idiots, I need to be alone. I just couldn't go there again with children and marriage.'

My eyebrows shoot up. I have heard many reasons for staying single but this was a new one.

Over the six weeks we have been seeing each other I have discovered a lot of things about Ross, things I have never encountered before. He has been known to swan around in Edwardian garb, he thinks carefully and deeply, he's a musician and he doesn't like cars or phones, and takes every opportunity to avoid using them. Fishing is very disagreeable to him due to the terrible state of the ocean's fish stocks, and despite wooing me with Kiss he has an aversion to '80s pop music.

'I lived through it the first time around. We mocked all those commercial bands. I just can't go there. Even in jest,' he had told me earlier.

'Your cheekbones look great when you're angry,' he says, trying to change the subject.

I glare at him. He is too handsome to be cross with for long.

'Come here,' he says, putting his arm around my shoulders and kissing my cheek.

He is leaving in two days, sailing south to the city where the Dalai Lama refused to get off the plane. I have never been a fan of Christchurch. It is too flat, too cold and has the highest number of intravenous drug users in New Zealand. Even if he wants me to, I'm not following him there.

'We've had fun, haven't we?' he says.

'We sure have. Nothing like a summer fling to kick-start the year.'

When the time comes for it to end (in approximately forty-eight hours) I am determined that I'm not going to descend into the pit of despair. I'm not going to pile on the pounds by downing litres of cheap booze and eating my body weight in Mövenpick maple walnut ice-cream while lying on the couch watching *Midsomer Murders* on the telly. Oh no, I am going to be a fortress of stoicism where heartbreak is not a guest.

'What are we going to do?' he asks, holding my hands in his.

'What do you mean? You are going home and I am staying here. It's OK. It's been fun. Maybe we can catch up when you come to town next.' I am surprising myself. I honestly am OK about it. My Thailand tan no longer has its golden glow, I have neglected my friends, the Bank and the Bitches for the last six weeks, and it is time to refocus.

'The thing is, Ange, I really like you and I don't want this to end,' he says slowly.

'Eh?' Have I heard him correctly?

Ah, so that is what all this is about! I nod my head slowly. Mr 'I don't want a girlfriend' has been coming up with ridiculous statements so that I would find him too exasperating to be around and ditch him, making it my fault and not his that it didn't work out.

'I like you — a lot,' he continues, picking up his chopsticks and stabbing the last octopus ball.

My heart starts pounding. I think about that first night down at the wharf, and how I allowed myself to imagine sailing around the harbour with him. Is this actually going to be a possibility?

'What about the fact that you don't want a girlfriend? How does that work within the context of "I don't want this to end"?' I ask, genuinely confused.

'I got you this,' he says, handing me a little box. It looks like it came from a jeweller's.

Sweet baby Jesus . . . what is going on here? My mind is whirling. I run a dating agency — I am meant to be up with the play! But now I have *no* idea.

Slowly I unwrap the paper and prise open the lid. Inside is a thin gold necklace. I take it out of the box and hold it up to the coals of the yakitori fire for a better look.

'Is this a parting gift?'

'No, it's a "do you wanna go round with me?" gift,' he says, laughing.

I can't believe it! Ross has done a three-sixty in the time it took to eat six takoyaki balls and drink a tiny cup of sake. This man is something else. And that is why I am falling for him . . .

'Umm, yeah,' I reply, imitating the speech pattern of a fifteen-year-old.

He takes the necklace out of my hand. 'I'll put it on for you.'

I move closer, holding up my hair and arching my neck the way I have seen movie stars do. Ross fastens the clasp. It feels cool against my throat, delicate and subtle. So unlike myself.

'Hopefully this won't turn your neck green,' he says, kissing me.

I smile. He has remembered the story I told him about getting a crappy gold chain from a guy at school and how it had turned my neck green.

'Thank you, Ross, it's beautiful.'

The waitress appears at my elbow.

'More sake?' she asks, offering us the dark brown pottery bottle.

Ross and I grin. 'Why not?' And we hold up our cups for her to fill.

Oh my God, I now have a boyfriend! A forty-five-year-old boyfriend with two children and a yacht, who lives in another city. Shockingly, he has no time for the neon glory of the 1980s but given that he has just pulled out a gold chain, I am prepared to overlook that.

'Here's to the summer of 2007,' I say as we clink cups.

'And here's to many more,' Ross murmurs.

Walking back to my place as fully-fledged boyfriend and girlfriend, we start working on the logistics.

'I could fly down on a Friday night and take the early commuter flight first thing on Monday,' I suggest.

'I won't be flying. I hate travelling by plane, it is so excessive,' he says.

Little did I know just how those words would come back to haunt me.

'OK, so how are you going to visit me?'

'I'll hitchhike to Picton and take the ferry.'

'Could you sail up?'

'It takes three days to sail from Wellington to Christchurch in *Astra*, she is not the fastest boat. By the time I get here I would have to turn around again. Oh, and I have a job on the weekends,' he adds.

My heart is sinking. 'I guess we will just have to play it by ear then. Hopefully we can see each other once a month.'

'Darling, we will work it out,' he says, pushing me against the wall and kissing me. It is romantic, not creepy. 'We can write letters.'

Two days later, Ross leaves. I tidy my room, wash the sheets, put on my new pink g-string leotard complete with butt ruffle and get down to business. Real Hot Bitchin' business — we have a twelve-hour dance-a-thon and an attempt at the world record for the largest synchronised dance routine to prepare for. Boyfriends have to take a back seat. We need all bitches on deck if we are to pull this off.

7

Chance to Dance

—————

'OK, Bitches, listen up. For this year's Fringe Festival we are hitting the streets of Wellington for a totally electrifying dance-a-thon,' I call over the excited chatter of forty Lycra-clad Bitches warming up at the Island Bay Surf Club.

'**O**h my God, that is soooo awesome!'

'I have just got this amazing new 'tard,' says Tiffney Jovi-Harket, holding up a yellow g-string leotard with mesh insert under the boobs. 'It'll look bitchin'.'

Debrelle Van Haller, the meanest Bitch in the whole troupe, sucks hard on her rolly and shouts over everyone else, 'Fuck yeah!'

I have decided that our stereo is not cutting it. We need a kick-arse ghettoblaster loud enough for us to sing over. We need to raise some cash.

Leroy Swayze, one of only three male Bitches, agrees. Today is he wearing a pair of blue knitted undies and a cropped yellow T-shirt with the words 'Danger Zone' emblazoned across his hairy chest. He looks fabulous.

Complete with sponsor cards, support crews, Snickers bars, legwarmers, glucose drinks and many changes of Lycra, we will begin our dance-a-thon at 1 p.m., bust out our moves at the newly opened Dowse Art Museum in Lower Hutt, carve up the sand on Oriental Parade, tear up the tarmac on Wellington streets and finish this celebration of dance at the San Francisco Bath House for the Dance Floor Emergency. It will be epic and no doubt exhausting.

'That is totally insane! I love it,' MaXine HendriX squeals.

MaXine has on her signature yellow g-string and blonde wig.

'What songs are we going to do?' Pearl Lusta asks. 'We have to do Poison — our fans love the bogan hits!' she adds. Pearl is from the Hutt and has great tits.

'Obviously "Pour Some Sugar on Me" — it is a great mix of filth and allows us to plumb the depths of our sluttier selves,' Leroy pipes up.

'We gotta do "Push It",' Debrelle calls out, 'for the crotch work.' She is right — the crotch work is phenomenal (some may say offensive, we say bitchin').

'Do we have anything that has transport in the lyrics? You know, if we are going on a train . . .?' Mystique asks, ever mindful of working the angles.

The angle we will really need to work is tits and teeth. The dance-a-thon is the weekend before we attempt to break the world record for the largest synchronised dance routine and we need numbers. We need hundreds, ideally thousands of people in the streets, dancing in unison to Bon Jovi's 'You Give Love a Bad Name'. We need to recruit madly. I remind the RHBs that not everyone is as comfortable as us with dancing like the world is watching. Somehow, Rosie and I have created a monster, a fame-hungry stampede of show ponies.

Luckily, the world-record attempt will take place during the Cuba Street Carnival. There will be lots of people around to coerce into watching us and shaking their booties. The beer tents will certainly help.

'Can we go in the parade?' Megatron says, clapping her hands together in her excited nineteen-year-old way.

'The parade!' Pearl breathes, her eyes gleaming at the thought of dancing down the main streets of Wellington in Spandex.

'I've done a lot of parade work before,' Randi Nights informs us. We look at her, surprised. 'I used to be in a brass band,' she explains.

That is something I am learning — the Bitches is full of very interesting people with colourful pasts.

'I can confirm we will be in the parade. We'll be with the firemen and — wait for it, Bitches — their foam cannon!'

An ear-piercing shriek rings out across the surf club.

'Hot, that is sooooo hot!' Bonnie Lee says, adjusting her mesh thong.

'We can warm up on their poles,' Bambi says. We are all looking at her in mock horror. 'You can't fight your nature . . . I don't deny it, I love hot firemen!'

Debrelle slaps her thighs and pelvic thrusts to the sky. 'When they put on the siren we can bust out our signature bitchin' crotch move!'

'We are going to have to pace ourselves, Bitches — it will be a big day,' Tiffney reminds us. 'Make sure you keep hydrated and bring some snacks.'

We all know what happens when Tiff's blood-sugar levels drop.

'Just out of interest, what is the world record for the largest synchronised dance routine?' pipes Leroy.

'According to my research, which admittedly was a quick Google search, there isn't one.'

'Really?' Coco La Chanelle questions. In her real life she is a doctor, so is used to double-checking facts.

'I am not counting a mass Highland fling in a Scottish village as our competition.'

'Too right,' Gem Wilder agrees, flexing her canary-yellow dance tights.

'In order for us to be considered for the *Guinness Book of Records* we will need to get everyone to register.'

'Awesome — that means we get to interact with our public,' says Donna Manley, arriving late.

'Exactly.'

'But so many people are scared to dance. Do you think we will get enough people to join us?' CJ Luvtodance asks the tough question as she take off her beige overcoat and reveals a purple crushed-velvet frilled leotard.

'Bitchin' 'tard, CJ,' MaXine notes as we collectively gasp at such a covetable item of clothing.

'Yip. We will buddy up with people and help them through the moves. In fact, come to think of it, it's a perfect opportunity for the single Bitches to meet men.'

'Ace, I am going to target the hotties and get my girls out,' Bambi says, squishing her ample bosom up around her chin.

'It is so great to think that through the power of dance we, the Real Hot Bitches, can change lives,' Tiffney sighs.

'Fuck yeah!' yells Debrelle. 'Less chat, more bitching!'

'OK, let's dance!'

Putting down pies and beers we make our way into the centre of the room. The floor-to-ceiling windows look right out over the beach to the dynamic Wellington South Coast. Sometimes, in winter, the rain and spray force their way through the fittings and into the club. Today the sun streams in and the room is hot. Real hot.

'Mystique, can you come to the front? I need to stand behind you and copy your moves,' I ask as we get into position for our first choreography of the afternoon. It seems some things never change. Despite running a dance troupe, I am still crap at dance.

'Let's do a run through of "You Give Love a Bad Name" first, then go back and work on the problem areas.'

'Nothing like a classic bogan anthem to get you going,' Leroy says as he makes his way to the front row.

'Eyes down, Bitches,' commands Tiffney. As the choreographer, her word is law.

Jon Bon Jovi starts singing and Tiff starts yelling instructions. 'Hands up like you have been shot . . . hands on your heart . . . You have just been shot, Bitches, so give me some eyes . . . OK, in the instrumental, stagger to your left . . . stagger right . . . stagger three-sixty degrees . . . now punch the air, like you are breaking out of your coffin . . . On the wah-wah-wah, gyrate your hips . . . OK, get ready for the first verse!'

'What you lack in technique, make up for in passion!' I call over the singing and the music.

Dancing with the Bitches always makes me happy. For two hours on a Saturday afternoon we joke, laugh and compliment each other on how fantastic our arses look in g-strings. Who cares if we are delusional?

'OK, remember the James Brown move as we die!' The song's finishing and we are dying slowly, in a heap on the ground, occasionally shaking our legs and arms to add authenticity to our death throes. (Our choreography often ends in us dying. Sometimes it is 'jazz-hands-style tableau' or, if we are really adventurous, a 'pulsing tableau'. This is extremely dramatic and always wows the fans.)

'Nice work, Bitches! That is a world-record-breaking choreo if ever there was one,' I say, clapping my hands and struggling up from the dead. 'Let's work on the other songs we need to go over for the dance-a-thon.'

We spent the rest of the afternoon perfecting our head rolls, kick-ball changes, squashing dwarfs moves, Douglas Wright sways and Wembley stadium arm-lifts.

'See you on Saturday at ten a.m. in full costume outside CJ's building. Love your work, Bitches.' I wave goodbye and lock up the surf club.

My handbag starts ringing. Ross has been away for a week and I haven't heard anything from him. He warned me not to expect daily phone calls or emails but a week . . . seven long, lonely days. I am trying to be cool but every time the phone goes I get all excited and think, Maybe this time?

I rummage around in my bag, tossing damp Lycra onto the pavement.

'Hello?'

'Hi, darling.'

'Hi! Oh, it is so good to hear your voice. How are you?'

'I'm great. I'm at work so can't chat but I am coming up next Saturday for a few days.'

'We have our dance-a-thon on — you can see me in full Bitch mode.'

'Fantastic. I look forward to it. I gotta go, I will meet you at the San Fran Bath House around nine.'

'OK, bye.'

A huge smile makes its way across my face. I look out towards the ocean. The sea is dark blue, and in the distance I can see the snow-capped Kaikoura Ranges hazy on the horizon. My boyfriend (yes, I really do have one) is coming to see me!

I flick my g-string up off the tarseal, mount my bicycle and pedal home.

Make-up is running into my eyes, my feet are aching inside my shimmery blue boots and my wig is slowly slipping off my head. We are ten hours into the dance-a-thon and I am halfway through Prince's 'U Got the Look'.

Debrelle is hollering on her loudhailer 'You're hot!' to any even vaguely attractive man who dares to cross our path. Gem Wilder's boom box is chewing through the D batteries, and she is developing ghettoblaster shoulder. 'Come on, Bitches — only two hours to go. We need to have ten bitches dancing at all times,' I say, trying to enthuse the exhausted troupe. We aren't used to dancing for longer than twenty minutes at a stretch.

'I need a drink,' Leroy sighs, saying out loud what we are all secretly thinking.

'Let's drag-run to Mighty Mighty,' MaXine suggests.

'Yeah, great idea, ready, let's go!' the troupe choruses, taking off down Cuba Street.

'Thank fuck for that!' Gem says as she swings the ghetto-blaster down on the bar. We order a round of tequila shots, slug them back and head to the dance floor. The intro starts for 'I Was Made for Loving You'. This has become my new favourite routine, as it reminds me of Ross and that night on the boat. I throw myself into the moves, lip-synching for all I am worth, then I feel someone staring at me — not the usual fan worship but a softer, kinder, more 'checking me out' kind of gaze.

Scanning the crowd, I see Ross. I can't believe my eyes — he isn't due to arrive for another two hours! I wave to him but, ever the semi-professional dancer, I finish the song and then race to the bar.

'Wow, that was scary — you guys are crazy,' he laughs.

'I think you mean we look amazing!'

'Come here,' he says, pulling me close and planting a kiss on my lips. 'You look great, Ange — the wig really works for you, and the Lycra, wow!' I can't tell if he is taking the piss or not.

'I've gotta get back, but I'll catch up with you in a few hours. I'm so pleased you're here!'

'Who's that, Ange?' Desiree Knightshade asks as I return to the sweaty bosom of the troupe. 'Is that Ross?' Desiree is one of my oldest friends and when she isn't dressed in Lycra she answers to Gabe.

'Yeah, that's him.'

'He looks like a great match for you. I love the tie.'

We look over at Ross, who looks like a man from a bygone era. A frock coat will do that. He is now sipping a beer and watching the spectacle of ten women in wigs, leotards and piles of make-up slapping their butts. A bemused look creeps across his face.

'I think he's a keeper,' I answer.

The dance-a-thon finally ended with aching limbs and bloodied heels. But it wasn't until three years later, outside the Christchurch Cathedral, that we actually broke the world record.

8

Saddle Up

—✦—

'We'll be at World's End in half an hour,' Ross says, looking up from the chart. A light breeze fills the sails as the pine-covered hills slowly glide by. I am sitting in the stern of *Astra*, Ross' yacht, holding the tiller.

'Watch the wind indicator, Ange — you want to be just on the wind. Bring her round a little to starboard.'

This is the start of our first-ever holiday together. We are on our way to Ngawhakawhiti Bay in the Marlborough Sounds for two weeks of good times — before Ross heads off to circumnavigate the South Island.

'Which side is starboard again?' I call back, getting flustered. Steering with a tiller is confusing. It isn't like a car — you have to push it in the opposite direction to the way you want to go.

'Pull it towards you, Ange.'

'Thanks, sorry . . . these nautical terms are tricky. I promise I'll nail them by the end of the holiday.'

He raises his eyebrows in disbelief. I have never been on a boat (unless you count the *Spirit of Adventure* when I was fifteen, which I don't because I was too busy ogling the boys from exotic places like Auckland). It is like learning a foreign language.

'Fizzboat fine on the port bow,' Ross says, alerting me to the speed boat ahead of us. 'Hold your course, speed gives way to sail.'

'Aye aye, Captain,' I call back. Earlier he had told me that poor communication sinks ships. I don't want that on my conscience, plus it's a great laugh saying 'Aye aye, Captain.'

'To think that only a hundred and twenty years ago all this land would have been covered in native forest,' Ross says. Now, the steep hills are places where a few scraggly sheep eke out a meagre existence.

The Marlborough Sounds are rich with stories, Maori tales of great daring by chiefs who waged raids on other tribes and of maidens swimming across bays to visit their lovers. Enormous schools of whales used to migrate into the sheltered bays to give birth. That was before greedy whalers decimated them, before European settlers arrived and introduced pigs and rats and disease.

Ross knows the stories, and as we pass coves and bays and rocks he tells them to me. I fall even more in love with him.

The sun is frying my back as I lie on the deck. Squinting out of one eye I can see the clear turquoise sea as it slaps against the hull. The white topsides of the yacht make my eyes smart. I pull my hat down further and slink under the beam of shade the mast has created.

Braving the glare, I survey the bay. Tiny translucent jellyfish occasionally break the surface and undulate slowly away. There's no one else here, just Ross and me. Down in the galley the sound of corn fritters sizzling in the pan makes my mouth water.

'Do you want some of these? Classic boat food!' Ross calls up the hatch.

My stomach is grumbling. All this relaxing is making me hungry.

'You bet.'

He appears, holding the beaten-up frypan in one hand and a cask of wine in the other. A 2-litre box of Country Red, to be exact.

'That wine had better taste like mother's milk,' I laugh.

My thighs and butt are aching from bike-riding 60 kilo-metres the day before. Our booze supplies were depleted and in desperation we had made a foray into the nearest town of Rai Valley, via the Opouri Saddle. I have done a fair bit of cycling in my time, but Ross is better than me (he is better than me at everything, except finding things). He was hardened to the near-vertical hill that lay between us and booze.

Arriving five minutes late for the supermarket, we have been reduced to begging at the local pub.

'Do you have any bottles of wine I could buy off you?' I ask the well-muscled barman, my grubby bike shorts making an shwak-shwak sound as I walk in. He looks me up and down.

'Nope, sorry — we don't have much call for wine round here,' he replies, casting his eyes down at his copy of *Best Bets*.

'Thanks anyway.' I glance up at a huge deer's head looming over the top shelf, its amber eyes keeping watch over rows of beer mugs engraved with names like 'Killer', 'Speck', 'Moose' and 'Ghandi'. I can see his point — not many delicate wine-sippers there.

'Al, does the sheila want wine?' a woman's voice hollers from out the back.

'Yeeep,' Al squeezes out of the corner of his mouth.

'I've got a cask here of some red stuff,' she yells back. My eyes light up. After three hours on the bike in the hot sun I am determined not to go home empty-handed.

'How much do you want for it?' I ask the faceless voice.

'Fifty bucks,' she says, coming around behind the bar, her tobacco-stained fingers holding up the cask.

'Are you serious? Fifty bucks for a cask of Country Red?'

'You can take it or leave it.' She is a hard arse, a no-time-for-city-folk country woman.

'Hang on.' I start fishing out sweaty notes from inside my bra. Ross has the wallet and is down the other end of the street trying his luck at the service station.

'I can give you twenty,' I say, counting out the notes on the bar.

'Fifty bucks or you can bugger off,' she says, sizing me up.

'All right, keep your hair on.' I pull out one of my father's favourite phrases and look her directly in the eye.

She gives me a sideways look. Perhaps I'm not the city slicker she thought.

'Where you from?'

'We're out near Duncan Bay, on our boat.' I consciously don't use the word yacht.

'Doing some fishing?'

'Um, not really.'

'There's that crazy ban on the blue cod round there, eh?' she says, opening a new packet of Rothmans. The thin plastic covering falls on the ground.

'Yeah, we are having a break from fishing.' Fudge the truth — she doesn't need to know that, given the state of the world's fish stocks, we find the thought of fishing abhorrent.

She nods. 'How much ya got here then, love?' she says as she begins picking up the sweaty money.

'Twenty bucks.'

'All right, that'll do. You fellas biked a long way for it.'

'Thanks. We've gotta get back before dark.' I grab the cask before she has time to change her mind.

'Have a good one — I wouldn't want to be on that road at night.'

Safely outside and feeling triumphant at procuring the booze, I wheel my bike to the road and wait for Ross. This 'holiday' is more like a boot camp. So far we have run the Nydia Track six times, regularly swum across the bay, kayaked for whole days to secluded beaches, and now we have to turn around and bike 27 kilometres back to the yacht! Despite being totally knackered I can't let this forty-five-year-old beat me. It is on this 'holiday' that we become competitive exercisers. I do it to get thin, Ross does it because he likes it.

Two hours later we are carrying our bikes over gnarled roots in the gloaming. As we negotiate a slippery creek I see for the first time in my life a bird whose song I had often heard. Ruru was heralding the darkness.

'Ross, look!' I whisper. 'Just there, on the branch.'

'Wow.'

'It's so much smaller than I imagined.'

'Ru-ru,' it calls again. Ross and I stand perfectly still, grinning, our teeth white in the half light.

'It'll be dark soon. We better keep moving.'

Five minutes later we are at the water's edge, slapping away the namu attacking our ankles and piling ourselves and our bikes into the dinghy.

The thought of a glass of wine had kept my spirits up on the long ride back, but now, as Ross rows us home, all I want to do is sleep.

That was yesterday. Today we are relaxing: no running, no biking and the only swimming is around the boat to cool down.

'*Salute*,' Ross says, taking a large swig of wine. 'Phew . . . that is rough.'

I look at the cask. I look at my watch. It is 11 a.m. . . . . too early for wine?

'Ah what the hell, we are on holiday. *Salute!*'

Corn fritters and red wine on our very own pleasure craft. I could get used to this.

'So, Ange, what are your hopes and dreams?'

I am beginning to understand that Ross isn't one to shy away from the big issues.

My stomach flips. I don't have the courage to say that my hopes and dreams revolve around him. Instead, 'I want to live in Scandinavia' comes falling out of my mouth.

'Saunas, flaying yourself with fir branches and eating gravlax, great design . . . and the people are all gorgeous.'

'Scandinavia?'

'Yeah.' What have I just said? Even though we are on holiday together, the words 'I don't want a girlfriend' are never far from my thoughts. I am being cautious, perhaps too cautious. Time to get the heat off me.

'OK, so what are your hopes and dreams, Ross?' I challenge him.

'I want to have a child, with you.'

Eight words. That's all.

I thought I had been so careful. I had never spoken about babies and wanting them. I kept news of friends' pregnancies to a passing comment. How had he read my mind?

'Really?' I say, my eyes suddenly pricking with tears.

'Yes, Ange. I love being with you, I want you in my life, you're kind and generous and funny and I know you would be a wonderful mother.' Years of worry and anguish begin melting away. I feel sick with excitement. At last, I could actually start imagining my life with him in it . . .

'I would love to be with you—' I can't believe I am saying out loud the words I had practised saying in the mirror. '— have a child and share adventures,' I say, crying happy tears.

'What about Scandinavia?'

'Plenty of time for that,' I say, standing up and dive-bombing off the side.

Unlike most people who share hopes and dreams, we go our separate ways. I go back to Wellington and Ross ups the anchor and sets sail for a three-month circumnavigation of the South Island.

9
Masculine Ego-Building

'The cockpit's blue,' I shout
into my headset.
'Are you sure he's here?'
the pilot shouts back.
I am on a tiny float-plane
flying into Doubtful Sound
to meet Ross.

'No, no, I'm not sure, but we made a plan two months ago to meet here so I am holding up my end of the deal,' I say, trying to make a joke. If he isn't here this is a very expensive wild-goose chase.

'I dropped some hunters off here earlier today and I didn't see any yachts, love.'

My heart sinks. I don't have a back-up plan if he isn't here. Trev, the pilot, seems like a good stick — maybe I can stay with him. In the thirty-minute ride from Te Anau we have discussed, in great detail, the dismal state of his love life: nasty divorce, dramas with caravans and the new girlfriend.

The landscape is full of dark green valleys and sheer running cliffs. It reminds me of the opening shot of *The Piano*. Looking down at the black sea, I imagine Ross sailing into the long sounds and anchoring in one of the arms, out of the wind, and waiting for me to arrive.

'What's that?' I say, pointing at a tiny speck of white and blue below us. 'Is that a moored yacht?'

'Yeah, it is. It wasn't here earlier — is that your bloke's?'

My breath hits the icy glass as I peer out the window and it fogs up. 'Ummmm, I don't know . . . Does that look like a thirty-three-foot yacht to you?'

From 10,000 feet up it's difficult to tell. 'I'll take a closer look.'

'Great, thanks.'

My heart is pounding. I haven't seen him for two months, and a lot can happen in two months, like I could have lost five kilos and he could have totally changed his mind. I had done what I could and spent the time exercising like mad, trying to shave off inches. Fingers crossed he hadn't changed his mind.

'I think there is someone on deck, love,' Trev says, turning to me with a big grin.

'Yes, yes, that's him! He is here!' I turn to the pilot and give him a high-five.

'OK, I'll bring her down.' We swoop and come in to land gracefully on the water. I feel like a movie star, like Katie Holmes going to see Tom Cruise on location. Deep Cove is home to an adventure centre, a few fishing boats and a top-heavy vessel with three masts that takes tourists on overnight excursions around some of the most spectacular scenery on earth. It is full of good southern men, who go for days without seeing anyone other than their dogs. They wear muddy-green bush shirts that come down to their knees and don't suffer namby-pamby fools. Thousands of tiny black sandflies make their attacks religiously at dawn and dusk. Only the hardiest can survive.

Ross is rowing towards the float plane. His back is straining as he pulls on the oars. It is cold, clear and incredibly beautiful. I have been imagining this moment for weeks, and have dressed accordingly in my multi-coloured adidas trainers. However practical polar-fleece-lined hiking boots may be in the subantarctic, I am seeing my future husband for the first time in two months and I intend to make an impression.

With one last heave on the oars, Ross makes it to the plane. He throws me the painter. I fumble about with it and attempt to tie a bowline around the float.

'You look wonderful,' he says as I throw my backpack into the dinghy and attempt, unsuccessfully, to get in after it. I really must work on that if I am to spend my life with a sailor.

'You look shattered!' I say, leaning across the thwart and giving him a much needed hug.

'Thanks, Trev! I owe ya. Good luck with the ladies, and remember, dating before mating!' I call back to the pilot as we row towards *Astra*.

We get on board, crack open one of the three bottles of wine I have brought and Ross holds me close. 'Everything I said in Ngawhakawhiti is still absolutely rock-solid, baby.'

'Same. But Ross, if we are going to have a family, I want to be married.' I had made a promise to myself years ago that I wasn't going to move in with anyone or have kids with anyone who wasn't prepared to marry me.

'Are you asking me to marry you?'

'No, I'm just saying that is what I would like.'

'OK, I'll think about it.'

Ross had spent twenty years married to Stephanie. He had much more experience with marriage and kids than I did, and he knew what he was getting into. I could understand his desire to think about it. Me, I am all white dresses and cute cosy cottages with his-and-hers bath towels.

Bang . . . bang . . . bang . . . this is no alarm clock or shag-fest.

'Are they gun shots?' I say, opening my eyes. I begin patting the bed, searching for my watch. I don't know why I need to know the time — gunshots are gunshots irrespective of light levels. My watch reads 6.50 a.m.

'Bang! Bang!' They sound much closer.

We are anchored in Crooked Arm, with ten metres of water and a cloud of sandflies between us and the shore. What is going on?

I go straight into worst-case-scenario mode. Is someone shooting at us? We could easily be murdered out here in this incredibly beautiful yet very, very isolated place. Are wild mountain men plotting to come on board, overpower us with the smell of their unwashed, unshaven bodies, strip us naked and leave us outside to the mercy of the sandflies? I take it further. We would have to beg for bug spray. Then, in our weakened state they would rob us of ... um ... cans of tomatoes and bags of pasta?

'Ross, wake up — I think someone is shooting at us!' I say, shaking him awake.

'What?' He sleepily rubs his eyes.

'Listen!'

Bang ... bang ... bang.

'Oh, that. It's the roar. It's just some hunters in the next valley — the sound travels for miles here. It's OK darling, lie down.'

I lie back down, pulling the heavy feather duvet up under my chin, and snuggle into Ross' arms. Despite my overactive imagination I love being out here. When I returned from London I promised myself that I would spend more time outdoors, hiking, horse riding, camping. An old boyfriend once described me as a peppermint tea and pumpernickel kind of girl (he, of course, was a champagne and cocaine man). At the time I thought he was being a total wanker, likening me to some washed-out hippy, but now as I lie next to the man of my dreams in a part of the world that few people have ever had the privilege of seeing, I am pleased I'm not snorting lines of coke off a shitty loo in South London. I slip back to sleep happily.

Before long, the buzz of sandflies wakes us. I crawl out of the tiny forepeak cabin and open the hatch. A brilliant blue sky and crisp, chill air greet me. The cliffs look like an Ansel Adams litho print, with their huge shadows and stark white crevasses. It is my last day, and again I am saying good bye. Each day we spend together makes me love him more. This voyage of masculine ego-building had better be worth it, I think.

'I love you, Ross.'

'I love you too, Angela. I will be back in May and I'll have had enough of the sea by then. I'll be well up for the comforts of home.'

'Think about what I said, about marriage,' I say quietly.

'I will.'

On the plane back to Wellington I stop myself from imagining him being swamped by an enormous wave and drowning. I am so close to motherhood and marriage.

10
Strawberry Letter 23

—————

'I am engaged!' I squeal down the phone to my mother.

'It would have been nice if he'd asked your father.'

'Mum, we are not living in the fifties!'

'We don't even really know this man, Angela, and isn't he divorced?' my mother replies, less than impressed.

'Mum, I am engaged, I am very happy!' I repeat. Ever since I was a girl I had prised her rings from her fingers and imagined the day I would have my own.

'He came back, I take it.' She can't help herself; she has to get the knife in.

'Yes.' There was a long pause.

'Congratulations, darling, I am happy for you,' she says through what I hope are not gritted teeth.

'We'll be up over the weekend and we can talk more then,' I say, ready to finish the conversation and determined her less than enthusiastic response is not going to spoil my mood.

For the last hour I have been an engaged lady. Ross' voyage of masculine ego-building is over. He is back from circumnavigating the South Island and the first thing he did was ask me to marry him. I am ecstatic.

'What did she say?' Ross asks.

'Oh, you know, she is concerned you're divorced.' My mother is Catholic, not a feast-day-and-funeral Catholic but an every-single-Sunday Catholic. 'Divorce is fine for other people, but I think the fact that her eldest daughter is marrying a divorcee who is thirteen years older than her and doesn't have a job is a bit to take in,' I explain, trying not to make my mother sound like an old-fashioned prude. (She isn't — she is an absolute darling, but she is not good with surprises.)

'Ange, I am not getting married in a church. Absolutely no way. The thought of it sends shivers up my spine.'

Ross is an atheist. He can debate the non-existence of God for hours in an erudite, extremely convincing way. I, however, grew up doing liturgical dance on the altar of St Patrick's Cathedral to John Farnham's 'Age of Reason'.

Liturgical dance often involves tie-dyed scarves, tambourines, long, flowing robes, and a slightly mental look in your eyes. Back in 1990 I was a believer. I was a Eucharist-eating, reconciliation-receiving, scripture-reading, altar-serving girl. (Interesting factoid: I was one of the first *ever* girl altar-servers in Australasia.) I spent fourteen years saying night-time prayers which started 'God bless Mummy, Daddy, Charlotte, Emily and Alice, and Sam King Arthur Meyer Pebbles John, the cat.' It didn't occur to me to not believe in God.

So, when Father Vince, the new young priest in town who drove a Volkswagen VW, had frosted hair and liked going surfing, was putting together a youth group, I signed up. Palm Sunday was the first event on the youth-group calendar and Father Vince wanted something spectacular to wow the congregation.

'Right everyone, listen to this,' Vince says, hitting play on the tinny stereo. (He was so cool we didn't have to call him Father.)

Tick . . . tick . . . tick . . . tick . . . The sound of a clock ticking filled the parish lounge. What was this song? Some new-fangled Christian rock. Does the ticking symbolise counting down the days until the Second Coming?

Then John Farnham begins to sing 'Age of Reason'.

I look at my friend Heidi and we snicker. John Farnham? Please, I may be a believer but cut me some slack. John Farnham! 'God, I hate it when adults try to be "hip",' I whisper to her.

'What do you think, kids?' Vince says as the song finishes. 'Great lyrics, great beat — I think we can work up a really grouse dance routine.' I cringe; more 'trying to be cool' from a man of the cloth.

'Come on, let's get started,' he says, bouncing up from his cross-legged position on the floor. We drag ourselves up off the couches and soon Vince has us in position on the altar.

'We will start from a rock pose, everyone down.' That's more like it, I think, striking a rock-star pose. 'No, Angela, I want you to imagine you are a rock . . . on the ground.' Why oh why does every liturgical dance have to start by pretending to be a rock?

'On the tick-tick in the music, I want to see trees . . . palm trees,' he instructs us. We slowly 'grow' from the rocks (surely we should have been seeds) and as the lyrics kick in we extend our arms above our heads and wave them around. (On reflection, the tree and rock motif are big in biblical literature — it is no surprise they made their way into this choreography.) Heidi and I exchange glances. She is a legendary giggler, so I bite my cheeks to stop myself laughing . . .

'OK, stop, that is not working. We need something more dramatic,' he says, taking off outside. We watch him through the stained-glass windows as he runs about searching frantically for something. (Another religious motif?) Finally he picks up a fallen Phoenix palm frond and heads back to the church. We race back into position as he comes through the side door.

'Here, try this,' he says, handing the half-decomposed frond to me. 'Wave it above your head in big sweeping moves.'

I do as I am told and lift up the heavy frond. Bits of dirt and insects come falling out and scatter all over the pale green carpet. (St Pat's had a makeover in the 1980s and to this day sports an attractive pastel colour scheme.)

'Ewwwww, yuck, I don't want to put this over my head!'

'Just try it, Angela. I want to see what it looks like. Remember, it is Palm Sunday, after all.'

I'm in the house of the Lord and I don't want to fight with his emissary on earth.

'All right,' I say, lifting it up and waving it around. There's no denying it, it looks dramatic.

'Wow, that looks great, don't you think, kids?'

'Umm, yeah,' mutter my fellow liturgical dancers.

'We are all going to have palm fronds, I'll bring them on Sunday. But first we have a dance to rehearse!'

Two hours later, John Farnham's 'Age of Reason' has been transformed into the parable of Palm Sunday. Oh yes, now we have Jesus arriving on a donkey, fronds being laid down the aisle, and eight fourteen-year-old girls dancing on the altar. It has all the ingredients to go horribly wrong.

Which is exactly what happens four days later at the packed 10 a.m. Sunday Mass. Vince is dressed in his priestly robes, his hair freshly frosted. I have on my new stone-washed jeans, and my family are all in the front pew. Everything is going well . . . until liturgical dance time.

We move quietly out of our seats and assume the 'rock' position on the altar. Suddenly the utter ridiculousness of what I'm about to do dawns on me, and I start giggling. I can see my mother out of the corner of my eye, giving me 'the glare'. This only makes it worse. A snort escapes out of my nostrils.

Oh shit, the music has started. Now I have to pretend to be a tree. I look to my left — Heidi is shaking. Oh no, there is no stopping Heidi once she gets an attack of the giggles. I keep my eyes forward and try to breathe through it. I am sucking my cheeks for all they were worth but it is no good. I *have* to laugh . . .

There are two hundred people looking at me while I attempt to grow into a Phoenix palm . . . I can barely stand up straight, let alone pick up a frond . . . Pwerfffffffffff . . . I double over trying to disguise my laughter.

I can see my mother. Oh my God, I am going to be in so much trouble. It's as if I have been possessed by . . . um . . . the devil? Oh shit . . . now Father Vince is looking at Heidi and me.

The thing about liturgical dance is that there is no backstage — you can't drag-run off to the side, you are on the *altar* — and we still have two minutes thirty-three of the song to go.

Somehow we manage to muddle through Jesus' triumphal entry into Jerusalem but as we slink back to our seats the spirit of forgiveness is nowhere to be seen on our mothers' faces.

Remembering this particularly embarrassing moment, I concede. 'I don't care if we get married in a church or not, darling.'

'Great, so long as we have a big party.'

'Maybe the Bitches can dance us down the aisle!' I say, getting excited.

'I'll get the champagne!' Ross says, making his way to the fridge.

Two hours later we have set a date for 25 October 2008 and are well on the way to planning our 'Ladies a Plate, Men a Crate' wedding.

'Ange, try this on,' Mum says, holding up my grandmother's wedding dress, a beautiful champagne-coloured 1930s style gown. 'My sisters and I used to play dress-ups in it when we were kids. There are a few tiny holes in the train but I am sure we could get them repaired.'

'Oh I don't know, Mum, it looks tiny. Nana was hardly a fat chops.'

'Just try it, darling.'

'OK, why not?'

'Apparently it wasn't just Nana who wore this dress — three other women in the district wore it too,' Mum continues as I gingerly slip the beautiful embroidered dress over my head. 'Money was tight, and there was little sense in getting only one wear out of it.'

I love this idea — it is totally in keeping with our theory of positive poverty (see page 115).

The seventy-year-old satin feels cool on my skin. 'It's beautiful,' I say, smoothing down the fabric.

'Oh, Ange, you look gorgeous!'

I can't believe it. It's a perfect fit, as if the dress had been tailor-made for me. Sure, I have more junk in the trunk than Nana, but actually, it works.

'I would love to wear this, Mum, it would be an honour.'

'You should, darling, you look lovely.' We hug and I breathe in the wonderful comforting smell of my mother.

'We can pick out some support wear later,' she says, giving me a gentle pat on my guts.

The wedding day arrives; I get up early and jog along the beach. Looking out at the ocean the sea is flat, the air clean and bracing and the sky slightly overcast. Today's the day. I'm getting married, and I know from now on large portions of my life will be spent on the sea.

Friends and family had helped us the day before, decorating the hall with streamers and balloons and flowers. The banner I have embroidered is hanging on the stage: 'Cherish Till We Perish' is our touchstone and is the first thing you see when you walk into the Paekakariki Hall.

Ross is going to sing me down the aisle, to his version of Madonna's 'Cherish'. Charlotte has spent hours making our wedding cake, which is finished with a pirate ship. We have about one hundred and fifty people coming to celebrate our wedding, and instead of speeches we have asked friends to perform in a cabaret-style showcase. We have even met Mum halfway and have a renegade Catholic priest lined up to officiate. This is a team effort, and we are very, very grateful.

'I, Angela Maree Meyer, take you, Ross Alex Humphries, to be my lawfully wedded companion. To have and to hold from this day forward; for better, for worse; for richer, for poorer; in sickness and in health; to love and to cherish, till death do us part. To you I pledge my love.'

And with that we are married.

The opening chords of 'Strawberry Letter 23' begin and the stage area that is doubling as an altar swarms with Bitches. They dance us down the aisle as the champagne corks pop.

Ross and I beam at each other. Our life together is about to begin.

11

A Slap
on the
Hand

There are three of us in our marriage: Ross, me and *Astra*. I have underestimated how demanding his mistress will be.

'**I** have to get off the boat. Can you come and get me?' I beg down the phone. 'We are anchored in Scorching Bay. It has been terrible — I haven't stopped vomiting for the last nine hours. Can you bring me a lemonade ice block? I am going to swim to the shore, please . . .'

The phone drops from my hand as I flop back onto the bunk and dry retch. Again.

Ross is on deck. Whitecaps are breaking all over the place and I feel like dying. I have had my fair share of vomity hangovers but this is a new level of dehydration. At five months pregnant I am starting to despair. Maybe I am going to be one of those women who are ill for the whole nine months? Maybe this is God's way of punishing me for being pregnant on my wedding day.

Earlier in the week I had decided to ask my midwife for help. On my walk to work I realised I knew exactly how many steps it was between rubbish bins: I knew the discreet, out-of-the-way bins for a quiet spit; I knew the path through the university that had particularly lush bushes to hide any upchuckings; and I had a stash of loose change in my desk drawer for emergency purchases of lemonade ice blocks.

And it wasn't just the mornings, it was all day.

'Angela, we wouldn't give you anti-nausea pills if they were dangerous. You need to be able to eat — your baby needs you to be well,' my midwife tells me as I lie on the bed with needles poking out of my head and wrists.

Images of Thalidomide babies haunt me, acupuncture does nothing, homeopathy's a joke and no amount of ginger tea can settle my stomach. In fact, it churns it right up.

The familiar feeling of nausea is beginning its next wave and, exhausted, I give in.

'OK, pass me the pills,' I say weakly.

I pop the little white pill on my tongue and, with my fingers crossed over my belly, I swallow it down. Twenty minutes later I'm hungry. I'm cured!

That was four days ago. Armed with the pills I'm full of hubris, full of 'I can still do everything I want to even though I am pregnant. I don't need to slow down. Sure, let's catch the ferry across Cook Strait to the Marlborough Sounds, bike 20 kilometres in the dark, pick up the yacht and sail her back to Wellington.'

Now, lying on the bunk, I'm going into ketosis.

'Get the wetsuit out for me please, Ross. I have to get off the boat.'

'You can't swim to the shore. I know it is not far but you can't stand up, let alone swim anywhere. Once the wind dies down I will pump up the inflatable and row you to shore.'

I crawl up the companionway and sit in the cockpit. The Chocolate Fish café is so close I can make out the signs on the toilets (yes, I'm looking wistfully at toilets). If I can only get to land I know I will feel better.

I grip the side of the cockpit and try to stand up. I retch again, horrible foamy green stuff. I honestly do not care; it dribbles down my chin and onto my top.

'Oh, darling, come on, lie down here.' Ross hugs me and wipes the beads of sweat off my brow with the back of his grubby sailing glove.

Suffice to say, the crossing had been a nightmare.

We had arrived at *Astra* two nights ago. She was anchored in Port Underwood, waiting for us to sail her back to Wellington. We went to pull up the stern anchor. It wouldn't budge. The winch was grinding as hard as it could but nothing was happening.

Ross peered into the water. 'I'll let the mooring go and turn her around, see if that makes a difference,' he called to me. *Astra* came around and again we tried the winch. Nothing.

'It must be stuck down really deep in the mud. I'll keep trying, maybe that will loosen her.'

The morning ticked by. We kept trying the anchor, it kept not moving. Finally, at low tide Ross was able to dive down into the murky water to check.

'It's not mud, it's fishing junk,' he called from the water. Old lines, bits of net and rusty chunks of metal had caught around it and were in no hurry to let go.

I handed him a knife and offered moral support from the deck.

I watched as he dived down and thought how happy I was to have married a capable, able-to-fix-most-things kind of man. He made me laugh, he made me think and he loved a challenge. This was a man on which a woman could safely lean. I was excited about having a baby and, as he came up for air and handed me the knife, I day-dreamed about all the adventures we would have together.

I'm not a born sailor but I figured that with practice I would overcome the seasickness and be able to stand shoulder to shoulder with Ross as the winds blew us across the world's great oceans. Our children would grow up with the sea as their playground, their skins bronzed by the sun. I would spend all day in a bikini and our bank accounts would always be in the black.

Eight hours later, we finally managed to manually haul up the anchor and motor out of Port Underwood. As we turned north I took the first watch. It was a beautiful clear night, with lots of stars, and the tiller wasn't too heavy. I kept my eyes on the horizon and at any signs of chunder I sucked in large breaths of good, cold sea air. But my body betrayed me.

'Sorry, darling, I'm really tired, I need to lie down,' I called down to Ross at 10 p.m., two hours before I was due to come off watch. I was losing my battle with nausea. I went down below and braced myself on one of the bunks.

I don't really remember much about the night or the following morning; I know I felt terrible and that the only thing that made me feel better was to lie very still with my eyes shut. I couldn't hold anything down and I was counting the hours until we got to Wellington.

But when we came into Wellington Harbour the wind clobbered us. It was gusting 45 to 50 knots, creating a confused, rough sea. Morning sickness melded into seasickness.

'Get on deck *now*, Angela!' Ross bellowed at me.

I woke up, dazed and groggy.

'*Now!*' he shouted again.

I stumbled onto the deck.

'Take the tiller. Push it over to you *now!*'

I looked up; we were about 200 metres from the shore — and not a nice sandy beach but *rocks*. The wind was so strong it was pushing us onto them.

Ross had been desperately trying to gybe; the sails were flogging everywhere and even with the motor going full tilt he couldn't get her to come around. He needed me on deck to hold the tiller while he tried to get the mainsail down. I summoned all my strength and leant heavily on the tiller. We were getting closer and closer.

'Brace yourself, Ange,' he instructed me in a captainly fashion.

I was still vomiting uncontrollably. I thought maybe the adrenaline would cancel out the nausea but it only made it worse.

We were so close to the shore that I could see the faces of the people in their cars as they went for a Sunday drive around the bays. At least there are people around to help drag me out of the water, I thought.

'OK, Ange, get ready, brace yourself!' Ross shouted back at me, still struggling with the main.

And then, just as we thought our boat was going to be bashed onto the rocks, he managed to haul the sail down and we headed back out into the middle of the harbour. Ross clambered into the cockpit and took the tiller.

'Fuck, Ange, that was really close.' His eyes were wide and he looked like he does when I know I should just shut up and keep out of the way. All I could think about was lying down again. 'We are going back towards Scorching Bay and I'll drop the hook there. We can't get up the harbour in this. It's too strong.'

Oh, thank God, I thought as I lay down again. Not long now . . .

Charlotte arrives just on dusk. I am sitting on the bench outside the toilets, waiting. Ross, dressed in his foul-weather gear, sits next to me as I rest my head on his shoulder. Already I am feeling better.

'Ange, you look terrible. I think you need more than lemonade — here, have some Gatorade,' Charlotte says, handing me the blue liquid. 'Come on, I'll help you to the car.'

I wave goodbye to Ross as he rows back out to *Astra*. He's going to spend the night on board and bring her round to Chaffers Marina in the morning.

We drive very slowly home. Charlotte pushes in one of her mix-tapes and Stevie Nicks starts playing.

Alice, my youngest sister, opens the door to the flat we all share.

'Right, into bed.' She ushers me into my bedroom, helps me undress and puts a bowl next to the bed.

The soft, clean, cool sheets are bliss. I sip on the Gatorade.

Alice is studying nursing and while she is very compassionate she doesn't put up with any silly nonsense.

'I feel OK now, Alice, just sore and tired.'

'Right,' she says in a disbelieving way.

'I just need to sleep.'

'Right,' she says again.

I know she thinks I am crazy for going sailing when I am pregnant. I shut my eyes.

'Call me if you need anything in the night,' she says as she gives me a kiss and turns off the light.

Instead of a deep, restful sleep, I got vomiting with a vengeance.

By 9 a.m. the next morning I'm lying on the couch, doubled over. Alice takes one look at me and says, 'You think you're fine but actually you're fucked,' and calls my midwife.

'Yes, all night, yes . . . that's right, nothing is staying down . . . OK, I will bring her in. See you in an hour.' She hangs up. 'Ange, you are going to hospital.'

Forty minutes later I'm sitting in a cubicle in Wellington Hospital as a nurse slaps me on the wrist. She's trying to find a vein.

'So it has been thirty-two hours of non-stop vomiting.'

'Hmmm,' I say, sucking my teeth as she gives my hand another slap.

'Why didn't you come in sooner?'

I didn't want to admit to being so stupid as to have gone sailing. 'I kept thinking I would come right,' I say, which wasn't an all-out lie.

'She has been sailing, across Cook Strait,' Charlotte announces.

I glare at her. The nurse raises her eyebrows 'Oh . . . I see . . . one of *those* mothers.'

No one has called me a mother before; I hadn't really thought of myself like that. I thought of myself as a woman who happened to be pregnant. It was another four months before I'd be a mother.

I don't bother to ask what she means. It is obvious: I am a selfish cow who is putting her own desires before the needs of her child.

She gives my hand another slap, harder this time, and jabs a needle into the vein.

The drip is in and I am moved into a room. Six litres of fluid are pumped into me. With each millilitre my skin plumps up and I begin to feel better.

Ross arrives in the afternoon.

'Hi, hon, check it out — my own room!' I smile, trying to be chirpy.

'Nice, Ange.'

'Did it go OK, getting *Astra* into the marina?'

'Yes, she's fine. But how are you feeling?'

'Better, but all my muscles ache. I'm still not hungry.'

He sits on the bed and puts his hand on my stomach. 'And the baby?'

'It's fine. They say this sickness business is a good sign and it looks like I am going to be sick for the whole nine months. I can come in once a week for a fluid top-up, though,' I laugh.

We hug. His strong, warm arms hold me tight and then he has to go. He is catching a plane to Christchurch in an hour and he will be there for the next six weeks.

Six weeks seems like an eternity. Ross has never been one for mobile phones so it isn't as if I can give him a quick call when I am missing him — and I am sure I am going to really miss him. This is my first baby and I obsessively check on the developmental milestones . . . This week the baby is growing . . . eyebrows! . . . Next week the heart and lungs! I know Ross isn't really that interested in all that, though; he has two daughters and has been through all of this before.

'Okay, darling, I will call you tomorrow. Get some rest,' he says as he backs out of the room.

'Give my love to Doreen.'

His mother is having heart surgery the next day and he is going to help her recover.

While I spend the next six weeks growing our baby, Ross starts planning an adventure.

Next to the photograph of Holly and Nina in the salon of *Astra* is an old chart of the Pacific. Someone has drawn swaying palm trees on it in coloured pencils. It is the record of someone else's dream. Carefully ruled lines mark the passages, by both date and nautical miles travelled. They made good time in 1964.

I had entertained the idea of 'going sailing around the world, OMG wouldn't that be *amaaaaazing*' in my early twenties. This was when I was busy hitching around Japan, taking slow boats to China and smoking opium in Vietnam. This is when I was young, carefree, childless, and didn't worry about mere trifles like money or personal safety.

Going sailing with Ross is my way of holding on to this adventurous side while I negotiate the transition into being a wife and mother. The map is our the reminder that the Pacific is there, waiting to be sailed. And to do this we have a plan; well, actually, we have three plans:

- Plan A — buy a boat in America or the Caribbean and sail it via the Panama Canal across the Pacific, stopping at tropical islands along the way and then eventually, once we are all very tanned, make it to Brisbane, tie up on the poles in the river, live on board for a while then sell the boat for twice what we paid for her and live happily ever after.
- Plan B — reconfigure *Astra* and sail to the Pacific. A good second option but *Astra* will need at least $20,000 sunk into her to get her up to Category One standard for sailing offshore.
- Plan C — reconfigure *Astra* and sail around New Zealand for a year. This is the easiest and cheapest option but the least attractive. Ross has already circumnavigated New Zealand and, frankly, the weather is a bit shit.

All we know is that come 2011 we will be sailing. Now we just have to do it, make it happen.

Mrs Blacksmith's Guide to Positive Poverty

Positive poverty is about having enough cash to get by and being OK with that. (By comparison, people in slums don't have enough cash to get by — they have no opportunities and fuck-all to eat. And that is not positive.)

Positive poverty (in theory) is liberating. Kinda like third form economics, it's all about needs and wants. I have a terrible time differentiating between the two. Often I have this debate going on in my head: I *need* a new custom-made leotard versus I *want* a new custom-made leotard.

Currently I have more than thirty leotards in my bitchin' costume bag, so no, I don't need one, I want one. The idea with positive poverty is that I say to myself instead, 'I don't need *or* want any more custom-made leotards. I am happy with what I've got.'

Tricky.

But I also want to go sailing. I want to live a life full of adventure. I want my days to be less about predictability and more about spontaneity. I want to bring my son up in the sunshine. So I have to look very carefully at my needs and wants lists and try to save as much money as I can in 500 days.

Here's how I am attempting to do it:

Don't have a car. Cars are hunks of metal you throw money at. If I don't have one, I can't throw money at it. Tick. One thing off the list. So far so good.

Walk. Easy! I do this every day. Also, I chucked on the pounds when I was pregnant so this is a good way to kick them into touch. Plus, it's free entertainment. While walking from A to B I can throw in a quick game of hopscotch and read all those brass plaques on heritage buildings, thus expanding my mind and enriching my local historical knowledge.

Grazia, Vogue, Marie Claire, Cosmo, NW *and other such magazines.* Don't buy them. Ange, put them down and step away from the rack. They will only make you feel like shit and make you think you need things you don't. Reading them is junk food for your eyes.

I have always enjoyed a flick through the glossy pages of a trashy mag, and at times it has bordered on an addiction. Weaning myself off these is going to be hard. But it is a cornerstone of positive poverty, so I have to do it. I must not buy things I don't need. (Will try repeating this as a mantra.)

Embrace simple food. This one is going to be a breeze. I am over the way every second show on the telly has people licking their chops and exclaiming 'I just looove the googy-oooyness of double cream'. It's food porn and I don't like it. I am trying to eat good food so I will feel better which means I can walk further which means I can have more adventures which means I won't get too fat which means I can continue to wear my clothes instead of having to shell out wads of cash to buy a bigger size.

Say 'I don't think so' to Plastic. Again, this one should be OK. I am really going to try to limit the amount of plastic I bring into my daily life. Do I really need to buy pre-cut carrots sitting on a Styrofoam plate wrapped in plastic? No. No, I don't.

Drink wine. I'm a realist. Being a member of a minority is going to be hard work. People will mock me, laugh behind their hands, tie me to the railings . . . I'll need to kick back and congratulate myself on belonging to the next great social movement. What better way to do that than with a $10 bottle of Banrock Station? If I walk to the shop, take my cloth bag and don't swig it down with fancy cheese while I read gossip mags, this will make me very positive and the poverty will be easier to bear.

Go to sea. This is probably my only hope of actually fully embracing positive poverty. There is only so much room on a boat and there are no shops in the middle of the ocean. It seems the best way to embrace positive poverty is to head miles away from temptation.

12

Enter Dashkin

I spent the last three months of my pregnancy making up for lost time. I wolfed down everything in sight. Self-saucing chocolate pudding? Why not? Cream cheese bagels? One won't hurt.

I replaced the small change in my top drawer at work with a giant block of peppermint chocolate. 'Oh hello, what have we got here?' I would say to myself as I snapped off an entire row of brown minty goodness. Morning tea? Pass me the muffins!

Like any first-time mother, the thought of giving birth was a mixture of excitement at meeting the little person who had spent days kicking me in the ribs and abject terror. My due date came and went and I was still pregnant. At thirty-four I was considered an 'older mother' and needed supervision. I dutifully trundled off to the hospital and instead of being told I could go home and wait for nature to 'take its course' the scan revealed that the baby was losing weight. This was not good.

'We can slot you in this afternoon for a c-section,' the doctor told me. I felt suddenly cold. I couldn't believe it. I had been feeling fine — how could my baby be in any kind of danger?

Ross had dropped me off and was going to meet me at home. 'I need to talk to my husband, can I come in tomorrow instead? I need to think about this.'

'Sure. There is no immediate danger but the baby needs to come out.'

I heaved myself off the examining table, reached down to uncomfortably squeeze my swollen feet into my shoes and waddled out to the bus stop. Buses with 'Sorry' where the destination should be whizzed past me.

I was scared. I tried to calm myself. I rang Mum.

'Trust your body, darling. Women have been giving birth for thousands of years.' I felt calmed by this and after consultation with my midwife booked myself in for an induction the next day. Ross and I had been luxuriating in getting up at 10 a.m. but on this day we were to be at the hospital at the ungodly hour of 7 a.m. I set my alarm.

The next morning Charlotte dropped us off and we went inside the newly refurbished maternity wing. Nowadays it is all soft lighting, birthing pools and whale music — if you want it. It was heaps flasher than our flat.

Then it began. Straps were fastened, heartbeats monitered, fingers shoved up my lady bits. It became about dilation, contractions, deep breathing and the sneakers. The registrar on duty wore oversized grubby white sneakers. He pushed back the double-curtained access to the birthing suite and all I clocked was peroxided blonde hair and the sneakers.

Oh great, I am going to be given birthing advice by a gay man, I thought. It turned out he was in fact one of the top neonatal doctors in New Zealand and over the long eighteen hours I spent in the birthing room I came to trust him implicitly.

I huffed and puffed; I tried but it wasn't working. After almost thirteen hours the midwife told me they were focused on positive outcomes as she removed my wedding rings and gold necklace and helped me into a gown.

During the caesarean I was terrified. I was trying to be brave, trying to rationalise everything that was happening, trying not to be disappointed that my journey into motherhood had been taken out of my hands. The only thing that calmed me was saying the Hail Mary over and over again, but skipping the last line about the hour of our death.

Into the blinding white light of the operating theatre, Dashkin entered the world. The surgeon's size-eight hands lifted him out of the gore as Ross said, 'It's a boy.'

'Welcome to the world, my darling,' I said through my tears. Oh. My. God. I have a son.

Then he was whisked away to be rubbed clean of his first home and prepared for the oxygenated air of the world.

'Go with him,' I said to Ross. Strangers were holding him, my precious little darling, before I had had the chance. I couldn't bear him to be surrounded by people whose names I didn't know in his first minutes.

His tiny body was lowered onto the scales, all jerky legs and arms. Finally, once all the checks had taken place, he was swaddled and handed to Ross, who held him so carefully. 'Is he OK? Is he OK?' I kept asking. I couldn't believe he was finally here, that we had a perfect tiny baby.

Ross laid him across my chest, and through my tears I choked, 'Hello Dashkin, hello my darling.' At the sound of my voice he opened his eyes and turned his head towards me. I was desperate to wrap my arms around him, to hold him to me, to feel his skin against mine. But my arms were stretched and strapped like a modern-day crucifixion, my utcrus sat on my stomach and I had a blue hospital barrier erected from just under my breasts, so I could only follow him with my eyes. His perfect head had scratches where the hook had nicked him during the membrane sweep. We both bore the scars of the day.

We had imagined a dark-haired child; he was golden, yet despite this he seemed so familiar, so perfectly himself.

Once my uterus had been returned to its proper place and I had stopped shaking, I was finally released from the restraints and Dashkin was tucked into the crook of my arm as we were wheeled through to the recovery room. Finally we were able to have our first hug. He wriggled and even though he was so tiny I knew exactly how to hold him.

I felt the weight of his body against mine as his little mouth turned towards my breast, nuzzling, looking for his first ever taste of food. The nurse was concerned his blood-sugar levels were low so gave him 30ml of formula.

I was hungry too — I had been in labour since 8 a.m. and it was now 4 a.m. I asked for a cup of tea and a piece of toast but the Filipino nurse told me, 'No food until you fart.' I thought she was having a very badly timed gag with me . . . I mean, it was 4 a.m., I had just given birth, I was covered in blood and all I was asking for was a nice cup of tea. I called the other Irish nurse over who confirmed that it was true — no food until I had let one rip. Ross and I laughed.

Dashkin was lying wrapped up, asleep in his arms. I remember looking over him at Ross and thinking, now we are a family.

Ross and I had agreed on his name earlier. Dashkin is a bit of a mash-up of Dakshin Ray, a mythical Bengali tiger god. We had also decided that he would be a Blacksmith — that we would start our own family name instead of having a really long hyphenated one.

We arrived in the ward and Ross laid out Dashkin's clothes. His clothes swam on him — his tiny legs only came halfway down the leggings and his singlets looked like nighties. Finally, after almost twenty-four hours, we were alone in the early-morning stillness.

I remember being so overwhelmed with love, so happy to have him here, so relieved that he was perfect. But we were in a public hospital and the moment was soon interrupted by the nurse telling Ross how to get out of the hospital after hours.

I held Dashkin in my left arm and we slept. I had forgotten to swaddle him and his tiny, jerky limbs woke him. Our eyes opened together and at the moment I understood what people meant by 'a deep, profound love' as Metallica's 'Nothing Else Matters' played in my head.

13
Yacht Porn

—✦—

Yacht porn, we call it. Ross is addicted. What started as a bit of good fun has turned into a fully fledged obsession. He spends hours trawling the internet looking for the perfect yacht to take us on an adventure. Luscious images in high resolution of smooth, curvaceous lines fill the screen every night.

'**T**his one looks good: a centre cockpit steel ketch for under thirty grand,' Ross says as the computer screen casts a blue light onto his face. I walk back into the lounge having put Dashkin down for his nap. Rubbing my eyes, I look over his shoulder.

'Where is it?' I ask.

'Aruba.'

'As in the Beach Boys song? It sounds exotic and warm.' It's freezing in our flat.

'Hey look, Ange, it's called *Summertime.*'

'Sold!' I laugh. We are stuck in the middle of endless winter. The heater we affectionately call the 'psychological glow' sits in the corner of the room pumping out retina-frying rays. I pull my big pink polar-fleece dressing-gown closer and wriggle my toes in my Warehouse Ugg boots. I'm committing multiple fashion crimes and I blame motherhood. Instead of thinking how hot I look in clothes I now find myself rating tops based on the ease of breastfeeding access.

'Click through and let's have a look at the interior,' I ask Ross as I sit down next to him on the same dining chair. One of my butt cheeks hangs off the side.

An image of the saloon comes up. It's stuffed with books and tools and has an air of filth about it.

'Oh look, a tasteful plastic flower arrangement.' We both giggle at the fake red roses on the table.

To be totally honest, I don't actually know anything practical about boats, things like chainplates and sails and engine configuration. What I'm looking for is comfort.

We had agreed that *Astra* wasn't the boat to take our now expanded family sailing. Sure, other people have done it in 33-foot boats, but I am not a sailor, I'm a new mother — and I need cabins fore and aft if I am going to spend a year on the ocean.

'What about the stern cabin? Any photos of that?' I ask.

Ross clicks on another image and we wait for it to download.

'Oh my God . . . there is a TV in there and . . . weird blow-up toys . . .' I say as the image begins filling the screen.

The cabin is huge. Dolphins leap across an ocean-coloured duvet, frilly cream curtains cover the portholes, an extensive video library with titles like 'Irritable Bowel Syndrome — a Sufferer's Guide' takes up one corner, and an inflatable globe jostles with a blow-up boat in the other.

'It needs a good clean — but it could work,' Ross says.

'Yeah, I reckon. Put it on the "possible" list.' So far we have three boats on our list. One is a 42-foot Vagabond in Baltimore, one is a 40-foot ketch in the British Virgin Islands, and now *Summertime*.

Like all good porn, our yacht viewing feeds a fantasy. It's providing much needed relief and escapism.

We have a little baby and no money, and it hasn't stopped raining for months. Imagining us sailing around the Caribbean in our very own pleasure yacht is the perfect way to stop us from going crazy.

The problem is cash and our lack of it. Ross' commitment to positive poverty means we live hand to mouth, we have no savings to speak of and the only asset we have is *Astra*. My student loan and globetrotting twenties mean I have some debts to pay. To make this dream happen, we need a plan.

We need a five-hundred-day chart.

Ross goes into his studio and pulls out a big sheet of white paper.

'It is going to be a twenty by twenty-five box chart. We can mark in key dates and cross off the days as we go,' he says, picking up the ruler and drawing up the grid.

I have never been big on counting days and marking things off. This is probably one of the reasons I can never stick to diets or save money. Ross, however, uses charts to great effect. When he was two-thirds of the way through his year in Christchurch he had made a one-hundred-day chart to count down the days until he moved back to Wellington. There was the forty-five-day chart he used to track his marathon-training progress, and now we had the king of all charts.

'There,' he says, sticking the chart to the wall. 'That should keep us focused.'

You can't miss it. An A0-size piece of paper with five hundred squares is now resident on our icy-cold hallway wall.

Dash begins crying. I squeeze past Ross and go to soothe him.

'Hush a bye baby, don't you cry . . . go to sleep my little Dashkin,' I sing in the dark as he slowly calms down. As I sing I think about the chart. Five hundred days seems like a freakin' long time (which it is), but as I keep singing I realise that it is exactly the right amount of time you need to extract yourself from one life and plan and equip yourself for another. 'When you wake you will find all the pretty little ponies,' I whisper as I back out of Dashkin's room.

'Right Ross, it is time to put our family motto into action. We need to go at it "Hammer and Tongs",' I say, coming back into the lounge, ready to make this boat buying happen.

'Great . . . We have to have arranged finance by Day 130, and all viewing of internet yacht porn has to be completed by Day 198.' Ross is on a roll.

'How much are we going to need?'

'OK . . . thirty thousand for the yacht, five grand for flights, twenty grand for living and another fifteen for repairs etc. Eighty grand should do it.'

He made it sound so simple. 'OK, I'll talk to the bank and see if we can get a loan. Do they do mortgages for boats?' I ask, trying to be helpful. I am totally out of my depth here. At thirty-four I have only just got a credit card and the only time I ever speak to the bank is to beg for overdraft extensions.

'No, Ange, they don't, but we should be able to sell *Astra* for around fifty thousand and we have five hundred days to save thirty grand,' says Ross, fired up.

'If you look after Dash I will go back to work four days a week,' I say, doing a quick calculation and realising that there would be no money for any kind of treats for the foreseeable future.

'I'll work on the weekends and paint maps and prints.' This is Ross' other passion: painting antique maps and prints and framing them up for sale. 'We might just be able to manage it,' Ross says, giving me a high-five.

'So long as I can Bitch on Saturdays, go running three times a week and share a bottle of wine with you on Friday nights, I'm up for it.'

Married life was not quite what I had imagined. There were no cosy fireside chats and I wasn't baking cookies, but it was way better: we were planning the adventure of a lifetime.

We cross off the days until finally, Day 204 arrives.

'Are you sure you've got your passport?' I call after Ross as I balance Dash on my hip. The taxi is tooting more urgently now.

He stops on the rickety path and opens his swag bag. Ross is going for the 'poor look' to act as a deterrent to potential robbers. He has a change of clothes, a camera, a stash of money and a book.

'Yes, it's right here.'

'OK, darling. Take care and good luck — buy us a boat!'

'Bye-bye, Papa.' Dash raises his little hand and waves as Ross gets in the taxi and heads to the airport.

He's on his way to Los Angeles, San Diego and Aruba. Yacht porn is about to get real. It's going to involve international travel, hotels, sunscreen and some pretty fast talking. We have cobbled together our $30,000. Who will win him over?

I go back inside. The place is a real mess — there has been no time for housework in the last two weeks. I have only just hung up my leotard after a sold-out season of the latest Real Hot Bitches show *The Fierceness*. We had wowed not only the crowds but ourselves in our most ambitious show to date. Based on *A Chorus Line*, Cynthia Sashay (played by me) put a host of wannabe dancers through their paces. I wore a specially made tuxedo leotard and pranced about the stage with a glittering stick, striking fear in the heart of Geraldine, my long-suffering sidekick. MaXine HendriX had been lowered from the ceiling while she sang 'Total Eclipse of the Heart' and the final number was Iron Maiden's 'Run to the Hills', where all thirty of us piled on the stage, galloping like horses and slaughtering each other. It was glorious.

14
Countdown

LA turns out to be a bit of a waste of time, San Diego offers up a floating bachelor pad that has never done any blue-water sailing and doesn't even have an anchor winch. Aruba is our last hope.

Ross emails me:

The Aruba yacht is filthy . . . but very strong and much larger . . . though only a little wider than *Astra* . . . interior feels about the same size as *Astra,* maybe a little larger but has a large cabin with double bed in the stern, small, tight walkway to get to it . . . forward cabin would need a bunk built in but quite easy to do . . . she has quite a pointed bow so should sail well . . . she just needs a really good clean . . . old guy is OK but has two small dogs and suffers with back pain . . . lots of small jobs to do around the yacht but nothing major, large engine looks well cared for and has a large generator . . . the yacht also has large solar panels and wind generators . . . she smells and is truly close inside if you get me, as is very hot here, 34 degrees . . . but is very cheap and is a much better buy . . . and doesn't require all the heavy expensive gear . . . also the cockpit is much better for us, with hard, built-in doghouse . . . we can live ashore for a few weeks and clean her out as a motel is close . . . very cheap to have her at the jetty, only US$30 a week though few facilities . . . I'll take some photos . . . will take her out sailing in the few next days and see how she points . . . she will be some hard work for a couple of weeks but I feel we can make his happen darling . . . but tell me how you feel about this . . . hope all OK with you baby . . . so much love to you and Dashkin — Ross x

I feel like it is now or never. I email him back with BUY IT in the subject line.

The next day, I am at work and surreptitiously checking www.aruba.com while imagining myself lying on the white sands as the waves gently lap at the shore when I get his next email:

Summertime is ours. The yacht is big and heavy . . . she is steady in the sea and does not plunge up and down . . . but is no ocean racer! But we are used to this I feel . . . she will motor at at least 5 to 6 knots which will seem quick to us . . . and here the wind is so, so warm . . . we will have our own steel battleship! And if we hit the submerged container we will sink it and if we hit the coral reef we will bounce! There will be issues as she is very cheap but we shall be safe and Dashkin can play in the cockpit . . . right, on to the next stage of our adventure, mainly sell *Astra* and make money! Loving you and Dashkin . . . see you soon — Ross x

We work like mad. Seven days a week. I go back to work full time, Ross works at the bookshop three days. We save every-thing we can. There is lots of interest in *Astra* but no one buys her. We crunch the numbers and realise that if we can get to Brisbane and sell *Summertime* then we should just be able to pay off the loan within the year.

There is so much to do, so many things to think about, like freighting our stuff to Aruba, getting the best insurance for blue-water sailing, getting a radio operator's licence, learning Spanish, ordering all the charts and courtesy flags and, my favourite, planning colour schemes for the soft furnishings.

'Floods, shootings, strange vomiting episodes — the first two months of 2011 could rival a chapter in Revelations for the drama and intrigue,' I say to Charlotte over our regular Saturday-morning coffee. 'In fact, I reckon those doomsday cults who have predicted that the world is going to end in 2012 might be on to something.' Charlotte lives in a separate flat downstairs and we usually have a good gasbag on a Saturday morning.

'So with that in mind, Sis, there is even more reason to be going sailing,' I continue, plonking Dashkin on the floor and adjusting my always-on-even-though-it-is-supposedly-summer woollen jersey.

'Or is it, Ange?' Charlotte asks, raising her eyebrows over her coffee cup.

'You know me, I'm a catastrophist. When I go running in the hills I spend most of my time planning what I would do if a wild pig suddenly appeared on the track.'

'In the highly likely case that this would occur, what would you do?' she says sarcastically.

'Well, I couldn't kill it with my bare hands — did you know Pearl Lusta once bashed one into submission with a sandshoe? Legend! Anyway, I would have to escape being mauled to death or disfigurement by climbing a tree.'

'Remember that strange death in Palmerston North when we were teenagers — you know, the one where the girl's body was found in a field and there was all that speculation that some terrible killer was on the loose?'

'Yes!'

'But then they discovered she had been gorged by a bull?'

'Exactly! You never know what could happen. I'm having an absolute field day thinking about the coming months,' I confess. 'A small child, an unpredictable natural world, a high potential for illness and accidents, sinking, running into large sleeping mammals . . .'

'Really deep water,' she adds.

'The possibility of tsunami — you know that is my biggest fear, eh?'

'Mmmm,' she says, nodding her head and passing Dashkin the wooden toy car.

'I have recurring nightmares about being swept up onto power lines by an enormous wave while I watch my family drown — and yes, I do know what Freud says about large bodies of water appearing in your dreams.'

'It's the thought of submerged containers that freaks me out,' Charlotte says with a shudder. 'I can't bear to think about all the man-made objects lurking about in the ocean.'

Charlotte has always been very specific about her phobias.

'And then there are the stats. Apparently 80 per cent of couples who go sailing together end up divorced.'

'What? Eighty per cent?'

'Yep! Supposedly Tahiti is full of abandoned boats, a floating graveyard of broken dreams. Once they make it across the Pacific the wives leave, totally fed up with shipboard life, and then the captains are left with no crew.'

'Well, you will have Dash on board to diffuse any dramas,' Charlotte adds hopefully.

'I mean, I get so seasick, I don't know how to sail. I am trying to learn as much as I can but with a full-time job, Dash and the Bitches there is just not enough time!'

'Angela Meyer, take your cue from the Bitches. What you lack in technique, make up for in passion.'

'You are absolutely right. I have actually done something — I am happy to report I have just become a marine radio operator.'

'Great! Do you have to know the phonetic alphabet? Alpha, Bravo, Charlie, Delta . . .' Charlotte says excitedly. 'I learnt it because there are always pub-quiz questions about it.'

'Echo, Foxtrot, Golf, Hotel . . .' We are both reciting it now. 'Whiskey, Yankee, Zulu!' we chorus at Dash, who is looking at his mother and aunt and giving us a toothy grin.

'More! More!' he says, clapping his hands.

I pick him up and squeeze him. He snuggles into my neck and begins playing with the skin under my chin.

'So what do you have to do to become a marine radio operator?'

'Talk to Dave.'

Armed with *Safety in Small Craft*, a pamphlet about the ionosphere and a Grade 8 Speech and Drama Certificate, I met Dave and four other wannabe operators on a wet and windy night in a hexagonal building at Evans Bay Marina. We made our way past the rescue boat and up the steep steps to the control room.

'You must be Angela.'

'Yes, and I take it you're Dave.'

'Sure am. Kettle's over there.'

Dave had big mugs and an ample stash of chocolate biscuits, which he dished out generously. Once we had finished our buckets of tea it was time to get qualified.

We Maydayed, we Pan-Panned, we learnt about the revered Channel 16, we had more tea, we got our heads around radio waves bouncing all over the earth, we had the importance of speaking clearly drilled into us, and then we learnt the most important lesson of all — how to turn your radio on.

'It is surprisingly tricky, and I had to sit an extra test for the single side-band radio, which we will be using when we are in the middle of the ocean,' I explain to Charlotte.

'Well, that makes me feel a little better,' she says.

It is now Day 460 and our preparations have cranked up. All of the charts for the Caribbean, Panama Canal, Galapagos Islands and the Pacific Islands have arrived. We spread them over the floor.

'It's a long, long way,' I say to Ross. 'Look — from the window all the way across to the couch and back it's ten thousand miles.'

Seeing the charts is making it all a bit more real. We can't pull out now. Seven boxes of books, ropes, bikes, a depth sounder, a GPS system, linen and all the things you need for a year at sea while en route to Aruba. I had handed in my notice at work, the Bitches are going on ice. We are about to up sticks and head out into the wild blue yonder.

Mrs Blacksmith's Guide to Upping Sticks — how to go sailing with a toddler and bugger-all cash

Marry a sailor. By far and away the best way to ensure large parts of your life are full of adventure is to marry a sailor. Hooking a sailor can be a bit tricky, as a nomadic life on the sea makes long-term commitments difficult, but if you can grab one while they are in port, you have lifelong travel sewn up.

Have a baby. This is great training for the four-hour watches. If, like me, you haven't spent much time on the sea, having a baby is a great way to prepare for the long, hard nights, relinquishing control to the captain, and having faith that things will get better.

Create a five-hundred-day chart: Even if you think charts are for disorganised losers, get a sheet of paper and mark out five hundred days. Do it now. Put it up in the hallway, and on the five-hundredth day write *Go Sailing*. You can write this in crayon, ballpoint pen — hell, go crazy with the glitter! Mark in other milestone goals like *purchase boat, save $10,000* and *book tickets to Aruba*. Stick to it, consult it often and mark off those days. The chart will keep you focused.

Read books. Children of Cape Horn by Rosie Swale is inspirational. She sailed with her two very small children around Cape Horn in a catamaran in the early 1970s. She has amazing tips for keeping kids entertained, washing nappies on board, what to do when weevils attack the stores, and she does all this with very little money while looking like a total fox.

Jill Dickin Schinas' book *Kids in the Cockpit* is full of great, practical advice about breastfeeding in oilskins, keeping harnesses on toddlers, making your boat child-friendly and has a whole chapter on safety. This is *gold*. Whenever I think 'What the bloody hell are we doing?' I pick up Jill's and Rosie's books and am instantly soothed by their wise words.

Tell people. Saying out loud that you are going sailing across the world with your family has the remarkable effect of making it real.

Hammer and tongs. This is how you must go after your dream. Other people will think you are mad, they will be jealous, they will think that taking a toddler sailing is tantamount to child abuse, they will try to dissuade you, but stick to your dream. Have some facts at the ready, like 'It is more dangerous to drive in Auckland than sail across the Pacific.' Hammer and tongs are also handy bits of equipment on a steel yacht.

Plan, plan, plan. Become a marine radio operator, do your Boatmaster's, study charts, read other people's blogs and forums, learn a bit of the local lingo, eat only beans and rice for a month, practice shitting in a bucket, get your capsule wardrobe together, get your toddler used to wearing his harness, bulk-buy Sea Legs and get used to doing exactly what the captain says, because poor communication sinks ships.

Cash. Save as much of this stuff as you can. Try to arrange some income while you are sailing, sell all your land-based stuff and have credit cards at the ready.

Positive poverty. Embrace this concept (see page 115). It will make being poor so much easier to bear.

Get fit. Don't be afraid to go pink in this pursuit. Sailing is physically hard work and looking after a toddler is physically hard work, so having good core strength is a sailor's best friend. Make the time.

Finally, *Do it. Make it Happen.*

15
Earthquake

There was just one more thing we had to do: go to Christchurch and paint Ross' eighty-five-year-old mother's house.

Dash and I landed at Christchurch airport at 9.45 a.m. on 22 February 2011. We made our way to Doreen's house to wait for Ross, who was scheduled to sail into Lyttelton Harbour on *Astra* around 11 a.m.

At 12.51 p.m., a 6.3 magnitude earthquake hit Christchurch, killing 185 people.

It is the dust; it gets stuck in the back of my throat and pulls me up mid-sentence. I have to stop, cough and start over again. My hair is thick with it. It coats the car in a thin grey film, it seeps into the house and tries to fill the cracks the earthquake has left.

We are the lucky ones. We have water and power and we have each other. Many other people have nothing. Where Doreen lives, it hardly looks like an earthquake has hit, aside from tumbled-down walls and gaping holes in houses.

Dash and I had just arrived from Wellington. Dash was having his morning nap, Doreen was hunting for her heart pills and I was on the phone to the travel doctors about getting yellow-fever vaccinations when suddenly the earth bucked.

The noise was incredible. Doreen and I just managed to cling onto each other. Dash was screaming in his bedroom. Things had fallen everywhere and I had to bash the door to get in.

He was terrified; I have never seen a look like that on his face. He was standing up in his cot howling, 'Mama, Mama!' I grabbed him and we managed to make it back into the lounge and collapse on the couch.

Doreen and I looked at each other. I asked her if this was a usual aftershock and she said this earthquake was much worse than the one on 4 September 2010.

We got out the radio and listened. The enormity of it all became more real. We had cupboards flung open and vases and glasses smashed but when we heard the cathedral had lost its spire and buildings in the central city had collapsed and people were killed we realised just how lucky we were to be alive and OK. We couldn't believe our eyes when I pulled back the sliding door: I don't even remember hearing it fall.

Then there was another huge aftershock. Dash went white and Doreen and I tried to make our way to the table. We had no idea whether it was going to get worse or if it would stop.

Our phones were down so we didn't know where Ross was, if Holly (Ross' daughter) was in the rubble of the central city, or if his ex-wife Stephanie was OK. I had expected Ross to be on a bus making his way to us. Then I heard that two buses had been crushed by falling masonry and I felt sick.

We got a few text messages, and finally at around 7 p.m. the phone lines were open. Steph called to say that she had heard from Ross, and that he was walking over the Bridle Path to us. I burst into tears, knowing that he was safe. Dash kept calling 'Papa, Papa!' and running to the door.

Holly and her boyfriend Matt arrived and told us how people were dragging others out of rubble and about the huge traffic jams as people were desperately trying to get home. I just wanted to see Ross and hug him.

I thought that if we could have a cup of tea things would be OK. At 10 p.m. the power came back on and just after another huge aftershock, Ross arrived, totally dishevelled and dirty. I can honestly say I have never been so happy to see him. He looked more handsome than ever and the cup of tea did make things much better.

Ross had just arrived after a two-day sail from Wellington into Purau, which is across the harbour from Lyttelton and was the epicentre of the quake.

He said he and his crew were sitting on the yacht and that suddenly it felt like thousands of jackhammers were pounding the hull. He thought that someone had run into them or they had run aground. They raced on deck to see the hillside sliding into the water. A tanker truck on the pass road had stopped and they could see the driver running for his life. The sound kept echoing around the hills and the harbour.

As the phones weren't working and he didn't know how bad it was in Christchurch, he decided to walk over the Port Hills. Standing at the top, he saw great clouds of dust and fires. He managed to hitch a lift and saw cars that had been swallowed up by the liquefaction. People were walking around carrying suitcases and desperately looking at their phones. He got to Steph's and helped her move the hot-water tank in the roof, which was about to fall through into the lounge, then she brought him around here.

The first night was awful. Ross was exhausted, Dash was traumatised and there were some pretty big aftershocks. We all just held each other tight.

The next few days were a bit better. We were squatting in a makeshift toilet in the backyard while only 3 kilometres away, in the central city, teams of people were pulling bodies out of the remains of buildings.

We filled our time helping other people pick up rubble and talking to strangers, asking, 'How's your place?' Most people said, 'We were lucky', but one guy I spoke to said 'I've lost everything'.

The next day Ross and I went over to his ex-wife Stephanie's on the east side of the city. Here it was like a war zone. There was liquefaction everywhere, more dust, tankers with water, people looking like zombies. I kept expecting to see Bruce Willis coming around the corner in combat fatigues. Stephanie had a hole in her roof so we covered that with tarps.

On the way back we drove over great bulges in the tarmac, past shops that were now piles of bricks and through suburbs that felt like ghost towns.

A supermarket was open. We stopped and got a few things. It was so eerie, going into a place that is usually ordered and clean and was now covered in dust. Shelves were empty and the usually pristine floors were smeared in dirt. There was a horrible smell from frozen foods going off and people were loading up with booze. The police were outside.

I felt totally powerless. Even if you want to go into the city centre and help you can't — there are checkpoints everywhere, lots of army trucks, police and so many high-vis vests.

Instead of painting the fence, we pile it up on the sidewalk. Now Doreen's peeling windowsills are in full view of the neighbours. Despite most of the city being in ruins, we run a paint brush over them because when you are eighty-five a freshly painted sill matters.

It feels like we are being held captive. The motorway north is clogged. Flights are full, with waiting lists of people standing next to the check-in counter. I want to leave and get back to Wellington.

The entire city is strung out and exhausted. With every aftershock I go white and dive under the table. Bob Parker, the mayor, wears his black turtleneck and bright orange lanyard and tries to soothe the frayed nerves of the shattered city with his smooth, media-trained vowels. Something about him riles me, though. I switch off the telly and pour out the brandy. Ross, Doreen and I sit and sip. Doreen lived through the Blitz. A bit of shaking doesn't faze her.

Five days later it is our turn to escape. As our flight lifts off the runway the plane erupts in an impromptu cheer. Even with its 150 kilometre per hour winds and major faultline, Wellington feels safe.

We spend the next three days making trips to Palmerston North to put our belongings into storage in one of Dad's many sheds. On our final night in the city, Pearl Lusta makes a trip over from the Wairarapa, and we sit on our friend's veranda, eating fish and chips and drinking champagne. This is it. Tomorrow, 3 March 2011, we are leaving. We are going to a tiny Caribbean island to take possession of a yacht, clean her up, then sail her to Columbia, through the Kuna Yala in Panama, into Colon, through the Panama Canal, across the mighty Pacific Ocean to the Galapagos, onto to Nuka Hiva, the Tuamotus, Raratonga, Tonga, Fiji and then to Brisbane, where I am sure I will be in need of a flat white and a lie down.

Our chart has kept us on track. We have been working seven days a week for the last nine months and have $17,000 in cash and another $8000 on our credit cards. Barring anything really bad going wrong with the boat, or our health, we should be OK. It will be tight — it won't be cocktails at the Copacabana or high rolling at the casinos but still, at least I won't be forced to drown myself in the paddling pool at barbecues where people talk about property prices and the PTA. I am sure that if we stay this will be my fate.

I haven't been able to procure a stash of Phenergan, a sedative used to calm children on long journeys, so spend the last hours in New Zealand ensuring I have enough books, games and toys to keep Dashkin entertained on the plane.

Charlotte drops us off. I am wearing a loose-fitting orange kaftan. I feel a little bit like a movie star at home, only much fatter. My plan is to get off the plane in LA, immediately adopt an American accent, ensure that my sunglasses are permanently glued to my face and act famous. Luckily babies are in fashion, so all I need now is an oversized takeaway coffee cup. This, I think, is the perfect ruse to stop us standing out as tourists and being fleeced by unscrupulous characters.

I have this international travel thing all sewn up. Aruba, here we come.

Mrs Blacksmith's Tips for Flying with Toddlers

Hope that you are seated next to a retired Jewish mathematician from Chicago. Unless you have the means to purchase a seat for your little one, you will be jammed next to some poor person whose idea of flying next to a toddler is the universe playing a cruel trick on them. It pays to be nice from the minute you sit down. Jewish mathematicians from Chicago who love kids and have a back catalogue of nursery rhymes are gold. Mildred, you were a star!

Don't do it alone. Attempting anything longer than a two-hour flight alone with a toddler is, in my humble opinion, madness. Husbands have their uses, and this is one of them. Aeroplanes call for active parenting — there is no room for 'just play quietly in the corner while Mama does the washing'. Oh no, this is the time to bring out the big guns, i.e. Papa. You will need to have your back-up well briefed and ready to step up at any time. More than anything, you need an arsenal of activities to keep your toddler entertained. Think books, toys, stickers, whatever it takes.

Bribery and corruption. How bad can a lollipop be?

Run them ragged. When I had my son, Bambi Du Bois of the Bitches told me to 'Run him like a dog, little boys need it.' As a new mother I was horrified that anyone would suggest I treated my precious angel like a dog, but as this precious angel has grown I often hear her advice ringing in my ears. She is right! Little boys need to raise merry hell for at least three hours a day.

   Airport departure lounges are just the place for this to happen, with long corridors and no way to escape! With a two-hour wait you can really run your little man ragged. Do this and I guarantee he will be begging you to sit on the plane.

Keep your hand luggage light. There is nothing worse than wrestling with a wriggling toddler, balancing four bags and having to wait in an official queue. Have one backpack filled with nappies, snacks and your entertainment arsenal. And, dare I say it, use a fanny pack. This is great for stashing all of your important docs. This way you won't have to swing bags and toddlers from shoulder to shoulder while you go through immigration. American officials have no sense of humour or compassion and sport a fanny pack as part of their official uniform.

Fly at night. They sleep!

Break out the Bloody Marys. These are the best boozy drinks to down on the plane, as they are the perfect ruse. I saw other parents ordering very obviously alcoholic drinks and getting 'the look', so avoid the judging eyes of your fellow passengers and go for the Bloody Mary — after all, it is just spiced tomato juice with a well-disguised kick!

Go to the toilet — for a break. Parenting makes you do things you never thought you would. This is one of them. I went to the loo just to have a bit of time out! On a plane there is nowhere else to go that is private, has a lock, is away from your toddler and lets you check your hair.

Dress smart. They say first impressions count, so dress your toddler accordingly. Put on their cutest outfit, brush their hair, ensure their nose is snot-free and make them practise their Ps and Qs. A smartly turned-out child will go a long way towards endearing yourself to your fellow passengers when the inevitable meltdown occurs. Shallow, I know, but it works like a charm.

Keep calm and carry on. Toddlers have an inbuilt radar — they pick up on how you are feeling. I have found the old mantra 'calm mama, calm toddler' to be mostly true. Remember, it is a just a flight — you are never going to see these people again, and every minute you are on that wretched plane gets you closer to your destination, where hopefully a deck chair with your name on it is waiting.

16

A . . .
Aruba!

We made it! After forty-eight hours, six bags, five international flights, four body searches, three Bloody Marys, two dodgy taxi rides and only one lost pillow, the Blacksmiths are in Aruba.

'Time check, Ross.'

'Eleven-thirty p.m.,' he says, looking down at his watch as the airport doors open and the warm trade wind hits us.

'Wow, it's the middle of the night and it is still really hot.'

'Trees, Mama!' Dash is wide-eyed and pointing at the row of coconut palms lining the road to Oranjestad.

We jump in a taxi and speed down the wrong side of the road. People are everywhere, grandstands are everywhere. This is as far away from sedate Kelburn as possible.

'What is going on?' I ask the taxi driver.

'It's Carnival!' he says.

Ross and I look at each other, our faces lit up by the momentary glow of street lamps.

'A carnival!' I say excitedly. Dashkin's nose is pressed up against the window.

'It's past the supermarket, on the left,' Ross tells the driver. We are trying to find the B&B we are going to stay in while we get our yacht ship-shape. 'Buffan's Tropical Haven, do you know it?'

'No, I take you to hotels,' the driver says as he begins to swing the car towards the glittering metropolis.

'It's just around this corner.' Ross knows where it is because he stayed there with hosts Rick and Sherrie when he came to Aruba last year.

Finally we find it, off the main road down a side street past a pack of stray dogs.

Rick is waiting at the gate. He takes our bags and the pushchair and we quietly make our way through the sleeping household.

'Here you go guys — we thought you would be comfortable here,' Rick says softly as he shows us into our rooms. There is a kitchen, bathroom and a cot for Dashkin. The smooth plaster walls are painted bright green. Ceiling fans, the kind I imagine Hemmingway writing under, blow cool air down on our yet-to-be-acclimatised bodies. Outside our door is a pool with sun loungers and tiny flesh-coloured laughing geckos.

'It's the middle of the night and we're in the Caribbean,' I laugh, unzipping the suitcases and getting out Dashkin's nappies.

'How about a Balashi?' Ross says, opening the refrigerator and handing me a can of icy-cold beer.

The can sizzles against my neck. It is *that* hot. The dogs begin to howl.

The next morning I put on my blue-and-white striped dress. I aim to project a nautical air over breakfast; this is, after all, the first day of my new life as a sailoress.

Sherrie and Rick have set a table for us on the veranda and we slug back much needed coffee. The dogs had not shut up all night. 'What are your plans?' Sherrie asks as she places scrambled eggs in front of us.

'We are planning to spend about a month here doing our own version of *Build a New Life in the Country* — you know, the show where fools buy cheap, dilapidated barns in the

English countryside and then spend years trying to do them up? Same thing, only on the ocean, and the yacht is apparently not dilapidated. She's more like a good state house of the sea with great indoor-outdoor flow. I haven't seen her yet, though,' I inform her.

'Wow! But you're not going to get much done in the next three days.'

Ross and I look at each other over our half-eaten breakfasts. 'Why not?'

'Public holidays. It's Carnival time,' Rick says.

I can't contain my excitement any longer: the thought of witnessing a real-life Caribbean parade is too much. 'Eat up, guys! Let's party's like it is going to be Lent on Wednesday!' I say, jamming food into Dash's mouth and running for my jandals.

I am no stranger to the concept of 'more is more'; in fact, I believe I may have had a hand in coining that phrase. Two hours later I am immersed in the true, bejewelled glory of it.

All day, costumes I have only dreamed of parade a mere metre away from me. Birds have been denuded, their feathers plucked from their soft bodies, dipped in brilliant dyes and glued to headdresses that would put a peacock's tail to shame.

'A golden butt chain!' I squeal. The sweaty crowd surges around us as one of their friends sambas past. Tall lust-struck teenagers pash right in front of me, blocking my view. I cough loudly. 'Hello . . . there is an all-in-one jewel-encrusted unitard walking past!' I shout over the music. They uncurl their tongues and look at me like I am an over-excited white lady at her first Caribbean parade. 'What?' I act surprised. When there are bedazzled boots, one-legged trouser suits and skin-tight satin so close to a recently retired Real Hot Bitch there is no time for niceties.

'Dash, look!' I mouth and point as one buxom lady wheels along her own personal float. 'Strut, pout, put it out — Pat Benatar, eat ya heart out!' I call to her in admiration. I wish I had thought of that — a personal float.

This is a *parade*. Old codgers sequinned up to their toothless chins mix with total foxes and ugly ducklings. Grandmothers shimmy with drag queens; young women eager to use the parade to show off their assets are upstaged by fat men in tight satin.

Combine the 32-degree heat and non-breathable fabrics and you have a sure-fire recipe for booze-a-rama group drunkenness. Each dazzling gang of show ponies has a mobile bar as its support crew. I love it.

The mere mortals on the sidelines clap and cheer and dance. Most families had set up camp the night before and are well provisioned with Portaloos, barbecues, ice-cold kegs, boom boxes and tiered seating. The party is set to go all night.

'Samba, shmamba — they are as in time as the Real Hot Bitches,' I say to Ross as we move towards the edge of the crowd for some fresh air. Dash makes a run for the beach.

'As a veteran parader — you know that aside from the Cuba Street Carnival, I was an elf in the 1988 Palmerston North Christmas Parade, eh?'

'I didn't, but go on,' Ross says, keeping a watchful eye on our son.

'Darling, I am suffering from parade envy!' I cry. 'I desperately want to shake my tail feather. I want to wear one of those flesh-coloured unitards with appropriately placed golden butt chains!' My heart is now beating in time with the extraordinarily loud sound system blasting its way along L. G. Smith Boulevard.

'Mama, look, shell?' Dash says, handing me a smooth pink shell that looks like a well-manicured nail.

I sit down next to my son and start digging with him. The beach is stunning: white sands, turquoise sea, fake boobs and itty-bitty bikinis with all manner of shapes and sizes squeezed inside them. Chilly-bins packed full of Balashi and unidentifiable snacks on skewers are guarded by dimp-ly women with smiling faces. There is more music, this time boom boxes blaring out a mixture of Genesis' 'Land of Confusion' and bad South American pop.

The sand is warm as it slips through my fingers.

'It may not be an hourglass, Dash, but these sure are the days of our lives,' I say. Ross raises his eyebrows, shakes his head and laughs.

'I think we should be heading back, it'll be dark in about an hour,' he announces.

'Really?' The sun is still burning my shoulders.

'In the tropics it's dark at six p.m.'

'OK,' I say. Dash is looking tired. He has been on his best behaviour all day and we are all beginning to feel jetlagged.

We start walking home past the Renaissance Marina where the luxury yachts are moored, past four cruise ships so enormous they dwarf the chocolate-box buildings lining the Oranjestad waterfront. A giant iguana stops us in our tracks; he looks like an Azerbaijani street fighter, complete with a tattooed tail, frilled neck, sharp claws and a fuck-off attitude.

'Hold it?' Dash says as he reaches for the tail.

'No darling, just look with your eyes,' I say, a little bit terrified. Visions of a badly scratched child fill my head. I find out later they are fellow vegetarians.

A truck roars past, blowing sand and glitter over us. The number plate reads, Aruba — one happy island.

17

Fight
the Filth

Today's the day. Today
I get to view the yacht we
have pinned our future
and meagre savings on,
the yacht whose siren-
like song has lured us
from the cosy confines
of Kelburn to the harsh,
blistering sun of Aruba, the
yacht whose name is so
obvious it is embarrassing:
Summertime.

As we get closer to setting sail I notice dramatic shift in Ross' description of *Summertime*. Six months ago it was 'She is a really solid boat — just needs a good clean.' Five months ago, 'It's a lot of boat for the price', three months ago, 'Think of her as the state house of the sea'. One week ago it became 'We will have our work cut out for us' and then, as we were about to touch down, the truth comes out. 'She's a dog, but we are up for an adventure, eh darling?'

We set off early, hoping to beat the blow-torch-like heat and begin to walk the dusty forty-five minutes to the bus depot. Even at 8 a.m. it is stinking hot. Dash sits in his pushchair slathered in sunscreen as we bump over mounds of rocks and rubbish that litter the side of the road. No pavement here, as no one walks. Only twenty years ago there were a handful of cars on the island, now hundreds of hulking SUVs with tinted windows choke the narrow roads. American package tourists hire dune buggies and quad bikes and roar around the streets, shouting to their buddies as they take short-cuts across roundabouts and off-road in the centre of town.

'I am sure the car is the emissary of the devil,' Ross says as we negotiate crossing the road.

A lifetime of looking left almost gets us killed. A car swoops over lanes of traffic towards us and just as I think 'This is the end' it pulls up hard on the brakes. The tinted window slides down and the driver says, '*Bon dia*! Where you go? I give you a lift?'

'Gracias, no, we are fine.' My adrenaline is pumping. After such a dramatic display of driving I figure I would rather take my life in my own hands than trust it to some well-meaning, mad-driving stranger.

'These Arubans sure are friendly,' I say as we finally spot a break in the traffic and madly dash to the other side. The pushchair wheels get stuck in the sand.

'Adventure, eh darling?' says Ross as he struggles to get all four wheels lined up. We walk past a derelict hotel, huge water towers, shipping containers and a light green- and white-tiled warehouse with 'Rum and More' written across the front in black old-fashioned lettering.

'Let's stop there on the way back,' I say, nudging Ross, the thought of an ice-cold rum making me salivate.

The sun beats down, frying my hair. What would the trashy mags say? I am going to need deep, deep conditioning by the time we get to Australia, but on the plus side I am going to be so brown and so thin! Ace.

We arrive at the brightly painted bus depot and collapse on the cool concrete bench. There are no timetables, just a hand-made cardboard sign propped up in the window of an idling bus. 'Sabana Basora' it reads.

'*Hola.*' Everyone here speaks Spanish, Dutch, Papiamento and a bit of English.

'Does this bus go to Bucuti?' Ross asks the hot-looking man sheltering next to us under the veranda.

He raises his eyebrows and shuts his eyes.

'I guess he is too hot to speak, but I think that means yes,'

I say to Ross as I wrestle with the pushchair and hold tightly to Dashkin's hand. Oh great, there is a turnstile on the bus. I attempt to slide the pushchair under it, lift my backpack over it, protect Dash from getting hit in the face by it and pay the driver all at the same time. Down the length of the bus blank faces stare at me. I smile. '*Bon dia!*' I am working on a warm greeting said in a pleasant tone to win me friends.

Dash loves the bus. Dash loves anything that is big and has wheels and a motor. He shakes with excitement and wants to sit in a seat all by himself.

The ex-Korean school bus kicks into life and we speed off with the doors open, past the pastel-coloured, white-trimmed buildings, past the scraggly dogs, past the 'Baby Back Ribs' shop. The driver yells out our destination at groups of people sheltering under trees and if anyone yells back he swerves madly to pick up them up. Bucuti, our destination, is behind the airport and just north of the rubbish dump.

We are dropped in a cloud of orange dust outside the Marco Polo Marina — a rather grand title for what turns out to be a fisherman's wharf.

Ross and I look at each other. This is it.

We walk towards the wharf. I can see her raked masts over the bleached wooden fence. I take a breath and squeeze Ross' hand.

We make our way down the steep steps. I lift my eyes from the rickety jetty and there is *Summertime*. She looks like a bag of arseholes.

I knew she was rough — I had pored over photos of her interior and the screen saver on our computer is a snap of her at anchor — but seeing her there with bits of frayed rope and rusty steel hanging off her, her bobbly seams oozing filler and with her name half missing, I feel like being sick.

I stand there very, very quietly.

'Angela, this is Reinhardt,' Ross says, introducing me to *Summertime*'s previous owner.

I find myself extending my hand while my eyes are locked on the bits of railing strewn around the wharf.

'Nice to meet you, I have heard so much about you,' I reply.

'All good, I hope,' Reinhardt jokes in his heavy German accent.

Thankfully, I can honestly reply, 'Yes.' Ross has regaled me with stories of the two of them playing chess and sharing meals. I dread him asking me what I think of the boat.

Luckily I am spared. Sparks from the welder start flying over the wharf, one narrowly missing my jandal. Ross picks up Dashkin.

'Don't let him look at the light, it will ruin his eyes,' Reinhardt says. Right now, looking at *Summertime* was hurting mine.

'This is Miguel — he is replacing the toerails and the chainplates. He is the best welder on the island,' Reinhardt says, introducing me to a wiry man squatting by the side of the yacht.

'This boat needs all the help she can get,' I say to myself through a false smile as I reply as cheerily as I can, 'Nice to meet you.'

I have nothing to say. Well, nothing I can say with Reinhardt and Miguel standing there. I can feel Ross watching my face for any trace of emotion. My sunglasses hide the *ice stare*. This face is reserved for severe cases of 'What the fuck have we done!'

'What do you think, darling?'

'Ummm, she looks bigger than *Astra*,' is all I can manage.

'Is it OK if we go aboard?' Ross asks Reinhardt.

'Sure, just try to look past the mess.'

I snap my head to look at him. What do you mean look past the mess? If the man who has been living on her for ten years thinks she is a mess, what hope is there?

Suddenly I have a flash of Kevin from *Grand Designs* doing a hushed piece to camera.

'I admire their determination but with only three weeks and a tiny budget I just don't know if they will be able to do it.' Cue long shot of ruined manor house.

'Be careful,' Reinhardt says, holding out his hand for me as I step over the freshly welded toerail and board my new home.

Bits of junk, including a garden-hose reel (this is a desert island, there are no gardens to speak off — what in God's name is a garden-hose reel doing on board?), clutter the deck, the cockpit has dog hairs stuck to it and there's a strong, fetid odour emanating from below.

Holding my breath I make my descent into the cabin. 'What's it like?' Ross calls from the cockpit.

'Beamier than I expected,' I call back, once my eyes have adjusted to the dim light. A smile of relief stretches across his face and he and Dash clamber down the companionway to join me in the saloon.

Reinhardt comes down too. It is suddenly very claustrophobic. He waves his hand towards the piles of books on the navigation table and declares in a way that only seventy-nine-year-old retired Germans doctors can: 'There is much more room without these.' No shit.

Pity the same can't be said for the galley. It is tiny. Even for a boat. The sink is outlined with green mould, a slimy cloth hangs over the faucet, plates and cups are jammed into an old dishrack and stuffed onto the shelf. A rope net, which if it was clean could add nautical charm, collects bits of food and grimy spoons. I slide back the cupboard doors. Cans with Dutch labels leak their contents over blackened anti-slip matting. I shiver involuntarily, like you do when you lick a lemon. Years of built-up grease, human and dog hair and skin shedding have created big dark stains on the wood. There's very little storage space and no gimballed stove. I don't want to put my hand on anything for fear of catching some flesh-eating bacteria. I can't help it, I gag.

'You OK, darling?' Ross asks, clocking me double-swallowing.

I cough 'Yes', squeezing the word out.

Continuing our tour, we take the required step from the galley into the equally repulsive saloon. It doesn't take a team of experts to realise that Reinhardt is a hoarder.

'I'd put money on the fact he hasn't thrown anything away for the last ten years,' I whisper to Ross. A heavy table with a collage of the Caribbean laminated onto it takes up all the floor space. The bunks are covered in strange pink and yellow candlewick upholstery, and more dusty books lie strewn around. Bits of rope and tools cover the portholes and block out the light. I spy the jazzy red plastic flowers under the machete. Not so classy now. Nothing is clean.

We inch forward and open the mirrored door into the head. The fittings have calcified and little bits of rusty metal crunch under my feet. I can barely bring myself to cast my eyes to the left. The toilet is grey with dirt, the pleated hoses are black. A bronze sign reads, 'Please only put things that have been eaten first down here', and to top it all off there is an outline of a hand on the wall.

'That must be where he puts his hand while he takes a piss,' Ross whispers.

'Holy shit . . .' I breathe.

I can just turn around. A door with another brass plaque, this time with 'Crew' on it, is in front of me. This is Dashkin's forepeak cabin.

I pull on the handle. With a tug, it opens. Bits of hosepipe, plugs, rope, more books and other filthy trinkets fall on top of me.

'I can't even see where the bed is,' I hiss to Ross. He quickly closes the door.

'That will be the first thing I clean out tomorrow, darling. Let's check out the stern cabin.'

I duck my head as we shuffle along the walkway under the cockpit and into the cabin.

This is where *Summertime* comes into her own. A huge bed stretches across the width of the yacht, portholes look out to the bright blue ocean and well-placed fans keep the stifling air circulating. But it smells like old man, the bedclothes are musty, dead flies litter any available surface, grease stains mar all the wood and piles of dust make me sneeze. Wires snake around the ceiling, running electricity to the TV. The blow-up toys are still there and, hanging on a hook, is a toy brass bugle.

'Just the kind of first home I have always dreamed of,' I say sarcastically to Ross as we come back on deck and breathe in less stinky air.

I look out to the Caribbean. Lines from Billy Ocean's 'Caribbean Queen' pop into my head . . . *sharing the same dream . . . two hearts that beat as one . . .* Marriage is about compromise and, for better or worse, I watch Ross as he helps Dash back into his pushchair. Despite the filth, I can tell Ross is excited. Really excited. This is our chance to live a different life, our only chance of sailing the world. I figure I had better buck up my ideas.

'Once I have removed those ugly curtains, repainted the ceiling, scrubbed the walls, thrown out the carpet, picked up the flies, sanitised every single surface and re-covered the soft furnishings, it will be lovely,' I say as cheerfully as I can.

Again I can hear Kevin from *Grand Designs*: 'It is repulsive. Yes, they paid a pittance for a yacht this size, but this boat is going to need a huge amount of sweat equity if she is ever going to leave this Aruban fisherman's wharf. Trying to do this with a twenty-month-old son seems . . . ludicrous.'

I hold Dashkin's hand and sit down, avoiding the prickles of the cactus trees, to wait for the bus. To my right, battered fishing boats are moored to the crumbling jetty and to the left, about a kilometre away, the rubbish dump smoulders.

18

Trouble in Paradise

— · —

I take a deep breath, squish Dashkin tightly and lift my right leg. This is no folk-dancing practice: this is boarding the yacht.

All I have to do is carry Dash along the gang-plank. Easy. I can use the self-steering system to steady myself, leap over the pile of ropes cluttering up the stern and be on deck in seconds.

I wait for the swell to be at its lowest and launch myself onto the old wooden plank. It's not steady, it wobbles. I lose my balance. 'Mama!' Dash calls, clinging to me. I suddenly have visions of Dash and I falling overboard, whacking our heads on the newly welded toerails and drowning in the drink. To top it all off, I am not wearing Goldie Hawn-style shoulder pads (*à la Overboard*) that can double as flotation devices. I stop, tensing every muscle in my body, exhale and inch my way towards the boat. I am determined not to get upset about this.

We make it on board, but there so many tools and bits of crap lying around the crusty deck I can barely pick my route to the companionway. Dash starts howling and Ross is just a wee bit too chipper for my liking.

'Isn't this great!' he says. He is possessed with sea fever. Ever since we met I had known he suffered from this most consuming of afflictions. We are here because he has to answer the call of the running tide. He lives for the wheel's kick and the wind's song and the white sail's shaking. I knew it was a wild call and a clear call that may not be denied. Luckily, I too am seduced by the thought of the vagrant gypsy life. But right now I am over it.

'I tell you, that John Masefield has a lot to answer for,' I say to Dash as I jiggle him on my hip. 'I'm not happy with the way we board her. It has to change,' I add, suddenly snapping.

'It's fine — there's no problem, it's how they do it in the Caribbean,' Ross reassures me.

'I don't care. I don't like it.' I am in rising drama-queen mode.

'Mama, Mama!' wails Dash for the hundredth time that day. He is hot and thirsty .

'It's fine,' Ross soothes.

'It is *not* fine!' I spit.

'MAMA, MAAAAAMAAA!'

'Here, you take him. I just need to sit outside for a moment,' I say, my eyes pricking with embarrassed tears.

'Umm . . . are you joking, darling?' Ross seems to realise things aren't going at all well.

'No, I am *not* joking. I don't know the first thing about sailing, I just . . .' and then the floodgates open.

I am a weeper. I get it from my dad. It is a well-known fact that Meyers are genetically predisposed to crying.

Mostly, I cry when I am happy, but seeing the yacht for the second time . . .

I thought I was OK with buying a filthy yacht and sailing around the world with a small child. I thought doing it on a very tight budget would make things more exciting, but obviously my subconscious has other ideas.

I desperately try to blink back the waterworks, conscious of the fishermen's eyes on me as they check out the gringa, conscious of Dash crying, conscious of how ridiculous I look weeping on the bow of a moored yacht.

But I can't stop.

The heat is exhausting and I am having a hard time adjusting to my new role as first mate. I sit on a pile of rotting ropes for twenty minutes, wetting my cheeks, thinking that this whole adventure is a disaster. I am pathetic! We haven't even left port and I am having doubts.

What kind of mother am I, to drag a little boy onto this flea-infested rust-bucket of a boat? After our visit yesterday I had noticed flea bites marching along his little legs and up his arms. Finally, once I can breathe without making that weird hiccuppy sob you do when you are properly crying, I hear my father's voice. Is that weird or what? He has two pearls of wisdom to impart. First, the '80s catch-cry 'Girls can do anything' (I guess that extends to sailing halfway around the world), and second, 'Do it once. Do it right', which could only mean stop snivelling and get cleaning!

I stand up, smooth down my frock, pull the halter-neck tie higher, which lifts my boobs into a pert position and, with John Meyer's words ringing loudly in my ears, I go below to face the filth, and the boys.

'Right, Ross, let's do this.'

'Mama, MAMA!'

'You OK, darling?'

'Yip, just a bit overwhelmed, but I am all right now.'

'Mama, MAMA!'

Soothing Dashkin's plaintive cries, I attack the disgusting galley with a new-found fervour. South American cleaning products (looking like brightly coloured sports drinks) are my arsenal against years of built-up human and canine filth. I squirt and scrub. I get out wire wool and scrub. My internal radio starts playing, and 'She Works Hard for the Money' comes on. I think about dancing to this song and winning the May Day cup with the Bitches in Palmerston North. We wore smocks and imagined we were cleaners instead of hookers. We used elbow grease, never seen before — or ever again— timing, laugh-out-loud comic gags and our incredible hot moves to blast our rivals, the Michelle Robinson Dancers, out of the competition. I sing as I remove the mould.

The head (toilet) cleaning takes a full eight hours of non-stop scrubbing, bleaching, rinsing, gagging, plucking and scraping to bring it to a level fit for human habitation. Pipes I honestly think are black are, I discover, *white*. It's worse than any shit-stained nightmare I have ever had. It's like being in a sauna breathing in toxic fumes while my skin is needled by thousands of Lysol droplets.

But the day does not end with a sparkling sink. Oh no. Dashkin lets us know he is *not* interested in watching his parents clean. Tired, hot, hungry (the yoghurt we had brought for his lunch had exploded in Ross' bag and there are no shops for miles), Dash shows up my feeble attempts at crying by letting out a murderous yowl. As if on cue, the sky turns black and a thunderous tropical downpour unleashes its fury.

'Quick, batten down the hatches!' Ross calls as he races to get the foam mattresses under cover. I am so pleased to be literally battening down hatches instead of the usual metaphorical kind that I squeal with delight. Amazed to see his mother leaping on the bunks, Dash stops crying.

Aruba is normally so parched that its drinking water is made in the world's second-largest desalination plant. But now there are flood-like rains. On land the sewers are overflowing, and when we get back to the B&B we find the pool is underwater.

Then, as suddenly as it started, it stops. The air is thick with humidity and we decide to call it a day.

I pick up Dash and step firmly onto the gangplank. We walk along the jetty and up the stairs to the bus stop.

'Well, darling, we've made a great start. There is no doubt about it, we still have a long way to go but if we keep this up, in ten days we should be ready to move on board,' Ross says.

'And just think, with every bit of cleaning we do, we are adding value. When we get to Oz we can put her on the market for twice as much.'

'Didn't Reinhardt knock seven grand off the price?'

'Yes, so we can put that money towards new soft furnishings.'

You gotta ask yourself why he did that, I think as the bus pulls up.

Damn those genetics.

19

Come Aboard

At 0930hrs on 21 March 2011 the Blacksmiths move on board.

Summertime is still pretty rough, with nothing to sleep on or eat off, but at least the grime and dog hair are gone.

'We're now "liveaboards"!' I announce to Ross. 'A fraternity I never imagined joining but oh, the twists and turns life takes . . .'

We drag our backpacks and provisions below. I'd had visions of Ross sweeping me off my feet and carrying me across the gangplank/threshold of our new home, but with six bags and a toddler he has his hands full.

We flop down in the saloon and stare at each other.

'Darling, we did it!' he says in a captainly tone.

I respond in an equally first-mate fashion, 'We sure did. To celebrate, I'll put the coffee on.' Dash, the ever helpful/ hindering cabin boy pipes up with, 'Dirty fly, yuck!'

'I think we should be proud of ourselves. In three weeks we have transformed this yacht into our very own Caribbean pleasure craft,' Ross continues, looking around at the warm oiled wood.

'I'll drink to that!' I say, pulling out the bottle of Aruban rum we had purchased from the famous Rum and More. Two days ago we had entered the showroom and were greeted by an overflowing tasting table. Bottles with photocopied labels were personalised with drawings of sunsets, dolphins and pirates.

Over the tannoy system, acid jazz played softly.

'Would you like to try?' a large Dutch woman asked us as she heaved herself out from behind the counter.

'Sure,' I said, as she poured coconut rum into a plastic thimble. I raised it to my lips and expected the smooth liquid to slide down my throat. Think again. This stuff was like paint stripper! Within ten seconds I'd turned bright red and was looking around for a discreet place to spit.

'It tastes like something you would slather on your legs in the eighties,' I spluttered. Ross wisely opted for the spiced rum, and while it was no Ron Abuelo it was smooth enough to justify spending US$8 on a bottle.

I splash a tot into Ross' coffee. Who ever heard of a boat without a stash of rum? In times gone by there'd have been a mutiny if the rum ration stopped.

'We are on a pretty tight schedule and we can't afford mutinies, so I guess this is only thing for it,' I say, filling up my cup.

We chink glasses. Dash climbs up onto the bare boards and snuggles into me.

We sip our drinks, the firewater mitigated by the coffee. The smell of old man is now replaced by a mixture of tea-tree oil, Pledge spray and dishwashing liquid. I can't believe we filled two skip bins with rubbish.

'I think we need some music,' I say, moving Dashkin onto my beautifully sewn red polka-dot cushions and making my way to the CD player.

Reinhardt literally walked off the yacht, leaving behind clothes, undies, pipes, every kind of tool imaginable, grime and grease, plates, pirate costumes and a very interesting selection of CDs. Titles include *23 German Hits from the Early '90s*, Ravel's 'Boléro', an informative CD on how to treat tapeworm and the granddaddy of them all, *Rod Stewart's Greatest Hits*!

I have always enjoyed Rod's husky tones, and while admitting my adolescent fascination with Rod Stewart is tantamount to social suicide, I challenge anyone not to acknowledge the poignancy of listening to 'We Are Sailing' while on your own yacht. With Ross in a pair of Stubbies it was as if Rod could read my mind when he belted out 'Hot Legs'. *This* is music to unpack to!

Dash agrees. 'Dance, dance!' he says as he waves his little fists around and dances with me in the saloon.

'It is the closest thing I've got to a living room!' I yell over the music.

Ross raises his cup. 'Go for it, darling!'

We spend the rest of the morning unpacking, and by lunchtime *Summertime* is slowly transforming into *Te Ikaroa*.

'Hello!' a voice calls from the jetty.

'Hello?' I call, coming up the companionway.

'Is your boy here?' A dark-haired boy is standing barefoot on the jetty, holding a fishing line.

'Yes . . .' I answer suspiciously. Who was this kid?

'What's his name?'

'Dashkin. What's yours?'

'Leendrick'

'Hi Leendrick. Do you want to come on board?'

'Yes.' He slides along the gangplank and is standing next to me in a flash.

'This is my father's wharf. That is his fishing boat,' he says, pointing to a yellow boat with the name *Nina* written on the cabin.

'Who's Nina?'

'She is my sister, she's a pain. Can I play with your son, Dashkin?'

'Sure. He is sleeping at the moment but as soon as he wakes up I will bring him over to the wharf.'

Rudi, Leendrick's father, is our landlord (or should that be sealord?). He owns the wharf and for US$200 a month is letting us live on board, use the water and washing machine, open-air cold shower and plumbed toilet. He played pro baseball in the '80s in Holland and now lives in Aruba with his children Leendrick (twelve), Nina (four) and his youngest daughter Genesis (two), living proof that Phil Collins is still a hit in Aruba.

'What is your boat called?' You gotta love the inquisitiveness of youth.

'*Te Ikaroa.*'

'Te ika roa . . .' He says the words slowly, trying to figure out if he knows them. At twelve, Leendrick speaks four languages. 'That's not Spanish, is it?'

'Nope, it is Maori. It means the long fish or sometimes it translates as the Milky Way.'

'Oh, a long milky fish.'

I laugh. 'You could look at it that way, I suppose.' I had wanted to call her *Le Coquesmith* (a combination of Candy Le Coque and Blacksmith) or *Wet Wet Wet* but the captain had far more romantic ideas and named her *Te Ikaroa* in honour of the Polynesian voyage we are taking her on.

I hear a little voice in the forepeak cabin. 'Ohhh, Mama . . .' Dashkin is waking up and soon his feet will be drumming on the board we jam across the door to stop him from falling out.

'Hang on, I'll just go and get Dash.' I peer over the board and look at my sweaty little boy. There is a wet stain where he has been sleeping. His eyes are sleepy and he reaches his hands up for me to lift him out. We look at the thermometer: 35 degrees Celsius. 'Hot,' we say together.

'Juicey, Mama?' he asks. I go to the icebox and get his bottle out. He sucks it back thirstily.

'Dash, Leendrick is outside. He wants to play with you.'

'Outside, outside,' he says, and heads to the steps.

I am still very nervous about Dash being on deck. One trip and he would be over the side. Even though we are at anchor I put him in his harness. We had trawled the internet for days looking for one that was small enough for him. Finally we found a Danish-made industrial-strength harness that I was sure would keep him tied to the boat.

'Why is he wearing that?' Leendrick asks, genuinely bemused. He's grown up diving off the jetty, swimming before he could walk and is supremely confident in the small dingy he whizzes around the bay in.

'I'm paranoid,' I answer.

He looks at me like I am a fool. 'OK,' he says, shrugging his shoulders.

I hand them a box of screws and nuts. 'Could you two sort these out for me please?'

'Sure,' he says picking up Dashkin and setting up a 'work station' under the shade of the wharf.

I go back into the cabin and keep cleaning. The bare boards where our squabs should be glow in the shaft of light beaming in through the hatch.

I planned to make my mark in the soft-furnishings department. I fancied myself a Martha Stewart of the sea. Much of my preparation in New Zealand was spent looking through *House & Garden* magazines, imagining a fresh, cheap new interior for my first ever home. As luck would have it, Mum had a bolt of drill cotton stashed next to the Christmas decorations which was perfect for the new 'look'. I enlisted the help of Gabe's mum, Christine, who is well known for her upholstery prowess, and she whipped up some covers for us.

A few days ago I had happily ripped off the old stale covers, only to find the foam rubber was a health hazard. Bugs had gouged out a hole the size of someone's butt cheeks and were forming tunnels in the remaining foam. Plus, Reinhardt had given Ross an approximation of the measurements of the covers as he couldn't be bothered moving all the junk! Disaster. My tasteful beige-and-white-check covers were useless.

There was only one thing to do. I armed myself with a copy of *Spanish for Cruisers*, enlisted the help of my new friend Sherrie, and went on a mission to find someone in Aruba who could make my soft furnishings.

For two days we crisscrossed the island, got caught in traffic jams and had the jalopy break down, until we finally discovered Hassan and his Orange Matrick Fabric factory. *Spanish for Cruisers* didn't cut it, as Hassan spoke Arabic! Luckily the age-old language of point, draw, sign and haul out a wad of US dollars worked wonders.

These guys were amazing. Not only did we have fantastic new squabs and mattresses, we had them delivered to the yacht within three days!

I reckon Kevin from *Grand Designs* would be proud. In real-estate terms, *Te Ikaroa* was 'a little slice of paradise, complete with a rustic charm and great indoor–outdoor flow. Perfect for those after the simple things in life.'

20
Glitterati

'Ross! Ross! Oh God!
Dashkin!' Blood was
running into his eyes,
down his nose and
dripping onto the wharf.

'**H**e fell into the bilge!' I hold him close and try to calm down. 'I don't know how it happened — he was standing on the squabs and then suddenly I saw him back-flip into the bilge. I thought he had broken his neck!'

I am in a *state*. I know that children hurt themselves. I know that as a mother of a little boy I have to expect lots of cuts and scrapes but this is the first time I have seen blood gushing out of my son's head. I scooped him out of the bilge, jumped off the yacht and run to Ross on the wharf as fast as I could.

'Sit down. I'll get the first-aid kit,' Ross says, running back to the yacht.

The white plastic chair sticks to my back as Dashkin's blood drips over my shoulder. His hair is wet with warm red blood.

'Darling, it's OK, let Mama see,' I say, soothing him.

He finally cries. Up until now he has been holding his breath. On his forehead I see a half-moon-shaped gash.

'OK, stay still, darling. Mama has to wash it.' The bilge is hardly the most sterile of environs and already I am imagining raging infections. I pick up the hose and try to turn it on with one hand and hold my screaming son in the other. The water rushes out and, to add insult to injury, sprays all over him. Dashkin hates getting his face wet. He is wriggling and screaming and the blood is still pouring out of his head. I can't see if it needs stitches or not.

I move us under one of the fluorescent lights. The white light makes everything seem surreal. Bugs swarm around us and huge moths slap into my face. I try to keep calm and carry on.

'Ange, sit down. Dash darling, I am going to put a plaster on.' Ross is back, the contents of the first-aid kit spilled out over the table on the wharf.

'We have to sterilise it,' I say, fumbling with a hygienically sealed packet of expensive wet wipes. 'At least Reinhardt left us a good supply of these,' I joke.

Ross puts one on Dash's head. The alcohol stings. I try to hold him still.

Luckily there is a towel hanging on our makeshift washing line. I pull it off and wipe Dash's face. He starts to cry a little less. Ross and I inspect the wound.

'I think it needs stitches,' I say.

'I agree, but we can't get him to a hospital.' Rudi and Leendrick had left an hour earlier, the buses have stopped, the Bucuti Yacht Club next door — which is really just an open-air pub — is closed and there are no phones for miles.

We keep checking through the kit. There are pressure bandages, syringes, masks, pills, splints, slings, intravenous drug kits, more sterile wipes, hundreds of sterile wipes, but where are the butterfly plasters? I packed the kit in New Zealand; Rosie from the Real Hot Bitches, as a newly qualified nurse, had acted as my professional health advisor. 'I know they are in here!'

'Ah-ha!' Ross exclaims, holding up the unusual-shaped plaster. We open it and, squeezing the wound together slowly, put it on his head. He finally stops bleeding. I wrap a cloth bandage around for good measure.

'I could use a Valium,' I say, leaning back and hugging Dash to my chest. Ross has a smear of blood on his cheek. We have a family hug.

'You can sleep in our cabin tonight, darling,' I say to Dash. He snuggles into me a little more.

I settle Dashkin in the stern cabin, then Ross and I sit in the saloon with a stiff drink.

'My only goal for this whole adventure is that we all arrive in one piece.' After tonight I mean it more than ever.

'Same,' Ross says, draining his glass and standing up. 'Ange, we need to keep packing. Tomorrow we set sail.'

Next morning the sun blushes its way into our cabin. Ross is jammed up against the port side, I am twisted into a strange 's' shape on the starboard side and lying spreadeagled, taking up three-quarters of a very large bed, is Dashkin.

'Good morning,' I whisper to Ross as he slowly moves his head from side to side. He sits up and clicks the fan to the top speed. Warm air blows across my face. Everything aches and itches. 'Rough night,' I say, attempting to stretch out my shoulders.

'Mozzies out in force.' We can't talk in full sentences yet.

'Ten past six,' I groan, moving my legs and wriggling over to inspect Dashkin's head. The blood has dried and it looks much better. A flash of light reflects off something white on the wharf straight into my eyes. 'What is going on out there?'

We look out the portholes on the stern and see three big men manhandling a fridge onto the jetty. Over the past week, under the cover of darkness, whiteware had been appearing. Three fridges, one with an unopened bottle of horseradish sauce still sitting proudly in the door, two small freezers and a coffee-maker had been loaded into a jet boat, which then sped off out to sea. Who knew an old fridge could fit so snugly into a speed boat? Turns out our neighbours are smuggling kitchen appliances into Venezuela. How rock and roll, I think — we are moored next to real-life Caribbean smugglers!

On a clear day, when the smoke from the rubbish dump isn't blowing toxic fumes all over us, you can see the Venezuelan coast. It is only 18 miles away but there is very little trade.

'Sorry for language, but they are fucken robbers,' says the racist barman at the yacht club where we are having a few drinks after a long day of grinding and painting. 'They come here and take our jobs.'

I sigh. Paranoia about immigration is the same the world over.

'Well, things are hardly fun in Venezuela — Chavez has seen to that. Good on them for trying to find a better life,' I say, thinking how much this small-minded idiot bugs me.

'Those guys in Venezuela are very skilled at fixing things. They'll have those old fridges going in no time,' Rudi says, signalling the barman to get three more ice-cold Balashis out of a huge chilly-bin.

'And the Colombians, they will try to kidnap your son,' Idiot says, placing the beers down and looking me in the eye. I glance at Ross, my temper rising.

'We'll take our chances,' Ross says, rubbing my back and giving me a kiss on the cheek to placate me.

The talk of kidnapping pricks my conscience. 'I'll go and check on Dashkin.' *Te Ikaroa* is moored at the next wharf, in sight of the bar, but still . . .

I jump through the chicken-wire fence, saying '*Hola*' to the hammock-dwelling stevedores Carlos and Levi. These guys are like human guard-dogs. Every night at about 5.30 p.m. they appear, eat their fried chicken and rice and take up residence in their hammocks. They like nothing better than watching *Dancing with the Stars — South America* on their enormous television. I swear glitter runs through their veins.

'*Hola*,' they call back, readjusting themselves in their striped cocoons. I sit and watch a few minutes with them.

The screen is full of yellows, reds, greens and purples. Arms and legs are feverishly whizzing around, while a cascade of mirror balls suspended above them shoots silver light into the camera. I am, of course, mesmerised.

'Wow . . . look at that move!' I say to Carlos. He nods enthu-siastically. '*Si, si.*' A drop-dead-gorgeous woman is being swung through her partner's legs and raised high above his head in an exquisitely graceful move. Carlos and I beam at each other. I laugh. Here I am sitting on a fisherman's wharf with an Aruban stevedore watching *Dancing with the Stars*. Fantastic.

He gets out his phone to vote. Drop Dead Gorgeous' number runs along the bottom of the screen as she smiles out at us. I give him an Aruban florin and he votes twice.

Dashkin! I get up and run to the yacht. I had been side-tracked by sequins.

I peer through his hatch. He is still there and, thankfully, sleeping soundly.

'I'll get the porridge on,' Ross says, as he climbs out of bed. The excitement of watching the fridge smuggling has worn off.

'Good plan. Then Dash and I will cycle down to the port authority to clear customs, while you get the final things ready for our maiden voyage,' I say excitedly, picking up Dashkin and helping him over the bulkhead. Our belongings had finally arrived after a six-week delay. Turns out the cargo ship had run aground on a sandbar in the Bahamas.

We spend the rest of the day filling up water and fuel tanks, double-checking the sails, stashing everything down below, ensuring the charts are lined up on the navigation table, sorting out nappies, frying sausages and hard-boiling eggs. Finally, at 5 p.m. on 21 April 2011, we haul up the anchor. My stomach flips. This is it.

Rudi, Leendrick and Nina sit atop their boat, waving until we are out of sight. My eyes well with tears — they have been great friends to us.

I turn to Ross standing at the tiller and see he has sneaky tears too.

'*Te Ikaroa*, keep us safe,' I whisper as we sail into the setting sun towards Santa Marta, Colombia.

21

Butt Cheeks of Steel

The silvery night is cool. *Te Ikaroa* rides slowly over the waves, leaving a trail of phosphoresence in her wake. The mainsails, mizzen and yankee jib are set for comfortable night-time passage, not to eke every last knot out of the light trade wind.

Below me, Dashkin and Ross are sleeping. I press the button on my watch and the fancy luminescence shows me it is 3.23 a.m. I scan the horizon for ships: nothing, just me and the sea.

I gaze out into the velvet blackness, breathing in the clean salt air. It is so peaceful, so much more serene than I ever imagined. I feel the stress of the last few weeks leaving me. I am alone for the first time in two months, there is no one sitting on my knee, no one asking me to hold this or paint that. It is blissful. It's the perfect time to do some squats.

'Exercise your way to Santa Marta!' I think as I hold the tiller behind my back, steady myself on the rolling deck and launch into a series of fifty squats. It is surprisingly enjoyable. I can check the compass, check for ships, adjust the tiller and tone my arse all at the same time!

30 . . . 31 . . . over halfway . . . 32, 33 . . . I am going to have butt cheeks of steel . . . 34, 35 . . . stay on course . . . 36, 37 . . . what is that on the horizon? . . . 38, 39 . . . is it a light? . . . 40, 41 . . . yep, it is a light . . . 42 . . . oh, hang on, get back on course, Ange! I swing the tiller to starboard. 43, 44 . . . hmmm, it's moving very fast . . . 45 . . . that is no cargo ship . . . 46 . . . oh my lord, maybe it's pirates! 47 . . . we *are* off the coast of Colombia, the drug-smuggling capital of the *world* . . . 48 . . . I can hear the throb of

diesel engines *and they are getting closer!* 49 . . . my thighs are killing me . . . 50!

'Rooooossss!' I whisper down the hatch so as not to wake Dashkin. Nothing. 'Ross! There are pirates heading towards us! It is only a matter of minutes before we will be shot to death!'

That wakes him up. Ten seconds later he is on deck.

'Yip, that is definitely coming towards us. Could be the coast guard. You're on communications — get on the radio and see if they are trying to raise us.'

I clatter downstairs — my legs have turned to jelly.

'Guarda Costa, Guarda Costa, this is the sailing vessel *Te Ikaroa*, copy.' Nothing. I peer out the porthole next to the nav table — the drug-smuggling pirates are about forty seconds away. I come back on deck, imagining Dashkin being taken away and sold into child slavery, and Ross and I begging for our lives.

'Shit, Ross, what are we going to do?' We don't carry a gun, it is totally against our pacifist ideology. In our safe, deep in the engine room, we have US$7000 wrapped in a blue-and-yellow-polka-dot scarf.

'I'm not sure, darling. We'll give them the money and the booze and see.' The light is so close we have to squint into it. My heart is going crazy; I feel like I am going to pass out. Then it veers away, turning further out to sea.

'Guess we weren't worth robbing,' Ross says, heading back to bed. There are still two-and-a-half hours left on my watch.

'Sorry to wake you. I tried to handle it by myself but I felt the captain needed to know.'

'You did the right thing. Call me if you need anything else.'

Sitting back down on the stern I take a few calming breaths and hum hymns. Whenever I am scared I find a quick rendition of 'Brother, Sister, let me serve you' very beneficial.

I check the GPS. We are making two knots. At this rate it will take us about five days to get to Santa Marta. We could probably walk faster.

Other than the almost-taken-hostage experience the voyage

is going well. Dash seems happy, the yacht is performing well and Ross is doing a marvellous job as captain. Before we left I stocked our tiny icebox with curry, rice, pasta and snacks in anticipation of being completely laid low with *mal de mer* but so far I am not feeling seasick. I am excited.

The bucket of nappies slops next to my leg. 'Phew . . . I'll rinse those in the morning,' I say to myself. The salt water combined with little-boy wee creates a rich brew, but once we have washed them six times, hung them over the railings and let the sun bleach out any bugs they are like new.

It feels good not to be using disposables. In Aruba, Leendrick thought nothing of throwing his little sister's nappies in the sea. I caught him one day and tried to educate him against doing this. He spent his life on the sea — surely he didn't want to be swimming next to pooey nappies? He just shrugged his shoulders.

It seems most people here feel this way. Instead of the pristine waters we hoped to find, the ocean is littered with Styrofoam cups.

We are about 60 miles off shore and I can just make out the silhouette of the hills, pitch black against the lighter black of the sky. We make our way slowly down the coast, pitching and rolling ever so slightly. *Te Ikaroa* is beamy and strong and rides the waves likes something that rides waves really well. I decide to ditch the second set of squats and enjoy the solitude.

A reddish light catches my eye. This time it is in the sky over the land. It seems to be tailing us. I'll give it ten minutes and then I'll wake Ross, I think as the light twinkles.

Straining my eyes and trying to keep my imagination in check I decide it is definitely a helicopter.

'Ross . . . I think we are being followed.'

Again Ross is on deck. 'Oh, that. Last night I thought it was following us too but then I realised it is just Venus.'

I am really going to have to get a grip or at this rate I will have an ulcer by Easter.

22

Deep-
Sea Dip

———

'Tie the rope around your waist,' Ross instructs. Dash is clipped onto the strong-bolt at the bottom of the mizzen mast and is crying loudly under the blue, yellow, red and orange-striped sun umbrella, which is acting as a makeshift bimini.

'Mama is just going for a swim, darling, I will be back soon.'

He is not convinced. 'No swim, no swim!' he demands.

Sometimes in life you have to block out the plaintive cries of your children and plunge into the seething blue mass of the sea. Also, my armpits reek. It is Good Friday and instead of watching *Jesus Christ Superstar* and eating Charlotte's home-made hot-cross buns I am about to plunge into the churning, possibly shark-infested water.

'You're on shark watch, Ross,' I say as I inch my way down the stern ladder. Three steps in and my toes are washed with salty water. Then, as we slide down a wave, I am up to my neck. With a scream, I let go. The rope pulls taut and I begin swimming furiously, trying to keep up with 16 tons of steel. This beats any ride at the Palmerston North A&P show.

While sitting on deck and gazing out at the azure sea it looked as if we were hardly moving; but now I am in the water I discover we are charging along. Who knew three knots was so quick? I can see how easy it would be to get lost overboard.

Below me are hundreds of fathoms of water. 'Fathom this,' I say to myself as I splutter and cough and attempt to impress Ross with my freestyle technique. I try really hard not to freak out but as *Te Ikaroa* rises and falls on the waves and I struggle to swim fast enough to keep up, I feel the familiar surge of adrenaline and forget all about my stinky pits. I scream and thrash about, which will no doubt attract sharks. Even though I know I am not going to drown or be left behind (I am tied on, for God's sake), I convince myself it is only a matter of minutes before my leg is ripped off.

As a special treat for Leendrick's thirteenth birthday, I had taken him to the movies in Oranjestad. We ate orange processed-cheese nachos and watched a film about a young girl surviving a shark attack. Flashbacks of her bleeding into the water are enough to send me into panic mode, and thankfully get my legs kicking fast. Super fast. I manage to grab the ladder and haul myself out of the water.

'That. Is. Really. Freaky!' I announce, dripping water all over our nicely scrubbed teak deck.

'I am sure it wasn't that bad. Here, you hold the rope while I have a dip,' Ross says. He bounds down the ladder and swims confidently along behind the yacht. Immediately I want to have another turn. Damn it, I tell myself, anything you can do, I can better. (This personality trait is unattractive and bloody annoying. It has got me into some dicey situations over the years and now it is about to get me back in the water.)

'I have to get back in. I have to face my fear and do it anyway.' Ross gives me the 'sometimes you are a bit of a dick' look as he towels himself off. It must be difficult being married to someone who quotes self-help mantras if you are a pretty cynical character.

Again I tie on the rope, smile at Dashkin and lower myself down. This time I know what to expect. I brace myself for the pull of the water, take a deep breath and let go. Waves whoosh past me. I try not to look up at *Te Ikaroa*'s masts towering above me, I empty my mind of shark thoughts, I count to thirty and then, when I am sure I have faced down my fear, I clutch the ladder, letting out a huge sigh of relief.

Dashkin and Ross clap as I return to the stern deck. They

know me so well. I take a bow and lie down on the warm wood to dry out. Dash gingerly staggers over towards me, sliding over the deck as the yacht rolls, and lands with a thud on my stomach, winding me. He is not amused. While Ross and I are having a great time sunning ourselves, high-fiving each other on our adventurousness, Dashkin has hardly left my lap. The poor kid has only recently learnt to walk and now, just as he has got the hang of it, everything starts bucking and moving on him.

'It's OK, sweetheart.' I hug him close. 'Can you see any dolphins?'

Ross and I look around expectantly. Dash perks up and garners enough courage to stand propped up against one of the gear boxes secured on the deck. I rearrange the cushions so he has something soft to press against and he seems happy to scan the horizon. He smells like sunscreen as he wraps his arm around my neck. I love him so much I want to cry.

'Right, I think I'll turn on the engine and recharge the batteries,' Ross says, getting up and making his way into the cockpit. We had filled the 400-litre keel tank with diesel in Aruba. My eyes had watered at the price, but we reasoned this would get us to Cartagena and maybe further if the trade winds held.

I could hear Ross counting . . . 'Eight, nine, ten . . .' Like any diesel engine, you have to prime *Te Ikaroa*'s before it will kick into life. He turns the key. It coughs but doesn't take. I look up.

'All OK?'

'Yeah, it should be. I'll try again.' He repeats the process. Again, nothing. 'I'll check the fuel lines. Could be an air bubble or something.' He disappears down below and I hear him moving tools. 'They look fine, I'll try again.' He tries again. Nothing.

The battery gauge shows that we are only on 11 volts — not enough to start the engine.

'OK, I'm going to leave it for a while, let the solar- and wind-power recharge the battery and then give it another go.'

Dash and I move into the shade as Ross tries to ensure that the starter battery is isolated from the mains. The control panel is all in German and the repairs Reinhardt has made over the years look like a bird's nest of black wires. As first mate, I come down to offer moral support.

'I think it is the pre-heating, Ange.' Oh heck, the pre-heating . . . I am not entirely sure what that means but I figure it is not good.

One of the reasons we had decided that this was the yacht for us was the engine. It is only 50 horsepower but it looked like it was in pretty good nick. We were yet to find out how very, very wrong we were.

The engine room is in the centre of the boat, accessed through the stern cabin. It reeks of diesel and is *very* hot. Ross goes back in for another look. I can't even poke my head in there; the very thought of it is enough to turn my stomach.

He checks everything and realises that it must be the solenoid switch that is broken. Which means that now we have to rely completely on the wind to get us safely to Santa Marta, which means patience. Lots of patience . . .

As a novice sailor (not that I am now in any way experienced), I was always looking at the clock, thinking, In three hours we will be around that headland, in four hours we will be in the lee of that island, and by dinnertime we will be dropping the anchor in some lovely bay. Being continually disappointed taught me otherwise. Sailing takes ages. (OK, OK, if you are in a flash boat and fancy yourself a bit of a Peter Blake then it is quick, but if you are in an old boat in light winds, believe me it takes forever . . .)

But once I 'let go' (self-help again) and stopped watching the clock I began to enjoy the slow passages. The constant need when you are on land to be connected disappears. You can't get emails so you cease to worry about checking them or sending them. Facebook and Twitter become face-time and conversations. I find myself quickly reading an Elizabethan love poem while Dash kneads the playdough. I prepare food, and Ross and I have wonderful long, rambling discussions. I learn how to read the GPS, plot us on the map and keep an active little boy entertained. Days morph into each other as we slowly, slowly inch our way down past the northernmost headland of South America, Cabo de la Vela, the lights of Bahia Honda and towards Santa Marta. I feel like a sailor of old.

Easter Sunday dawns and the wind freshens as we close in on Santa Marta. We are all very excited — we are about to make our first landfall. Dash and I creep out on deck as dawn breaks. The dark-green jungle-covered hills of the Parque Tayrona come into view as the sky lightens. The name makes me hum 'My Sharona' as I put the coffee on.

Finally, after months of reading and planning, the names in our cobbled-together cruising guide are coming to life. We get the binoculars out and look for the twin peaks of Simón Bolívar and Cristóbal Colón. Both have an altitude of 5770 metres above sea level, making them the tallest seaside mountains in the world. Unfortunately the cloud cover hides them.

I am keen to hike to Ciudad Perdida, the Lost City. It is a five-day hike from Santa Marta into the lost city of the Tayrona empire, which pre-dates Machu Picchu by six hundred and fifty years. It was 'discovered' in 1972 by a group of local treasure hunters who followed some stone steps they found in the jungle. The butt-busting twelve hundred steps led to an abandoned city made up of over one hundred and fifty terraces carved into the mountainside, complete with tiled roads and stone plazas.

Soon golden figurines and ceramic urns began turning up on the black market, raising the suspicions of the local police, and after some gentle persuasion the looters revealed their treasure store. In 1975 the authorities took over the running of the site but that didn't stop eight foreign tourists being kidnapped in 2003 by the National Liberation Army.

For the thirty years the concerns and claims of the local indigenous population were ignored, until finally, in 2009, the Global Heritage Fund begun working in Ciudad Perdida to preserve and protect the historic site. By all accounts the trek is a long, hard grind with mosquitoes nipping at any exposed flesh, but to me it sounds great. I may not be very good on the water but one thing I can do is walk.

'Half a knot, wow,' I say, checking the GPS and bringing out thick, black coffee to Ross. He has been on watch for eight hours, cat-napping when he could. I think he looks very handsome, like a man who could advertise an expensive sports watch.

The wind drops off as we get into the lee of the land, the bay of Taganga opens up to our left and in the distance we see the lighthouse of Santa Marta. We slop about and I continue to try to raise the Guarda Costa on the VHF.

By mid-morning a light breeze begins blowing from the east and finally, after five days at sea, we sail into the harbour. The Easter Sunday crowds promenade and frolic on the beach and boulevard, and keep an amused eye on the new ketch attempting to anchor in the bay.

'Come in, the sailing vessel entering the harbour.' Finally the VHF talks back to me — in English! I blush, embarrassed at my mangled attempts to speak Spanish.

'Yes, we are the sailing vessel, over.' Rats, I have forgotten all the protocol I am meant to use over the airwaves. We are advised by 'John' to anchor in the harbour and a mechanic will be sent to us.

The smells and sounds of a whole new culture are so tantalisingly close; through the binoculars I spy old men frying fish over barbecues, families playing in the sand, teenage boys fishing off the rocks, soldiers with AK47s slung over their shoulders, fruit-sellers laden down with pineapples, mangos and bags of ice, and people in traditional clothes sitting under the shade of a gorgeous yellow flowering tree with baskets and trinkets laid out before them. A huge, muscular statue of a group of Tayrona Indians stands slap bang in the middle of the promenade, keeping watch over the sea. Wafting over the water I hear car horns, snippets of Spanish and, cutting through it all, the tinkle of the ice-cream seller's bell as he bumps his way along the foreshore. I am ready to jump overboard and swim to shore for a taste of cool, creamy goodness when I remember we are still flying the 'yet to clear customs' yellow flag.

A fizzboat comes zooming out of the flash new marina and makes its way towards us. On it is Megan the mechanic.

He is dark and wiry and on the deck in no time. I try to explain that we have engine trouble, that it won't start and could he please have a look at it for us. I am still in my bikini and it has been a while since I've had the chance to sort out my bikini line. I suddenly feel very exposed. It is all right wandering around in bugger-all in the middle of the ocean but now, with a strange man on board, I feel stink. I grab a salt-encrusted towel off the lifelines and wrap it around myself. Ross is in his undies too but they look like tight togs.

Megan pokes around but can't find the problem. Through a series of hand signals and the occasional word of Spanish, it is decided that we will try to sail into the marina. Before we have a chance to work out a plan, Megan has pulled up the anchor and is back in his dinghy, ramming the side of the yacht.

'What the hell is going on?' I shout to Ross, who is equally panicked.

'I think he is trying to push her in.'

'In a dinghy? What the hell?' I run around the blistering hot deck tossing out the fenders. 'Megan isn't a mechanic, he is a maniac!' I call back to Ross, who is pushing the sails over and getting ready to gybe into the narrow marina entrance. *Te Ikaroa* has other ideas. She is not going to be pushed and gybed anywhere. She falls off the wind and we are right in the middle of the shipping lane. We drop the anchor to stop us drifting any further, and with that Megan throws up his hands and zooms off in a blaze of two-stroke fumes.

'What the hell was all that about?' I ask Ross.

'I don't know, Ange, but now we are in a bloody crazy spot.'

This whole deeply embarrassing debacle provides much amusement for the Easter Sunday crowd. I get back on the VHF and sheepishly request a tow . . . and who should turn up but the elusive Guarda Costa. Their dark grey boat pulls up alongside us. Two enormous 450-horsepower engines perfect for out-running drug smugglers hulk in the stern, but all I am focusing on are the four pistols and three AK47s.

'Are you OK?' A smiling face peers out from under a dark blue hat.

'Ah, not really. We have engine trouble,' I say, hoping that if I speak slowly it will make up for the fact I am not speaking Spanish.

The guarda, Nicola, asks for permission to board. (Another girls' name — for some reason, Colombia is full of guys with girls' names.) I grant it . . . as if I was going to say no! I am still freaking out about the guns.

Unlike Megan, Nicola is full of helpful suggestions. After some rapid-fire Spanish a thick tow-rope lands with a thud next to my foot. I tie it around one of the cleats, while Ross secures the bow. John from the VHF stands expectantly on the T-berth in the marina and, after a bit of discussion, *Te Ikaroa* is slowly towed into port.

The Blacksmiths' maiden voyage is over.

23

Pump
It Up

—·—

'Pump up the jam … pump it up …' Itty-bitty booties are pumping up the jam all right, right next to our star-spangled ketch. The marina is so new we are in time for the opening party. On a thick finger of broken concrete a mere 5 metres away from our deck, promotional girls shake and pump it and ensure all the rich old men who invested in Santa Marta's swankiest new development are suitably 'thanked'.

'Coming up next is the Miss Santa Marta beauty pageant,' a fat, greasy DJ announces over the PA. Dash loves pretty girls and stands expectantly on the starboard side, waiting for the show to begin.

I don't stand a chance. I can see that my stay in Colombia is going to be soul-destroying. The women here are stunning. Their breasts are amazing, their caramel-coloured skin well moisturised and their long, thick, dark tresses cascade down their toned backs. Great. In comparison I am a frazzle-haired, pink-skinned chubby.

Dash and Ross enjoy the show as I try miserably to 'rise above' my jealousy. It's no good. I crack open another can of beer. Take me back to Aruba with its obese flubbery American tourists! At least I look good by comparison.

I take another swig of warm beer. I know it is empty calories, but right now *I don't care*. Even when I was twenty-two my boobs weren't that high!

The pageant prances on and the contestants are soon narrowed down to the final five. Miss Perty Pert takes out third place, Miss Ridiculously Gorgeous with the flicky hair is handed the second-place-getter tiara, and just as the winner is about to be announced, the heavens open. It buckets down, sending the leering old gents running for shelter under flimsy tarpaulins. I smile. 'Ha — that is what happens if you are too hot! The gods send rain to cool you down!' No more Club Colombia for me. I am getting belligerent.

The deck starts steaming; we retire down below and turn on the fan. It is finally quiet. The rain shut down the PA too.

'Phew, I can actually hear myself think,' I say. Oh marvellous, now I am turning into a curmudgeon. In fairness, though, the music was insanely loud, so loud we had to shout to hear each other and after the wind at sea we were all craving a bit of silence.

'I'm heading to bed,' Ross says, dragging himself off the couch and walking towards the stern cabin. 'Sleep well, darling, I'll get up to Dash in the morning.' We have a day-on, day-off system as Dashkin refuses to sleep later than 6 a.m. According to Ross it is my genes that have caused this wakefulness — apparently Holly and Nina were never early risers. 'And you are younger than me, Angela — you don't need as much sleep as I do.'

The next morning — breaking the law, as we have yet to clear customs and immigration — we leave the confines of the marina and head into the city. Spanish-style houses line the leafy streets, which open up onto paved plazas. Baskets of ripe mangos, fresh coconuts and piles of limes jostle for space with 1980s-style blenders on the *jugo* stands. These Santa Marta icons are evenly spaced every 50 metres along the sea front. We stop and speak Spanish for the first time on dry land.

'*Hola, jugo per favor.*' I don't want to complicate things by throwing in a 'May I please have . . .' I decide to stick to the basics.

'*Qué tipo de jugo de lo que quieres?*' says the not very friendly woman behind the stand.

This reply wasn't in the guidebook! 'Ummmm . . .' I guess she is asking me what kind of juice I would like. 'Ummmm, *mango e maracuya per favor?*' I am secretly impressed I can remember the word for passionfruit under such stressful circumstances.

'Juicey!' Dash squeals, holding out his hands and straining to get out of the stroller.

'*Sin azúcar, señora?*' she asks.

Azúcar? Azúcar? I'm raking my brains. What is *azúcar* again? I know I have practised this word. I watch her lips as she asks me again. Ah-ha, it's sugar! Do I want sugar in the juice! '*No azúcar per favor, señorita,*' I reply.

As she scoops the ripe flesh out of the passionfruit, peels the plump mango and hits the start button on the blender I ponder how sad it is I am no longer a *señorita* but an ageing *señora*. The blender roars and crunches. She sets down two plastic chairs under the scrubby tree next to her stall and gestures for us to sit down. It is service but no smile.

I shuffle into the shade, eager to shield my skin from the sun's harmful rays, arrange the pushchair under a branch and wait. Two minutes later ice and pulp have been transformed into liquid deliciousness. This is the best juice I have ever tasted. We all share a straw and it is gone within seconds.

Handing back the empty glass, I begin the money talk.

'*Cuánto cuesta?*'

'*Tres mil pesos,*' she says. Holy shit. Three million pesos for a juice — that is daylight robbery.

'*Tres mil pesos?*' I repeat.

'*Si.*'

'Ross, I think we have been done!' I whisper to him as I get out our money and try to make sense of the foreign notes. I hand her a 50 mil pesos note and hope for some change. She shakes her head and before I can become indignant she reaches over the counter and plucks a 5000 peso note out of my purse!

'*Gracias,*' I say, although I am not sure why I am thanking her for helping herself to my cash. Five seconds later she hands me a 2000 peso note, tosses the glass in the bin and turns her back on us. I got it wrong. *Mil* in Spanish does not mean million in English, obviously.

Ross takes the pushchair and we head deeper into Santa Marta. Smiling gents with AK47s studiously guard every street corner. Policemen make me nervous. Once, while at a teenage party in Palmerston North, I was grabbed by the lapel of my prized 1970s-style black leather jacket and thrown into the back of the paddy wagon. Sitting opposite me, hiccupping and farting, was a drunk, fully patched Mob member who eyed me with lustful glee.

After a terrifying ride around the back streets of Highbury we made it to the station, where I was promptly released — a case of mistaken identity, it turned out. This brush with the law was enough to give me a lifelong distrust of cops.

Needless to say, these Colombian policemen with *guns* are making me very nervous.

'Imagine the conditions in a Colombian jail,' I say to Ross as we squeeze past a well-armed officer of the law. The footpaths are high off the road, potholed and only wide enough for one slim person to comfortably walk on. Pushing a stroller is hard work and my 'pushchair elbow' flares up. This occupational hazard is caused by pushing a cheap pushchair (not the big off-road ones most people have in New Zealand) over uneven surfaces for hours on end.

'Simón Bolívar.' Ross reads out the plaque under a statue of a man sitting astride a well-muscled and anatomically correct stallion. 'Liberator of Latin America from the Spanish Empire.'

It is truly magnificent. 'Look at the thighs on him! Powerful. What a total spunk!' I whistle, craning my neck to check out the handsome bronze Señor Bolívar.

'Agreed — he's not too shabby,' Ross says as we move back to fully appreciate the glory of this monument.

So who is Simón Bolívar, other than being the liberator of Latin America? We realise we have a gaping hole in our knowledge of South American history. Ross, as a history enthusiast, is ashamed and desperate to find out more. I'm keen to know if he has any good-looking descendants.

We spy a pamphlet on the grass and attempt to translate

the Spanish tourist brochure. 'Simón Bolívar led Colombia, Venezuela, Ecuador and Bolivia to independence — ah, that explains the investment in the statue.

'Despite coming from a family who had gained much of their wealth from sugar plantations, Simón was staunchly anti-slavery. He passionately believed in liberty, individual freedom, and was a huge fan of the French and American revolutions. He desperately wanted to create a constitution for South America.'

Unfortunately he had a hard time convincing the South American public of the benefits of his liberal philosophy and in 1830, at age forty-seven, after trying for many years to lay the foundations for democratic ideology in Latin America, he died in Santa Marta.

'He was younger than I am now when he died.'

'Do you have a hankering to be a revolutionary hero, Ross?'

He looks at me. 'No, but I do covet that waistcoat.'

'Big horsie,' says Dash.

'Yep, Dash, that is one very big horsie.'

24

Bile in
the Aisle

—·—

'Is your head made of cheese? Are you crazy?' I am getting a spectacular dressing-down by a toothless granny in the middle of the *supermercado*. 'What is wrong with you? Didn't your mother teach you anything?'

Thirty seconds earlier, Dashkin and I had been minding our own business, wandering around the air-conditioned supermarket picking out treats for dinner, when suddenly a stranger started shouting.

'What about the milk?' she yelled. At first I think she must be yelling at her husband but when she pokes her finger into my chest and starts spitting with rage I realise I am the problem.

I smile awkwardly and try to move Dash away.

'It is the middle of the day!' she fumes, following us to the frozen-foods section. I desperately look around, trying to catch the eye of my fellows shoppers. I need some support against this grey-haired attacker. But they glare at me like I am the devil incarnate.

What the hell is going on? Somehow I have managed to outrage all the customers of the Carulla supermarket.

I check that I am not inadvertently exposing my arse. Nope, I am wearing a pair of white respectable-length shorts, a black singlet top and well-worn Tevas. (I can understand that in some circles wearing Tevas would be enough to incite a riot but, judging by the casual approach to fashion in South America, I can't see that this could be the reason for the rant.)

'What is wrong?' I ask her.

'Look at your son!' she yells, pointing at Dashkin. I look at him. He looks adorable, sitting in his pushchair holding a red capsicum in one hand and a cucumber in the other.

'Look!' she barks again. Suddenly I snap. My blood boils. *No one* has a go at my son and gets away with it.

'Right, lady, back the fuck off!' I say in English. My eyes narrow and my jaw sets. I am ready for a fight. I stand up to my full 163 centimetres and get ready to face this granny down. 'What. Is. Your. Problem?' I yell back at her.

She's not fazed by my fighting talk. 'What are you thinking — taking such a white child into the midday sun?' she says.

'What?' As if verbal harassment wasn't enough, she gives me a good whack on the arm!

'Easy, tiger!' Is this nut job really arguing with me in the middle of the frozen-foods aisle about how pale Dashkin is? It seems she is. She has a point to prove and cranks up the Español to three hundred words a minute — way too quick for me to keep up. All I can pick out is '*Leche, leche*'. But why the hell is she talking about milk?

'*No entiendo.*' I give up. This is too weird.

'*No Colombiana?*'

'*No, Nueva Zelanda. Estamos aqui en nuestro velero.*'

'Ahhhhh!' She begins moving closer, puckering up ready to kiss Dash.

Dashkin is not amused. He has been getting more and more concerned at her ranting.

'NO NO NO NO!' He starts thrashing his legs and throws the veges at her. No one has a go at his mama and gets away with it. I smile at him. That's my boy!

'*Leche,*' she says again.

'*Leche?*'

'*Leche de sol.*'

Sun milk? Does she mean sunscreen? I reach into my bag and pull out a well-squeezed tube of 80+ sunscreen.

'*Bueno, bueno!*' And with that she is transformed back into a nice old granny doing her shopping, and shuffles off.

I stand there completely flabbergasted. 'What just happened?' I say out loud to no one. The other shoppers disperse, Dash asks for his cucumber and it is as if the outrage never occurred.

We make our way to the checkout. The Carulla supermarket workers are dressed in beige pants and crisp white shirts and all of them have manicured fingernails, shined and painted with a clear nail varnish to really set them off against the colour of money.

We pay, leave and head back out into the 36-degree heat. Dashkin and I put our hats on and we walk slowly back to the yacht.

On the way I can't help thinking how strange the whole interaction was. In New Zealand I wouldn't discipline other people's children, I wouldn't question parents if their kids were dressed inappropriately for the cold. We Kiwis keep to ourselves, we look the other way and we have one of the highest rates of child abuse in the developed world.

It seems that in Colombia, people have no qualms about taking you to task if they are concerned for a child. I am actually pleased that Granny cared enough about my little pale-skinned boy to stop her shopping and keep on at me until she was satisfied I was a competent parent. They say it takes a village to raise a child and I guess she was just doing her bit.

25

Riding High

———

As night falls the children come out kind of like they are in some creepy fairytale. The shaved-ice sellers line up their ancient trolleys, the man selling single cigarettes begins plying his trade, the mariachi band starts tuning their instruments and the parents of Santa Marta vie for a spot on the benches of Santana Square.

It's not really creepy — it is just finally cool enough to play. By 7.30 p.m. the ornate band rotunda is full of freshly scrubbed, laughing, squealing children playing catch or jumping off the balustrades. An impromptu game of tag starts up. Big kids chase little kids. Little kids forget they are meant to be running away and get side-tracked by the blue lights the council has installed in the paving. It is all good, clean fun. And it is a marriage-saver for Ross and I.

We are three months into the 'adventure' and it is quite hard work. It's hot and dry and the sun is ferocious. Ross has been stuck in the engine room for five whole days trying to fix the raw water intake and the impeller pump. He is worn out, thin and stressed, and our relationship is what a counsellor would call 'strained'.

I am finding the adjustment to ship-board life difficult. I resent not having any time to myself. I am sick of doing nappies by hand in salt water and the novelty of cooking with a single element is wearing off. I can't study the 12-volt system *and* build towers, draw tractors *and* read *Old MacDonald Had a Farm*.

As someone who did women's studies as part of my undergraduate degree I'm very surprised to find myself in a situation where the gender roles are so clearly divided. Back in

Kelburn I imagined myself learning to sail and being a useful first mate. Instead, I cook, clean and look after Dash while Ross sorts out all the boat stuff. It sucks. I'm sick of it. But there is no way in hell I'm going home.

We totally underestimated how all-consuming having a twenty-one-month-old on board would be. We underestimated how much work the boat would require. Sailing solo seems easy-peasy compared to hitting the high seas with your wife and child in tow.

I try to remind myself that there is no time for navel gazing — it's late in the season and we have to keep moving if we are going to make it across the Pacific.

In Santander Square, everything seems OK. I look around at all the other parents and know they have had challenging moments too. One woman is especially nice and each evening we chat in a strange mix of English and Spanish.

A man comes up and asks for money. I look at him, give him a 2000 peso note and know that my day has been better than his. Way better.

Dashkin is having a marvellous time kicking a neon-pink plastic ball around with three other boys. I catch Ross' eye and he takes my hand.

'Ange, adventures are great to plan, hell to do and wonderful to talk about later. Once this engine is fixed everything will be easier.'

'I know. It's just taking a bit of getting used to and I miss my sisters and friends. I don't really have anyone to talk to, you know, and you know how much I love talking!' I laugh.

'I know, darling.'

I feel like I am going to cry, so quickly change the subject.

'Tomorrow's Sunday. You won't be able to get much done, so why don't we get up early and bike to Taganga before it gets too hot?'

'Sounds like a plan.'

I am not sure why I added 'let's get up early' — we are up at sparrow fart. Every. Single. Day.

At 7.30 the next morning we are ready to hit the road.

Dashkin looks fabulously regal sitting in his special bicycle seat. He loves going for bike rides and is trying very hard to be patient.

We take off down the jetty and ride up to the gate. The security guards, who are normally smiling and joking, are all very quiet. Something bad has happened.

'What's wrong?' I ask Manuel, who can speak a little bit of English.

'Very sad. Marina is dead.'

'Marina the little dog? How?' It could hardly be old age — Marina was just a puppy.

'She was run over by a car, here,' Manuel says, pointing to a recently scrubbed spot on the driveway.

'Oh God.' I feel sick — the fact that it had to be scrubbed means lots of blood and guts. 'I'm so sorry, that's terrible. Who would do that?'

'The boat with the party last night — they are drunk, drive fast and kill her. They didn't even stop.'

'Those wankers!' I clap a hand over my mouth. No swearing round Dash.

'Where's doggie, Mama?'

I get off my bike and turn to look directly at Dash. 'Marina's dead, Dashkin. She was run over by a big car.'

'No big car, where doggie?' He starts to cry — not because he has understood she is dead but because she is not there at this precise moment.

'Shh, darling.' I have no idea what to say next. Normally I would say, 'We can see Marina later', or 'It's OK' but both of those would be a big fat lie. Instead, I go for the cautionary angle . . . kind of like a modern-day Grimm's fairytale.

'Naughty car. We must be careful near cars, darling. Always hold Mama's hand.'

That seems to work. He stops crying, but poor Manuel looks devastated. Ross shakes his hand and I give him a hug. Dashkin waves as we head into the traffic.

Down Carrera 2, into the Calle 5 and up over the hill to Taganga, a small fishing village about 5 kilometres out of Santa Marta. As we make our way north the quaint, leafy streets turn into rough, potholed roads, which turn into dusty dirt roads, which turn into a steep slum.

A group of old black women with white hair are sitting fanning away flies and mosquitoes with scrappy pieces of plastic. I watch their faces as they notice Ross cycle past; their looks are a mixture of amusement and incredulousness. They nudge each other and make sexual quips in what sounds like a mix of Spanish and Carib, a local dialect.

Then they spy me. Big throaty laughs spill out of their mouths. I smile and try to make the ride look easier than it is. Seeing me puffing and panting sets them off. They slap their huge thighs and call their family members to watch the crazy gringa.

Suddenly the laughing stops. '*Qué lindo! Muy blanco!*' The women are rising from their upturned boxes. They have seen Dashkin. I crank up the pace.

'Wave, Dash!' I command out of the corner of my mouth. Sweat is dripping into my eyes and my legs are screaming. The encounter with the concerned granny in the supermarket is still fresh in my mind — the thought of eight old ladies descending on me is frankly terrifying.

Dash waves. They coo, wave back and stay put. Phew.

At the top of the hill, policemen ask to see our passports. We chat about how beautiful New Zealand is, then whizz down the dangerously winding road into Taganga.

It's a little bit shit. The once cute fishing village has been overrun with hippies. There are stalls selling dream-catchers, tie-dyed MC Hammer pants and smoking paraphernalia. Down on the beach people are trying to make a buck. You can hire deck chairs, get your shoulders massaged, buy sliced pineapple with chilli or knock back a cocktail in a coconut — all for a price.

We wheel our bikes along the hot sands and spread out our towels. I perform the dance of 'getting into a pair of togs on a beach'. Success! No fanny flashing.

Dash and Ross run down to the water. In return for carrying Dashkin on my bike I get ten minutes alone. I lie down and shut my eyes.

The dark silhouette of palm trees fills my eyelids and I can hear backpackers talking loudly about their cocaine-fuelled night. I remember when I too had wild party nights, though mine usually involved a leotard and a vodka slide.

A man stands over me, blocking my sun. I open one eye. He is selling bad '90s sunglasses — the kind that make anyone who wears them look like a serial killer.

'No, gracias.'

The mother and daughter sitting to our left are squabbling. I note the daughter has the most fabulous squishy bum.

I feel much better seeing someone else with less than firm buttocks and jog — yes, jog — in my togs down to the water. Woohoo, I am basically Pamela Anderson! Then, I trip, fall and belly-flop into ten inches of water. Ross and Dash laugh uproariously and I figure if I can't beat 'em I might as well join 'em. We spend the next half hour pretending to fall into the sea. Dash thinks it is hilarious. We think it is pretty bloody funny too.

26

Rough as Guts

I have been ill for the last eighty-four hours. I have self-diagnosed giardia, complete with headaches that are like stabbing knives, stomach cramps like some evil foe is maliciously squeezing my guts, and explosive poo.

I am so exhausted that if I sit down, the only thing I can think of is lying down. Reading to Dash has me hallucinating with fatigue, and despite being in bed by 5 p.m. yesterday I am still shattered.

Manson's Tropical Diseases 19th Edition is a huge green tome left on board by Reinhardt. Reading it is like watching *CSI*, only much better. You identify your symptoms and away you go. There to help you make your diagnosis are hundreds of sepia photos of African men in the death throes of extreme threadworms, lockjaw, jiggers, malaria, yellow fever, leishmaniasis, cholera and, of course, the one that makes me sweat with fear, rabies! Thank God I am not foaming at the mouth.

Finally, after following a flow diagram entitled 'Parasites — Which One Have You Got?' I narrow it down to giardia. At least I will die thin.

When I was a ten-year-old I wanted to be a missionary — not because I had a deep desire to bring Jesus to the heathens but because it would help me lose weight. All that living under the unrelenting sun and scraping out a tiny existence with not a dairy in sight seemed like a bloody great way to get a tan and get slim. I also used to fantasise about lying on the beach and letting the sun melt the fat off my body. Clearly I was mad.

I had thought it was a bad case of seasickness. We motored

out of Santa Marta with a strong smell of diesel in our spacious, yet stifling, stern cabin. The sea was a sloppy, confused black mess — in other words, conditions were ripe to bring on my seasickness. And oh lordy, did they bring it on!

At first I was OK. I kept watch on the bow, finding myself a snug spot jammed between the fuel jugs and the dinghy, gazing up the length of the mast. To reassure myself I hummed my way through the soundtrack of *Les Misérables*. In my cut-off jeans, yellowing singlet and matted hair I could easily pass as one of the chorus. However, as we got further offshore I felt my stomach churn and headed down to bed.

I struggled through the night and finally, at 5 a.m., I staggered back on deck with Dash clinging to my neck. I sat in the cockpit sweating profusely and trying to breathe deeply. You know when you are really, really hung over and you are sure that if you could just lie on the cold bathroom linoleum you would feel better? I was like that, eyeing up the sea thinking, Just a quick dip and I'll be good as new.

Anyway, that set the scene for the whole voyage. Ross was on deck all night and then all day and then all night, despite suffering from a nasty chest infection. I hadn't prepared enough food as I thought, naively, that I had overcome my seasickness, meaning Ross had bugger-all to eat for three days. In the middle of the second night we lost all power. *All power*. The batteries had somehow lost charge as a dodgy Reinhardt repair meant a wire had come off the alternator.

Strangely, as soon as the motor died, Dash woke up for an instant and said, 'No motor', and went back to sleep! Such is his limbic connection with the engine.

I lay there imagining us being run down by huge tankers, like the poor family in the book *Ten Degrees of Reckoning*. As I was talking myself out of those negative thoughts, a huge wave doused Dash and I while we lay in the stern cabin. It swamped the deck and poured through the open hatch, soaking the bed.

'Ross! Ross, are you OK?' I am so paranoid about him falling overboard I can't really sleep when he is on watch.

'Just a freak wave, nothing to worry about.' I lay there with a racing heart and a dodgy gut as Dash rolled over and went back to sleep.

On deck Ross turned us into the wind, to charge the batteries. After about twelve hours we managed to get the motor started and continued on towards Cartagena.

Amid the nausea, there were of course some bright spots. Dash now 'plays' the harmonica. ''Monica, 'monica,' he says.

One night, when I had lost the will to live and had to go and lie down in the cabin, Ross and Dash serenaded me with a great little tune, with Ross on ukelele and Dash on 'monica. Heartwarming, I tell ya.

As soon as Dash sees land he brightens and no longer has to be glued to my knee.

Our first glimpse of Cartagena is extraordinary. Huge, tall, thin skyscrapers loom on the horizon. I get that butterfly feeling in my stomach (a welcome new sensation after the churning of the previous few days) as we approach.

Entering a city by sea is like coming in the back door — there are no glitzy duty-free shops or officials stamping your passport. Just fishermen and lots of slightly manky water. The bay of Cartagena is rich with history, choked with weeds and has a strong smell of sewage.

A large statue is mounted in the middle of the bay. Mother Mary no doubt, but I can't be sure as we didn't get close enough to eyeball her. I called up the marina, Club Nautico, on the VHS and got no reply. Surely my Spanish is not *that* bad?

At 10.23 a.m. we drop the hook and Ross and I sit in the cockpit, exhausted. Dash is knackered too and asks to go to bed. 'Mama, bed, sleepy.' I happily put him down. We pump up the dinghy and when Dash wakes up, we zoom into the shore.

By this time it is about 12.30 p.m. or 'slap bang in the middle of the siesta'. A surly looking 'trollop', as Ross so eloquently described her, greets us by raising her very made-up eyes (think baby blue eye-shadow with glitter eyeliner — Bitches, you would have been proud) from her Facebook page and wagging her finger.

'Noooo, you come back later,' she drawls.

'Ah, can we just quickly check in?' we ask.

'Who you want to talk to?' she snaps.

'Um, David?' we say, remembering that Romero, our immigration agent in Santa Marta, had recommended him.

'Humph, OK.' She makes a call and five minutes later an obese David turns up. He is so fat the plastic legs on the chair splay out when he sits down.

Club Nautico is a ruin. There are always six or seven guys who sit around the dock all day watching soaps on a huge TV screen that is protected from the elements by a bit of black plastic. The showers are cubicles made of slimy plywood, fitted with a hose. But at least there are showers.

John, the English-speaking dock hand we had heard so much about from the cruising guides and online, is nowhere to be seen. Instead, sitting at the long table are groups of sun-hardened old sea dogs who drink cans of Aguila all day, while painted Colombian ladies sit passively at their sides. Interestingly enough there are signs about respecting the 'standards' of Club Nautico, like wearing a shirt while in the (non-existent) restaurant and thinking twice about using hookers!

This is my first taste of the cruiser community and I gotta say it ain't pretty.

We always planned to get repairs done in Cartagena, and what do you know? As luck would have it, we have loads of repairs that need doing! So far the list looks like this:

- water in the 400-litre fuel tank
- leaking impeller
- no power
- overflowing head
- broken outboard
- new sail covers.

Ross is amazing but even he has his limits. I think we are at that phase in the journey where we ask ourselves 'Why are we doing this?' Of course, just as I am wondering this we have an incredible sunset and the full moon comes out as we are eating dinner on the deck. Dash starts singing, 'Twinkle twinkle little star', and I remember that it is for moments like this that we are doing it!

I can also report that, due to taking some incredibly powerful Colombian prescription drugs that turned my wee fluoro orange for three days, I am now able to down a cold beer at the end of the day and I no longer feel like death warmed up.

Slowly, slowly, we are getting there.

27

Beggars on the Wall of Love

Ooh là là Cartagena! You are a city in love. Step aside Paris — Cartagena beats you pants down. Courting Colombians leave no nook unoccupied on their four-hundred-year-old city wall — it makes the Eiffel Tower look positively prudish in comparison.

In this Ciudad Heroica, any time is pash time. We are not talking holding hands and a quick peck on the cheek — oh no, what I have witnessed, on my daylight walks with Dashkin, can only be described as erection-creating, panty-moistening heavy petting. Apparently, as long as you pucker up within spitting distance of a church spire you're not breaking any laws, religious or otherwise.

Lewd conduct — what's that? Fancy a pash? See you on the wall. Need to spice up your marriage? Take it out of the bedroom and find a nook. Flaunt it on the wall!

Lovebirds of the world — migrate to Cartagena de Indias!

I love it. I think it is wonderful. I want to drag Ross away from the fuel tank and get myself some pash rash.

This wall of amore was ordered by King Felipe II of Spain in 1586 to stop pirates ransacking the city. It took a hundred years and the blood, sweat and tears of fifteen million African slaves. Charming. (Not.)

But there is something about walls and romance and the bones of slaves. When I was twenty-two I met an Australian-Sicilian gent on the Great Wall of China. We pashed as the sun went down and romanced each other for years. Like Cartagena's wall, the Chinese wall is packed full of skeletons. Maybe they whisper to those in need of love, challenging them to kiss the person next to them as a way of honouring their sacrifice. When I die I hope my funeral turns into a smoochfest and my bones are buried in the garden wall.

Dash loves the wall too. Although he is at the adorable 'hugs and kisses' age, he is more interested in the wall as a vast running track.

All 11 kilometres of it are raised, paved and free of cars. Admittedly, there are some sheer 10-metre drops and the grannies of Cartagena have already given me a rap over the knuckles for letting him wander free. However, I was prepared for them and had my comeback sorted. 'Niño blanco' is growing up on a boat, he knows all about 'be careful, big drop, I don't fall down'. This boy knows when to hold hands.

As soon as we are through the imposing gate he leaps out of his pushchair and gallops off. As he jumps on the big beige flagstones, I try to teach him the rhyme about stepping on a crack and marrying a rat. 'Rat, rat, rat!' he chants gleefully.

Joining us on the wall are expensively dressed tourists carrying parasols and wandering at a sedate, sweat-reducing pace. Not us — we race about sweating up a storm in our faded salt-water-washed shorts and T-shirts.

If the turrets aren't occupied by lovers, Dash and I climb in them and peer through the gun emplacements. We stare out over the crowded streets of Getsemani, across to the island of Manga and out into the bay where the yacht is anchored. We wave to Papa on Te Ikaroa.

If we poke out our heads and twist our necks to the left we can see the Castillo de San Felipe de Barajas. It is very impressive, shaped like a trapezoid and full of secret tunnels. It has no vertical walls, and was designed to deflect cannonballs.

On a plinth, guarding the entrance to the fortress, is the one and only Don Blas de Lezo. If this man were alive today he would have ladies falling over themselves to shake his hand. I say hand because he only had one. And one leg and one eye, but he was brave and clever and saved the city from being sacked by the evil English Admiral Vernon. Honestly, I would date him. Think of the conversation over aperitifs.

'So, Don, tell me about the time you saved Cartagena.'

'Well, Angela, it was pretty crazy. Everyone wanted a piece of Cartagena. As you know we have a wonderful deep-water harbour — but what everyone really wanted was the gold and silver.'

'Oh, you mean the gold and silver that the Spanish had plundered from the Incas?'

'Yes, not our finest hour, I admit. But the dirty French and English pirates were constantly looting us. We could barely get a ship out of the bay before the cannonballs started flying. Even that supposed hero Francis Drake had a go. Nasty piece of work.'

'Great beard, though.'

'True. Anyway, up in Florida, one of the Spanish customs officers, Juan León Fandiño, went a little overboard and sliced off the ear of the English Captain Jenkins.'

'What? Why?'

'Found out he was smuggling.'

'Good God, that's barbaric.'

'You've got to remember these were bloody times. There was none of this touchy-feely business you have now. I mean, look at me, I'm half the man I was.'

'Sorry, Don. Please go on. More wine?'

'Why not, I love a good drop. So, this jumped-up official bragged that he would slice the English king's ear off too if he ever set foot in Florida. News travels fast, and soon the Brits were spitting tacks. Sir Vernon, who was a Member of Parliament, decided that enough was enough and convinced England to declare war on Spain.'

'Nice one, Juan — now everyone is *muy* pissed off.'

'It gets better, or worse depending on whose side you're on. Vernon, who has now become an admiral, conquers Portobelo with six ships, and based on this success manages to sweet-talk the monies to fund, wait for it, a hundred and eight ships, twenty-eight thousand men and twenty thousand cannons!'

'Wowee.'

'My dear, you forget gossip works both ways. Soon I found out about his plans.'

'What did you think? Were you scared?'

'Me, scared? Dear girl, I had been in many, many battles and always managed to survive. Once when I was in Genoa I surrounded the town and threatened to raze it if they didn't pay up. Believe me, I know a thing or two about being under siege. I knew that we didn't have the numbers — only three thousand men and a few local Indians — but we had the home-ground advantage.'

'So what happened next?'

'Vernon and his cronies arrived just outside the harbour on 13 March 1741 at nine in the morning. They got out the cannons and didn't stop firing for days. Sixteen days, to be exact. Jolly annoying, too.'

'Jeez, that is rough. I heard you sunk your own ships?'

'Yes, it was a last-ditch attempt to stop them entering the harbour — didn't work, though. All I got was another hole blown in my arm!'

'So Vernon just waltzed on in?'

'I wouldn't say waltzed. Did I mention he had help from Washington?'

'George Washington?'

'No, his good-for-nothing half-brother Lawrence. He supplied twenty-seven hundred north Americans and two thousand Jamaicans. These bastards were sent to take the La Popa Convent. Streets were falling, people were dying and smug old Vernon thought victory was in the bag. He even sent word to England saying Cartagena had fallen. Can you believe the arrogance?'

'But you didn't surrender.'

'Good grief, no! We sat up in the fort and picked them off. The bodies of the dead were piling up. Unlike miserable old England, Cartagena is a tropical city and it didn't take long before those bodies were decomposing and spreading disease.'

'Ewww yuck.'

'You asked how I saved the city. I'm merely providing the details.'

'I know, and I am really enjoying it. It is just that I am vegetarian and a bit squeamish. The thought of the bay being knee-deep in bodies grosses me out.'

'You should have smelt it.'

'Oh, please . . .'

'I could see that the Brits were faltering. We had been fighting for about six weeks — they were tired, we were tired, but this was our only chance. I sent out my remaining six hundred men and commanded them to bayonet the hell out of them. They were magnificent. They killed eight hundred and held another thousand prisoner.'

'Wow! I mean, that is great but still, lots of people died.'

'Get over it, girl! This was war!'

'Think of those poor mothers hoping their sons would soon walk through the door . . .'

'Really, I think you have drunk too much wine, this melancholy doesn't suit you. I haven't even got to the bit where they retreat, and have to sink their own ships because they don't have enough men to sail them home. Oh, and have a look at this . . .'

'A coin. "The Spanish Pride pull'd down by Admiral Vernon", and on the other side "True British Heroes Took Cartagena April 1741". Classic.'

'Ha! The fools had it minted before it was all done and dusted. I particularly like the way I am kneeling at Vernon's feet! Ha!'

'He must be so embarrassed.'

'I've heard there has been a bit of a cover-up — at the highest level. No one is to mention the war.'

'You have a beautiful eye, Don.'

'And you, dear girl, are far too young for me. Judging by all the fortune tellers who have been visiting me recently, apparently I die in September and mystery surrounds my grave.'

'Sounds like the perfect end to a remarkable life, wouldn't you say, Don?'

'Is does, my dear. Thank you for the wine and I'll see you on the other side.'

Dash and I keep walking for another 2 kilometres and stop next to a thin man with an insulated box to buy a drink. Condensation forms as soon as the bottle hits the 36-degree air. It is hard to know whether we should open the bottle or lick the sides.

By 2 p.m. the school kids are hard at work, licking the lips of their latest paramour. The stretch between the main gate and the market gate seems to be the Colombian version of 'meet ya behind the bike sheds'.

If only I knew then what I know now, The ManBank would have set up HQ on the wall! Business would have boomed. I would be rich. Dash and I could swan about in a horse-drawn carriage waving at the hoi polloi and, most importantly, I would have a yacht with a shower.

Instead, I clip Dashkin into his pushchair and we trudge back to the broken-down Club Nautico.

28

Bugged Out and Tanked Up

The devil is in the detail.
My natural tendency is
to adopt a 'she'll be right'
attitude but when you live
on a boat, that just doesn't
cut it. As Ross is constantly
telling me, 'You must think
very carefully, Angela,
about everything.'

There is a big difference between she'll be right and a detailed devil. In our case it is a 6-millimetre devil.

We have found an amazing mechanic named Elvis who is our lifesaver. He says, 'Friend, it is necessary to get a new fuel tank, I sure.' Dash adores him and stands on the deck calling, 'Elvis, Elvis!'

Our new fuel tank, all one million pesos of it, was due to be fitted last week. We had prepared ourselves for Big Wednesday (as we affectionately named it). We had formulated a plan: as soon as we saw the tank arriving, Dash and I would head out, enabling Elvis, Nestor and Eric to manhandle the tank into position under the starboard bunk.

Wednesday arrived and we were up early; I had the bags packed and the pushchair poised. We waited and we waited. Finally, at 5 p.m., we saw Elvis walking down the jetty.

'*Hola*, Elvis,' I called to him in a somewhat confused manner.

'Friend, there is a problem. Eric the man who makes your tank is hurt his eye. Friday, I sure,' reported Elvis.

Well, you can't argue with that. 'OK, no problem,' I lied through my smile. 'See you on Friday.'

Five days earlier, Eric had come on board in his stockinged feet and taken measurements for our 'in-a-very-tricky-position-no-room-for error' tank in centimetres. Ross, the ex-picture framer who works in millimetres, was less than impressed.

'I don't trust those measurements. I would have thought you would use millimetres. This tank must fit into this space,' said Ross.

'I sure, no problem, Eric has much experience, he is professional,' soothed Elvis.

We dutifully peeled off the 500 mil peso down-payment and hoped for the best. Two days later Elvis, not Eric, arrived back to take some more measurements. Ross couldn't hold himself back: he got out the ruler and measured the space himself, every last millimetre of it.

'Just so long as it fits,' he said as I secretly crossed my fingers.

Friday came and went and there was no sign of the tank. Just Elvis — who was as frustrated as we were. 'Tomorrow, I sure, at nine a.m.,' he said.

On Saturday we wake to torrential rain. Leaks are appearing all over the boat. With the hatches battened down, the cabins turn into mini saunas. In weather like this, we figure it is unlikely that the tank will arrive.

Then, out of nowhere . . .

'Arghhh!' Ross cries out. He has tweaked his back while checking the bilge. I have never seen him suck his teeth like that, and realise this is no ordinary pain. This is full-strength-Voltaren, keep-the-small-child away-from-me pain. Dash and I make ourselves scarce and spend the next hour splashing in puddles on the foreshore. Hours of fun can be had this way — if you are prepared to pick your way through the rubbish.

'*Mama, agua! Agua, jump!*' exclaims my newly bilingual child.

'*Si, si, agua,*' I confirm in equally bilingual fashion.

On our way back we meet Elvis on the jetty. 'Today we do the tank, in twenty minutes, OK?'

'Right, OK, great,' I reply, and then think, but it is raining and what can I do for five hours with a toddler in the torrential rain?

I swing into action mode. The pushchair is so sodden it's unpushable, so in desperation we bundle ourselves into a taxi and go to the Caribe Plaza megamall.

As any mother knows, going into one of these temples of temptation without a pushchair is insane. I follow the flashing neon signs to a promisingly named 'Playspace'. Dash is tired. He takes one look at the musical rides, smiling attendants and big, noisy kids and howls. It is all too much; he flops down on the floor and weeps.

Scooping up my tired darling, I think quickly. Movies! He can snuggle into me and go to sleep!

'No pero, blah blah, esta, no, no, no prohibito,' spits the extremely beautiful total cow at the movie theatre. It is 2.10 p.m., the children's movie started at 2.05 p.m. (what is that about, five minutes past the hour?) and apparently there is *absolutely no admission* after the advertised time.

Shit. No pushchair, one very tired, cranky little boy, Playspace is a no-go, pouring outside, we can't go back to the boat . . .

Then I look to my left and there, flashing before my eyes, is a giant neon soft-serve cone. I do what any mother would do in this situation: I cough up the 2 mil peso at Mimo's and get the boy an ice-cream. Crisis averted.

We find some steps (one of Dashkin's favourite things) and walk up and down them for forty minutes. Finally, after about two hours of wandering around, I am totally out of things to do and we taxi back home. Thankfully, the rain has stopped.

We come through the gate and Elvis is sitting watching Barcelona vs Man United on the giant plastic-covered TV. As I walk past he makes some strange hand gesture that I can't understand, but it doesn't look positive.

Dash and I pick our way gingerly along the 100 metres of slippery, broken wharf to the yacht. Ross is sitting in the dripping cockpit.

'All done?' I ask expectantly.

'They haven't turned up yet. I think a certain game of soccer might have slowed things down a little,' he replies.

WTF! I have just spent the last two hours in a shopping mall with a cranky toddler, walking up and down stairs! Then my thoughts turn dark. Oh Lord, we have been totally ripped off. There is no tank, it was all a scam. We are the victims of a very complicated scam! Dash is desperate for a nap and is asleep the minute his head hits the pillow.

As if by magic, the sun comes out. Struggling along the jetty I see Elvis, Eric and a light green coffin-shaped fuel tank.

And the comedy begins. First up, the tank has to be got onto the boat. This is no small task, as it has to get through the cockpit, down the companionway and then fit into the space.

Sweat starts dripping off Elvis the minute he lifts the tank. Lots of rapid Spanish is exchanged and after some fancy footwork across the gangplank, the tank is on the stern deck. It still has a long way to go.

Getting it through the cockpit proves a tad more difficult than Elvis or Eric expected. Ross smiles wryly. 'I told them it had to be able to fit through there,' he says. His back is still smarting and, as his ever-loving wife, I am determined that he is not going to do any lifting.

'Please, friend, I need some rope,' Elvis requests.

'Here,' says Ross, handing him the rope from Dashkin's harness.

Elvis loops it over the grab rail and with Eric in the cabin they manage to lower the tank down.

So far, so good. Ross looks a little dubious.

'I think the tank is too big,' he says as we peer through the hatch. Elvis and Eric are trying to devise a plan to squeeze the steel tank into the bunk.

By this stage everyone is slick with sweat. The humidity is at 100 per cent, it is 34 degrees outside and the mercury is climbing.

From the vantage point watching through the hatch I am

able to take special note of Eric's lustrous hair. He sports a fashionable wavy mohawk. It almost makes up for the dodgy measuring. Almost.

'Friend, I think you come here and look this, the tank it is too big,' says Elvis. 'We need to cut here.'

I have stayed silent and tried to keep out of the way but the thought of someone cutting into the bulkhead is too much.

'Ah, hang on, I don't think we should be cutting into the bulkhead,' I announce through the hatch.

Three male faces look up at me. I lose my nerve for a moment. 'Eh, Ross?'

'We cut this bit and then we can lower the tank in here,' says Elvis.

Out comes the measuring tape. If Eric has managed to make the tank too long, who says he hasn't also made it too wide?

I am trying to keep myself from going into worst-case scenario mode. Dash decides that something exciting is going on and the familiar wail of 'Mama, Mama' begins.

Only I can't get to him. The tank has blocked the entrance to his cabin.

Thinking like MacGyver, I wrench open the hatch of his cabin and lower myself onto his bed. I do this like the Dukes of Hazzard used to leap through the open car window as it sped away, but in a vertical way. Dash is so surprised he stops crying and stares open-mouthed.

'Hug, Mama, hug.' He wraps his sweaty little body around me. 'Juicey?' he asks. 'Please, Mama?'

I pick him up and lift him through the hatch onto the deck then, thinking I am much taller than I am, try to jump back up through the hatch. It is too high to lever myself up.

Dash is alone on the deck without his harness. I have to get out there now. So I do this strange crawl, bracing myself on anything I can, and flop onto the deck. I can feel the bruises turning purple already.

'Look, Dash, flying bugs. Look at their wings.' At first they seem like a welcome distraction, then suddenly the three or

LEFT
Candy le Coque.

BOTTOM
Bitchin', island styles!
Kuna Yala.

RIGHT
In fetching stripes, the sailor boys. Dash aged five months, Ross a bit older. Wellington.

BELOW
Jolly jumping in the stern. Ngawhakawhiti Bay.

BELOW
The five-hundred-day
chart, the start of it all.

BOTTOM
Te Ikaroa, in all her glory.

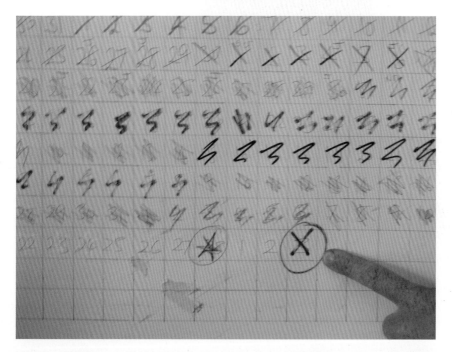

ABOVE
Ross in the engine room,
Santa Marta.

RIGHT
Me and Dash, Santa
Marta.

LEFT
Towards Cartagena.

BELOW
Fried fun in Cartagena.

ABOVE
Ross in the Kuna Yala.

RIGHT
Dash with a good-looking
digger, Portobelo.

RIGHT
On board the US Coast
Guard cutter *Active 3*.

BELOW
Me, Jan and Dash,
Panama.

four bugs turn into three or four *hundred* bugs, then three or four *thousand*. It is a plague of biblical proportions.

The air is thick with them. We are swatting them away but they keep coming. Their wings are falling off and littering the deck. They swarm all over the boat, up the mast, into the cockpit and down into the cabins and saloon. No other boat in the marina is affected, just *Te Ikaroa*.

It is no longer fun. I feel like I am going to inhale them. Dash starts crying and we flee to the wharf. The drama escalates as the jigsaw drill comes out and they start hacking into the bulkhead.

Then, as suddenly as they arrived, the flying bugs depart, leaving hundreds of strange earwig-type bugs in their place — their wings have dropped off. These suckers are all through our beds and the saloon. Even Eric and Elvis have no idea what they are.

'Friend, I not sure what these are.'

It is getting dark and tempers are starting to fray. After a quick discussion it is decided the tank will be removed, and Elvis will come back on Monday with a carpenter.

Darkness falls just as the light green tank is lowered back onto the deck.

Our home is a wreck: bits of wood everywhere, piles of wings in the corners and crawling bugs all over the place.

Order was sort of returned as I put up the makeshift table, opened a cold beer for Ross, fed Dash, washed Dash, put Dash to bed, read Dash *Old MacDonald* for the millionth time, and pressed play on the computer for the last episode of the second season of *The Wire*. Sometimes you just need to blob in front of the telly. Escapism is bliss, even if it is into the hell of the Baltimore drug scene!

29

Kuna
Yala

Ah, bliss — we have spent the last twenty days in the Kuna Yala and we are loving it. Inhabited by the indigenous Kuna people, these islands off the northeastern Panamanian coast are a welcome respite from the cut and thrust of the mainland.

Over one hundred years ago, after being thoroughly shafted by the Spanish, Scottish, British and Americans, the Kuna declared themselves independent from the Panamanian government and opted to maintain a traditional way of life. Think thatched huts, traditional dress, no intermarriage with non-Kuna, no TV, no radio and a very real belief in the spirit world.

The Kuna are dark skinned with large, wide-set eyes, incredible cheekbones, kick-arse attitudes and the best fashion sense this side of the equator. The women sport beaded leg warmers! They are also very short — not pygmy-short but very short nonetheless.

Getting to this 'almost paradise' was a three-day slog bashing to windward. (Most other yachts whizz down here from Cartagena laden with backpackers in one and a half days.) Not *Te Ikaroa*; as a steel ketch of uncertain parentage, she needs a nice breeze blowing on her stern to reach the dizzying speed of 6 knots. We trundle about at an average of 3 knots. At this rate it will take another eight months to get to Fiji.

Luckily I am enjoying being out at sea. I like the way we live during these passages. We are all together, rocking and rolling, *but* this seasickness business is a real bitch. If it had a name I reckon she would be called Chundara Biggy-Time-Time. She'd be very fat and eat tacos with heaps of sauce that drips all over her spray-on top. She'd pour her huge bulk into tiny faded denim short shorts, creating a camel toe of epic proportions, sit on a plastic chair and demand food. All. The. Time.

Seasickness makes me hallucinate. So far I have seen Tess of the d'Urbervilles, Sir Walter Scott, Lois from my old work and St Theresa, the little flower. I know it was her because there was a strong smell of roses, which may actually have been Dashkin getting into my moisturiser down below, but remember I am hallucinating.

During these trippy times I start blinking hard and thinking of the packets of NoDoz my sisters and I would find in the glovebox of Dad's Ford Falcons. Driven mad by curiosity, I once put a pill into my gob. It fizzed and foamed and tasted like licking the bench of the poison shed.

Anyway, we slowly make our way into Puerto Escoces. And there was paradise, minus the city.

'Look, a welcoming canoe,' says Ross, just as the anchor bites into the mud. They are still a way off, so I leap into the clearest, bluest, warmest water I have ever had the privilege of plunging into. I splash around, do a cursory freshen-up of my pits and bits and haul myself up the boarding ladder before they are too close to be offended by seeing me in a bikini.

'*Hola*!' we call. (Our pilot book had the Kuna word for 'lipstick' but not for 'hello'.)

'*Hola*,' the man and boy call back. Ho-la! I can't help but stare. The planes of their faces are the most chiselled I have ever seen. I stand wide-eyed while Ross and the man speak a curious mixture of English, Kuna and Spanish. Somehow we all manage to understand each other. We are to pay the chief $10 for staying in the bay, coconuts are for sale, we are not Americans and have a nice time.

And we do. The next day we wake to find dolphins jumping next to us, and instead of the usual avian dawn chorus we hear the terrifying calls of howler monkeys. Dash does a fantastic impression of them over his porridge.

Our Stone Age-style neighbours are up and at 'em at 5.30 a.m. I put my head out of the cockpit at ten past six and see the cooking fires are lit and the men and boys are in their canoes, paddling across the bay on their way to check the banana plots. To our left are nine thatched huts. Three are built on stilts over the water and in front of us, barely discernable from the jungle, are the three-hundred-year-old remains of a fort, part of the ill-fated Scottish attempt at establishing a colony on the isthmus.

Back in 1698, around twelve hundred Scotsmen and women were sent here to try to create a base on the isthmus of Panama. The idea was that Scotland would control the gateway between the Atlantic and Pacific, thus becoming a mercantile and colonial superpower. It didn't work. It failed. *Badly*. Spain was already here and had a pretty tight hold on the trade. And, let's face it, pasty gingers don't do well in the tropics — rolling hillsides, yes; tropics, no. The heat was too much and soon men were dying like flies. Eight months later the colony was abandoned. But . . . crashing across the waves in blissful ignorance was another boatload of fresh-faced recruits. You can imagine how annoyed they were to find the place deserted. Couple that with lots of antagonism with Spain and yellow fever and you had a recipe for disaster. I'd desert too! Only a few hundred people survived, and when they got back to Scotland they were shunned by their families and regarded as a disgrace to their country.

We, however, are enjoying the tranquillity of the bay. We decide to row to shore as the noise from an outboard seems gauche.

This is where it gets ugly. And this is where I get mad.

Strewn along the entire shore are plastic bottles, plastic shoes, bits of broken plastic, plastic children's toys, plastic lunch boxes . . . anything you can think of made of plastic is here and it is *revolting*. What is going on? It ain't the Kunas' rubbish 'cos these guys are living in thatched huts, cooking fish over a fire. This is rubbish that *our* culture generates, tonnes and tonnes of it every day, and it washes up on *their* beaches.

What are they meant to do with it? Pick it up and put it where?

I am ashamed. Really ashamed. The Styrofoam container is plain wrong.

'Mama, starfish! Look, shallow water, starfish!' Dashkin's excited little voice pulls me out of my dark mood. Our dinghy drifts over stunning coral, spectacularly coloured fish, slick stingrays and Dash's new favourite creature, starfish.

'One, two, one, two!' His pointy little finger counts them as he leans out over the dinghy, touching his pink nose in the water. 'I all wet!' Ross and I laugh and cuddle our crazy critter.

The wind picks up, causing the glass-like sea to become choppy. Ross hauls on the oars and the rowlock breaks. I feel very heavy and try to think light thoughts. It doesn't work. Dash senses things aren't going to plan and decides to squeal, setting off the howler monkeys.

We make it back, drag ourselves on board, knock back a coconut and, as we have about 8000 miles to go before we get home, haul up the anchor, flick on the depth sounder and head out of the bay.

30
Grounded

———————

'Oh my God!' yells Ross.

'Oh my God!' I repeat, terrified.

'Oh my dod!' Dash repeats, because he is still learning to talk.

A huge crunching sound stops us in our tracks. We have run aground. Hard aground, on a shoal. Looking over the side, I can see *everything* on the bottom. We are in half a metre of water.

'Try to reverse!' I call to Ross. He clicks the motor into gear and we gun the engine. Nothing. I look over at the mangrove swamp 5 metres away.

Alligators. *Salt-water alligators*. We are going to be stuck on a boat with flesh-eating alligators snapping at us. Sweet baby Jesus. We are in Bahia de Masargandi, a place that is described in our pilot book as *uncharted, unsurveyed, all yours*! The only sign of human habitation is a hut at least 2 nautical miles away. The occupants use dug-out canoes, not massive power boats — which is what we will need to drag a 16-ton steel boat off a shoal. We are *fucked* . . .

This is all going on in my head but on the outside I say things like, 'OK . . . Right . . . OK . . . Right . . . Dash, you go down below, Mama just has to help Papa on deck for a little bit.'

I know that I am a very bad mother but still I throw a handful of lollies at Dash, chuck him in the stern cabin and head back on deck. Ross is white.

'I thought I was in the channel — the depth-sounder said 10 metres. I was looking at that shoal over there. We were cruising at 5 knots. This is bad, Ange, really bad . . . what the hell was I thinking?'

I am to blame. I was distracted. I was meant to be on shoal alert. But I was blindsided by an enormous moth and a small boy.

'I am going to take the anchor and put it on the stern and see if we can drag ourselves off that way,' Ross says.

We are doing things the old-fashioned way, with charts, a compass, a small GPS and a fish-finder which doubles as a depth-sounder. Most other yachts have GPS systems showing the exact location of the boat in real time. Not us, we didn't have the money.

Our most treasured possession is Eric Bauhaus' *Panama Cruising Guide*. This book has become our Bible. We know exactly which pages to turn to for guidance and study it every night. Whenever we are making a passage it is on deck and is constantly being referred to.

'Right, OK, yip.' All I can think of is that I will have to get into the soon-to-be-infested-by-alligators water and push the boat off the shoal.

We heave the anchor around to the port side and swing it as far as we can. It grips onto a particularly grippy-looking rock and we click the engine into reserve. Fumes bellow out the exhaust, two agonising minutes later we move — a tiny bit.

'OK, we are OK, we can drag ourselves off here!' Ross calls from the bow. 'Gun it again, Ange.'

We come flying off the shoal and are suddenly cast into a labyrinth of shallow soundings.

'Zero point four metres, two metres, zero point six meters . . . How on earth did we get in here?' I ask Ross as I try to keep my eyes on the depth-sounder and look at the sea at the same time.

Sweat is pouring off us both, we have the look of the hunted in our eyes and we are getting further into the maze. Suddenly we hear the same crunching sound.

'Oh fuck!' we both whisper. Dash is within earshot and we are trying not to swear around him. 'Right, OK, right, let's reverse!' Luckily we approached this shoal at a mere 1 knot so we weren't as wedged into it we could have been, but we are still grounded. We reverse, we get off. My adrenaline is through the roof.

We work as a team, me spotting and Ross on the tiller. We head for the darker water in the middle of the bay as the wind blows up and tries to ground us for the third time.

When the depth-sounder displays 10 metres we drop the hook. We are bouncing around, but the anchor is holding. The last thing we need to do is drag.

Calming down, we sit in the cockpit looking at each other. Our sugary boy climbs up the companionway and parks himself on my knee.

'Every day is an adventure, baby.'

'You're not wrong. Imagine what we would have got up to today if we were still in Wellington,' I say, adjusting one of my soft furnishings behind me.

'Is there any of that rum left?' Ross asks as he wipes away the blood from his head. He had cracked it in all the 'excitement'.

'About two nips.'

'Pour it, baby.'

I am definitely a bad mother.

31

No-see-ums

———

'Welcome to our very own picture-postcard tropical island of Kuanidup! This idyllic coconut grove is surrounded by clear, azure waters teaming with all manner of marine life. On a clear day you can spot stingrays, sharks, turtles and pelicans — all from the comfort of the foredeck.

On shore, there are multitudes of crabs, starfish and, for those with children, your very own naturally occurring toddler paddling pool. You won't go hungry here, as Kuna men visit daily in dug-out canoes laden with bananas, coconuts and plump, delicious-looking fish.'

To entertain my family I am pretending to be a travel-show presenter.

'But be warned, not all is as charming as it seems in this part of the world. Like Milford Sound this place is home to the dreaded sandfly or, as they are called here, no-see-ums. Look, my legs are covered in weeping sores! I have been eaten alive! The tiny black smudges itch for *days* and the only way to stay sane is to grab a comb and feverishly scratch at your legs — your fingernails will be too split and soft from the salt water to offer enough friction. You will dread going ashore and you will wish for the comfort of a cold, rainy day in Wellington. Wind and sun damage and airless nights locked in the stern cabin will certainly age you but on the plus side, you'll be the thinnest and brownest you've ever been!'

Cabin fever. It's time for an excursion. Across the bay is a small island called Wasladup that we need to investigate. We row across and discover hundreds of conch shells lying on the beach. Their garish pink interiors remind me of a pair of bitching tights I once owned, and the next thing you know I am busting out long-forgotten moves to Pearl Lusta and Rex Carlisle's monumental choreographic debut 'Thunderstuck' by AC/DC. On cue, the massive grey cloud claps out an almighty belt of thunder while a lone pelican drying his wings atop the only coconut palm looks down his nose at me and flaps in support. This is Bitchin' island styles!

As I reach the bit where I have to grapevine across the sand, Dashkin joins in. 'Fun, Mama, dancing!'

Ross shakes his head in the 'oh, Angela' way that people who know me well seem to adopt as I scoop up Dash and raise him above my head in power pose.

It feels good to dance. On my own island. In the Caribbean.

'Here it comes . . .' Ross yells over his shoulder.

'Rain, Mama!' Dash says excitedly, holding out his hand from under the tree and trying to catch the drops before they pucker the sand.

'Come on! It looks like a good swimming hole here.' Ross has rounded the corner and is standing knee-deep in clear blue water.

Dash races and I pretend to race down the beach. We both squeal delightedly.

Ross is right — there is a natural toddler's pool on the far end of the island. The weeds and rubbish that choke the other islands in the Kuna Yala are miraculously not present.

By the time Dash and I get there, Ross is lolling in the water with his head just visible.

'It's hot!' I say as I sit down in the water. 'Can this place get any better?'

The rain teems — a true tropical downpour so heavy we can hardly breathe or open our eyes. It pounds the water, splashing onto our faces. We squint and turn our backs to the wind. Dash refuses to join us.

'Really deep water . . . be careful . . . harness on,' he says, slapping his chest.

'It's OK, darling, it's nice and warm,' I call over the rain. 'Mama and Papa are here, come on.'

'No!' He is squatting on the shore, looking for crabs. His blond curls are pulled straight by the rain and drip water along the bridge of his nose.

'Come on.'

'No, no get in water,' he says, standing up and waving his little arms.

Ross sucks himself out of the water, wades to the shore and gathers up Dash.

'No, no!' he screams, wriggling and trying to get free.

With a toddler, nothing is easy. One must possess the patience of a saint and my ambitions for beatification have long since faded. Sometimes living in a space the size of a game of hopscotch in 35-degree heat, twenty-four hours a day, with a forty-nine-year-old and an almost-two-year-old is like being flagellated with thorn-studded twigs. I am trying not to get too bitchy or frustrated but if one person is feeling antsy then it's impossible for it not to affect everyone. I am trying to *be kind*.

Ross gently lowers Dashkin into the water and the squealing stops.

'Warm water . . .' Soon he's lying on our backs, floating around the pool, cautiously sliding off, getting braver and more confident with each splash. The rain is still bucketing down. This is what I imagined. *This is more like it.* Private islands, isolated beaches.

I swim over to a large stick poking up out of the water. There are marks at regular intervals etched into the bark.

Back when I was a girl I had belonged to 'Spy Club'. Every Sunday after church we would meet and report on our weekly activities. We wrote notes in invisible ink and undertook covert surveillance operations on our neighbours. A fake nose could really take you places. Clues were everywhere, you just had to know what to look for and how to interpret them. One of the Spy Club members had a book on disguises.

This training came in helpful now as I examined the stick. Marks at regular intervals, hmmmm. Ten metres from the shore, hmmmm. Could be a Kunan torture device — people are lashed to it and as the tide comes up they are almost drowned . . .

'Hey, Ange, I think we should be getting back. Dash is starting to shiver.'

'Right, OK, just having a look at the stick.'

'Yeah, it's where they tie up their canoes when they come to check on the coconuts,' says Ross, drowning my theory of foul play.

Sometimes it is hard being married to someone who is much smarter than you.

At nine the next morning there is a loud rapping on the hull and a strange voice calling '*Hola*'. I look out the porthole and see two dark, menacing eyes peering out of the slit of a balaclava.

Holy shit! I look out again and see another four guys in camouflage gear, holding AK47s. Bravely, Ross makes his way into the cockpit, while I try to find some undies for Dashkin.

My heart is racing. We have about $2000 in cash in the safe in the engine room, they can have that . . . would they want my wedding rings? What about Dashkin? People have told us there is a lucrative trade in child smuggling. They can have my wedding rings but they would have to shoot me before they got anywhere near my son. I can hear Ross talking to them. It doesn't sound like they are making threats.

Hang on a moment . . . it is nine o'clock on a Tuesday morning, they said '*Hola*' not 'Give me your money' and they're not making any attempt to board our boat. If they are not pirates of the Caribbean, then who are these people?

Ross is in conversation with a man in a blue uniform.

'Did you hear a distress call, sir?' He asks in perfect American.

'No, sorry.' The truth is we never turn our radio on at anchor.

'Last night we received a distress call from a yacht named *Pilot*. We're looking for it,' he continues.

'*Pilot*? No, sorry, the only other yacht here was an American charter and I am pretty sure it wasn't named *Pilot*.'

'Thank you for your time, sir. Have a good day.'

And then they speed off.

Ross and I laugh nervously. Suddenly I remember Dashkin in our cabin. I pull open the hatch and a mischievous, smiling face looks up.

'Wee-wee, Mama,' he says, pointing to the large puddle on the bed. An undieless little boy in our stern cabin has proved to be much more dangerous than our unexpected visitors.

Later that day I sip my Kuna Colada (rum, lime and fresh coconut juice from a coconut which has been macheted opened by my own fair hands) on the foredeck and watch as the sunset shoots pastel peach fingers across the sky. Grey clouds hang low and the ebbing blue light creates a vision of an 1980s watercolour. Below me in the cabin, Dash and Ross are slumbering. I am happily alone. So very happily alone.

32

Portobelo!

Treasure hunters, pirates, the black Madonna, historic battlements, and *ice-cream*! We have arrived in Portobelo.

For the last two weeks, Dashkin has been demanding ice-cream. Now, finally, it is mere hours away. I will no longer hear a little voice plaintively begging 'Ikebeen, Mama, please?' Let's get that dinghy off the davits and row to the festering-looking shore!

There will be shops! And booze! And I won't have to whip up something tasty out of a can of beans. Yeehaa!

'Come on, Dash, let's get your shoes on,' I call out, trying to hurry us along.

'Look, Mama, trucks!' Dash spots the huge, brightly painted trucks as they wind their way along the bumpy roads towards the settlement. The jungle is thick and smells warm and earthy. I throw my 'good' orange sunfrock over my bitchin' gold leotard and the family descends into the dinghy. Ross sits in the stern and suddenly I am stuck by the fact there is more than a passing resemblance between Ross and Francis Drake. I can't believe I hadn't spotted it before — the beard, the brows . . . the cravat.

'Francis Drake lies in a lead coffin at the bottom of this very bay,' Ross says, reading my mind. 'We could be floating over him now.'

'Oh, charming. If he is in a lead coffin he must have had some pretty nasty disease, like yellow fever.' I peer over the side nervously. Instead of a ghostly-yet-strikingly-handsome visage all I clock is my wonky reflection in the dark, scummy water.

We pick our way past flash catamarans and spacious-looking 50-foot yachts and pull up next to a concrete jetty. This next bit is always interesting: getting out of the dinghy gracefully. Ross leaps out, looking like a panther. I, however, have Dash on my knee, a pushchair jammed into my back, a bag of rubbish between my feet and a pack filled with water bottles, nappies and sunscreen overbalancing me.

Dashkin's life jacket makes manoeuvring him bloody difficult, so we do this thing where Ross says, 'Hands up, Dash' and I inevitability start singing 'Hands up, baby hands up!' while poor Dashkin's arms are almost ripped out of their sockets as he is lifted onto dry land.

Unsurprisingly, as soon as he hits the sand, he wants to take off.

'Stay still, sweetheart, wait for Mama,' I call out as I hurriedly fling things out of the dinghy, haul myself up the jetty and flop onto the concrete. Today I am greeted by dog shit and fish guts.

'Ikebeen!' Dashkin is on a mission and takes off down the road. We pass damp houses covered in green mould. Mosquitoes breed before our eyes, leaf-cutter ants march next to us, and dogs snap and growl as we negotiate potholes, glass and murderous-looking roosters. Portobelo has fallen on hard times. Gone are the glory days of Drake with its industry, Incan gold and pirates. Now it's all corner boys sporting sparkling white trainers, Asian grocery stores and cans of coconut peas. We feel very white and middle class as we walk past a group of guys knocking back nasty-smelling firewater. Inside the 'shop' I find Estella Azura Pasas y Ron, which looks like ice-cream for one. Perfect. Dash holds it with two hands and takes it to the counter. Ross buys a cask of wine, US$2 for 2 litres. *Bargain!* Vino Tinto Clos, welcome to our world!

We head outside to eat the ice-cream. We sit down on a sixteenth-century bridge and Dash sticks his plastic spoon into the rapidly melting rum and raisin ice-cream.

'Yum!' I hover next to him, hoping for a taste.

'Try some, Mama?'

'Why yes, darling, don't mind if I do!' He scoops up a tiny bit and hands the spoon to me. Instead of reaching my mouth, it drops. Disaster! It is now down in the fetid, vulture-lined drain.

'Oh no, get it Mama!' Like hell! I'll be in a lead coffin by the end of the day if I venture down there.

'Yucky! I don't want to catch cholera, Dash,' I explain. And then, trying to distract him, 'Look at the big flesh-eating birdies.' There is a great flapping of black wings as the vultures rise up out of the drain. They are too much like turkeys for my liking and I am totally revolted by turkeys. It stems from the time I was twelve and had to pluck lice-ridden birds on my uncle's farm. Ross and I raise our eyebrows at each other.

'The big flesh-eating birdies?' Whatever it takes, right? Travelling with a toddler certainly changes your perspective.

We row back to the yacht and pore over the *Panama Cruising Guide*. Tomorrow we are going to Colón.

33

Power
Shower

— ❦ —

Described in the early 1900s as the 'pest hole of the universe, and the wickedest city in the Americas', it is surprising how incredibly excited we are to be here in Colón.

I swear I have lost 4 kilos in four hours. My nerves are wrecked from navigating tiny *Te Ikaroa* past colossal tankers and cargo ships. I have never been so 'up close' to such enormous hunks of metal, but I was certainly not interested in getting 'personal' with *any* of them. I needed to be on my game.

This is one of the busiest ports in the world. The officials are known for their bureaucratic adherence to details, so we could get fined shitloads of money we don't have or, worse, be denied access to transit the Panama Canal.

Ross is on the tiller and it is up to me to request permission to enter the eastern breakwater. I am taking it very seriously.

On the VHF, captains of all nationalities are requesting pilots and admeasures. There are no other ladies.

There is a break in the transmissions. Right. I pick up the hand-held and take a deep breath. 'This is the sailing vessel *Te Ikaroa*, requesting permission to enter the eastern breakwater.'

There is a *lot* of fast Spanish. Ross and I begin to get jumpy. I try again, and again. Nothing. We are approaching the breakwater. A fully laden 250-foot cargo ship, *Everdainty*, looms next to us.

'*Te Ikaroa* requesting permission to enter the eastern breakwater.' I am doing everything Eric Bauhaus told me to do.

'Excuse me, ma'am, please get off this channel. Cristóbal Control Tower manages the eastern breakwater. Go to channel nine.'

Oh God. 'OK, thanks, sorry.' I change to channel nine. Dash is waking up.

'Where is the gap, Angela, can you see the gap?' (Ross has called me Angela, so he must be getting stressed.)

Finally someone answers me: 'You may proceed.' I have the binoculars glued to my eyes. The breakwater is a line of huge boulders, and depending on the angle you approach them on, it looks like one continuous line with no gap. There is one thing for it.

'Follow *Everdainty*.' Ross swings the tiller around and we fall in behind. To the left is a busy cargo dock. To the right are the remains of a yacht club helpfully named, wait for it . . . Club Nautico! Steward's boats roar past at 10 knots.

We get as close to shore as we can and anchor in 10 metres. Three minutes later the thunderstorm that has been threatening all day unleashes its fury. In seconds we are soaked to the skin.

I bungle down below, grab Dash and the shampoo and we all stand on the deck laughing like monkeys, leaping like gazelles, having our first 'proper' wash for a month. Relief. We made it. The next part of the journey is about to begin.

And Tito is about to appear.

'I reckon we could out-run him,' I say to Ross as a rotund old man waddles towards us. He has that slack, slightly open mouth that really fat people get when they are trying to do any kind of exercise. 'What is it with fat port inspectors and rundown yacht clubs called Club Nautico?' Dash spies a crab and sets off to investigate.

'You want to transit the canal?' Slack-jaw asks, waving us over to a mosaic area next to a disused Members Only swimming pool. It is cool.

'Yes, what is the wait?' We have heard that sometimes you have to wait for up to six weeks.

'I think maybe the end of the week, you can go through.' We look at each other, surprised.

'End of the week! Great, that works for us.' This is much sooner than we expected. 'OK, what do we need to do?' The daily thunderstorms are a reminder of how we need to keep pressing on, of how late it is in the season and how we really need to be heading out into the Pacific in three weeks.

'You need an agent. I call my friend, Tito, he comes soon.'

Dash and I amuse ourselves spotting ants and iguanas while Ross makes his way through the mountain of paperwork. We are in the middle of a detailed study of some ants when two gun-wielding policemen roar up on a motorbike right next to us. They park under the ant tree, pull out greasy paper bags that they have tucked down under their ammunition belts and proceed to have morning tea. The ubiquitous sausage roll of New Zealand has been replaced by fried empanadas but the world over, 'smoko' is a serious business. Dash and I check out lizards elsewhere.

A rickety yellow cab pulls up next to the statute of the Blessed Virgin Mary. The front door swings open, the music stops. Tito has arrived.

'Get in, we go.' The Blacksmiths do as we are told. 'Sorry, but my city is very dangerous, you always take a taxi, and never go on the outside of Avenida Central. It is OK to walk from Club Nautico to Colón 2000 but no more.' I am always a little cynical about speeches like this — it sounds like a scam to get us to pay for taxis rather than walk for free.

'Last week one family got robbed at gunpoint by a taxi driver, he take them far away and steal everything. They had a children like you.' Hmmm, that blows that theory out of the water. 'You *never* go with a driver called Salista, he is bad man.'

I look out of the window. It is grim. 'Pest hole of the universe' doesn't seem to be much of an exaggeration. All the buildings are crumbling, the rain has blocked the drains and people are wading shin-deep in grey water. No one is smiling.

We fly down side streets, roar over intersections and pull up hard next to Tito's 'office'. Dash and I stay in the taxi while Ross and Tito go inside to photocopy our documents. South America is *big* on photocopying. They leave no form uncopied.

An injured man shuffles past us, his arm in a filthy sling; his amigo has a bung foot and hobbles alongside. Another guy pushing a trolley of used tyres disrupts the traffic, horns honk, people shout. A bus, painted like a bogan's wet dream, thunders along. Our driver gets out and heads to a street stall selling ripped copies of Shakira's greatest hits. I feel like I'm in a movie.

'Ladybug!' Dashkin exclaims, pulling my jaw to get me to turn around. And there, among the filth, grime and sweat-soaked seats of a crappy taxi cab in the middle of Colón is a beautiful, shiny red ladybug. 'Oh, tickly!' he giggles as the ladybug crawls over his palm.

The men arrive back, including the driver, and it's off to the port authority. Security is tight here: metal detectors, emptying of pockets, photo ID. But hang on, what do you do with an under two? A port is no place for a child, but you can't leave him outside alone? A big debate for the boys at the gate. He's allowed in but has to hold my hand at all times.

We march down a strange caged walkway, collect the contents of our pockets and gaze at a splendid rogues gallery. Papering the wall are hundreds of wanted posters. Bad boys, hot bad boys, especially Angel Herrera — woah, that is a smoking-hot mug shot. Smouldering eyes, stubble . . . 'This way, ma'am.' I am dragged back to the stifling heat of the port of Colón, bustled back into the taxi and taken down to the Cristóbal control station. Fingers crossed, I don't have to see the radio controller. How embarrassing.

More security, video surveillance this time, and no lifts.

We trudge up four flights of stairs and wait in the cool, air-conditioned office.

'You can have water,' Tito says, waving his hand towards a water cooler and a pile of conical paper 'cups'. Dash and I are parched so make a great game out of filling the cones with water and trying to drink as much as we can before it seeps out the bottom. Tito hands over our papers and passports; we smile sweetly, attempting not to look like the great unwashed, sun-frazzled sailors we are and more like the smooth city slickers of our passport photos. We leave with instructions to 'call this number at seven p.m. tonight'.

From the balcony we see The Flats, a bleak anchorage divided into three sections. If this was on land it would be like the badlands of some British estate. The phone call will advise us when to make our way here.

Tito drops us back to the yacht. We have just enough time to hit the shops of Colón and do some serious provisioning for the crossing of the Pacific Ocean!

34
Super 99

Super 99! Well, well, well, who would have thought food shopping in Colón would be such a delight? This is a cruiser's paradise. Tinned goods as far as the eye can see. Aisle thirteen — a marvellous selection of tinned ham, beef and sausages; aisles four to twelve are jam-packed with tinned vegetables. I audibly exclaim when I spot a selection of mixed veg.

Mixed veg in a can, imagine! This ingenious invention will slash our shopping bill in half, revolutionise our menu and save us from bleeding gums.

I pile twenty of the beggars into our trolley. So far we have forty cans of tomatoes, twenty cans of corn, thirty cans of beans (kidney, cannellini, navy), thirty cans of sardines, five cans of olives, twenty packets of pasta, ten packets of porridge, twenty packets of coffee, six 2-litre bottles of Ron Abuelo (it's only US$12!), heaps of Clos and a bottle of Moët for when we cross the equator.

Our young son reminds me of the need for some special treats by continually saying, 'Lolly, lolly, lolly.' I give in and spend the next ten minutes wandering around the kilometre-square supermarket looking for sweets. Dashkin's eyes are trained and as I whisk him past what I think is only the cornmeal aisle he makes a grab from his pushchair and snatches a pack of marshmallows. Squish, his teeth have bitten through the plastic.

'Dash, no!' But this boy is like lightning. He rips at the marshmallows like a hungry dog. 'Dashkin, stop it!' I pull at the pack. Please dear lord don't let an old lady witness this; I cannot handle another telling off by a granny in a supermarket.

'*Cut it out now*!' He is being a right little pain. We are in the throes of the classic tantrum. I eyeball him (Supernanny recommends this). 'You want the marshmallows?' I repeat back to him in a dramatic fashion. He is so stunned he stops shouting and stares at me.

'Yeah, Mama.'

I am tempted to say, 'You can't *handle* the marshmallows!' but instead I pipe up with 'OK, I will put them in the trolley and we'll buy them.'

Out of the corner of my eye I see the security guard coming towards us. He is carrying a gun and I can't handle the gun. We hightail it to the checkout.

Three hundred and fifty six US dollars later and we are taking Tito's advice. We are en route to the club in a taxi, being serenaded by 1970s Panamanian pop hits.

We unload everything into the dinghy, pick up 20 kilos of laundry, throw on six grubby tyres (we need to strap them to the side of the yacht for the transit), balance ourselves on top of it all and put out to *Te Ikaroa*. It is a treacherous 10 metres. Steward boats charge through without a care in the world for overloaded family dinghies.

'Hold on . . . here comes the wake!' Ross calls out as Dash clings to me, while I cling to the washing. All of my clothes are in these bags — there is no way they are getting wet and there is no way in *hell* they are going overboard. They may be faded, but they are all I have.

Six minutes later, safely pulled up alongside *Te Ikaroa*'s port side, Dash relaxes. 'Ahhhh, home.' He totters down below to continue drawing ladybugs. I get busy labelling the provisions: T for whole peeled tomatoes, T and a lightning strike for chopped tomatoes (I am a firm believer in comedy in the pantry). Tins of peaches labelled *durazno* (no time like the present to practise a bit of Español) take up the entire bottom of the locker, on top of which is Dashkin's favourite food, porridge.

While I am busy being a good little homemaker, Ross gives Dashkin a bucket bath on deck. Actually, it's more of a puddle bath, as we are on strict water rations; every couple of days he gets a 2-centimetre deep fresh-water splash to prevent nappy rash. If the Plunket nurse could see me now!

Another massive cargo ship passes 30 metres away. Dashkin waves his soapy hands to the figures on the bridge as they come into dock.

It is 7 p.m., time to make the call. 'Be at The Flats, anchorage B, at two p.m. tomorrow,' a thick Spanish accent informs us.

Ross puts the phone down and we sit quietly in the saloon. Tomorrow we are going to transit the Panama Canal. On our yacht. With our son. It's a dream come true — the realisation, for both of us, of a lifetime's goal. I, of course, get all teary-eyed and transport myself back to my happy place, the early 1980s.

Ever since the summer holidays of 1982, I have wanted to travel.

Charlotte and I had spent the afternoon making up dance routines to 'Physical' by Olivia Neutron Bomb at our grandparents' place in Longburn. Granddad appeared out of the smoky lounge and the clutches of my yellow-fingernailed Nana and sat down on the deck with a old metal tobacco tin in his hands.

'What's in there, Granddad?' I asked.

'This?' he said, tapping it on his knee and loosening the hinge. It opened, knocking a pile of small photos into his hand. We moved closer.

'What are the photos of, Granddad?'

'The war,' he said quietly.

We knew about the war. We knew he didn't like talking about it. Charlotte and I sat still.

He shuffled them.

'This is in Egypt,' he said, pointing to a faded sepia photo of a young man dressed in a khaki uniform. There was a pyramid in the background. We snuggled in, looking over his wrinkly biceps to get a better view.

'Is that you, Granddad, in the olden days?' I asked, amazed that he could ever have been young.

'That's me in Egypt.'

'Egypt,' I breathed. I had just finished a project at school on ancient Egypt and was well versed in scarab beetles, curses, hieroglyphics and of course mummies. And now, here was my grandfather telling me he had been there! He had been to the pyramids!

'Did you see Tutankhamen's tomb?' I asked excitedly.

'No, Angela, we weren't sightseeing.'

But 'Did you see any mummies? What about sphinxes?' I gabbled on. 'What was it like, being in Egypt?'

'It was very hot.' Granddad laughed.

'Like today?' I said, eager to appear knowledgeable even if it was just about the weather.

'No, Angela, *very* hot. Forty degrees. It doesn't get that hot in Palmerston North.' He smiled. 'And there was lots and lots of sand.' He was lost in his own recollections.

We continued looking through the photos, Charlotte and I taking turns to hold them very carefully on the edges while we squinted at our grandfather in exotic locations, surrounded by Jeeps and strange men.

Soon after, Mum, Dad and our baby sister Emily arrived in the turquoise Ford Falcon to take us home. Granddad slipped the tin into his trouser pocket. As we drove back into town, Joan Jett and the Blackhearts belted out 'I Love Rock and Roll' at a respectable volume.

That night I lay in my top bunk under my new brown and beige duvet thinking about the images Granddad had shown us. I wanted to have stories to tell; I wanted my own tin of adventure.

I knew that one day, when I was a grown up, I was going to travel.

That little tin had opened up the world.

35

Beef Cakes

The next morning, armed with the passports and US$1000 in cash stashed in Dashkin's backpack, Ross heads off to the bank. Tito and some 'muscle' escort him. We discover we have to pay the deposit for the transit before anything more will happen, and to pay the deposit you have to go to the City Bank in Colón. And to survive going to the City Bank in Colón you need some big motherfuckers by your side.

'Take care!' I call, totally jealous he has bodyguards. Now that I am the sailing equivalent of a 1950s housewife I have cleaning to do. Lots of cleaning. Our transit depends on it. This very afternoon an official from the Panama Canal is coming on board to check our loo. One skid mark and we might not be granted access, one leaky valve and our hopes and dreams could all be crushed like a bug.

Regulations state that all yachts must have a holding tank, which means a close inspection of the shitter. I am not taking any chances, because in Colombia the holding tank overflowed into the hand basin. Just think about what that actually means — disgusting, eh? It is no place for a child so I set Dash up in the saloon with playdough, raisins and a cardboard box and work like a woman possessed. Three hours and thirty-five playdough ladybugs later, *Te Ikaroa* is looking spic and span.

Ross arrives home, alive and intact. He pours himself a nerve-settling drink and we head around to The Flats. Past rusty old boats with great gouges out of their sides, past Korean fishing boats with deck hands dangling down the stern as they repaint the hull, following the markers all the way around. We anchor in the B Zone.

I call the control tower — finally something that doesn't involve a can of Pledge and a wet rag! They advise that the Admeasurer will be on board in 'one zero minutes' — just enough time for me put the jug on and arrange the ginger snaps on a plate. Apparently providing refreshments for the officials is mandatory. The better the biscuit, the better the service.

Out the porthole, a pilot boat churns up the sea as it makes its way towards us. With a bang, Chong leaps on board.

He's a preppy, podgy Asian Panamanian with lovely manners. He swoops on the biscuits and begins filling in forms. We cover off the gross tonnage, how much diesel we have on board, and then the one we have been waiting for, 'What is her top speed?'

'Nine knots,' we lie in unison. I almost choked on my ginger snap — we have never got her above 5.9 knots. Chong merely raises an eyebrow to indicate he is 'in on the game' and 9 knots is duly recorded.

Next, out comes the tape measure. Chong instructs Ross to hold one end and head down to the bowsprit while he leans over the stern and pulls it taunt across the davits.

'Forty-seven feet,' Chong says matter-of-factly. I start whooping, 'Forty-seven feet! We own a forty-seven-foot sailing vessel! Woohoo, that'll be great for the resale in Brisbane.' (Technically, she is still only 40 feet but when you include the davits and bowsprit it is 47.)

As Ross and I high-five each other Chong grabs another bickie and radioes for the pilot boat. Dash spends his time sneakily throwing bananas off the stern and as Chong departs sings out 'Bye-bye, man!'

Back at the rolling anchorage of Club Nautico, Tito is waiting with 100-foot lines. These attractive light green ropes lie curled around the jetty like strange tentacles. By law, each boat must have four experienced line-handlers, who stay on board for the two days it takes to transit. We are hoping for dry weather as there is no room down below for four big strapping lads.

At 6 p.m. we call Chong and are advised to be back at The Flats tomorrow at 2 p.m. to begin our transit. Woohoo!

I have given myself a black eye from over-excitedly folding nappies.

Emil is an ebony Adonis. He's all triangle back, bulging biceps, twelve-pack stomach and powerful thighs, and he has a lion tattooed on his chest. Dash can't take his eyes off him, nor can Ross, and nor can I. He is magnificent and, fantastically, he is one of our line-handlers.

'Hug you?' Dash says, sidling up to him. I suddenly wish I were almost two.

There are three other line-handlers: Gatto (the cat), Juan (very fat) and Sebastian (a thin boy). Tito has briefed me on the importance of providing them with food and Coke at regular intervals. I decide to make like Nigella and appear on deck with a plate-load of ham, lettuce and cheese sandwiches. They salivate and descend on the food like a pack of wolves and, like, I imagine a pack of wolves would, discard the scraps of wilted lettuce to lie limply on the deck.

That was the first of many, many rounds of sandwiches. I am eager to get going, but our pilot has yet to arrive. He will guide us through the locks and across the Gatun Lake and into the Pacific Ocean.

Ross and I are nervous: will *Te Ikaroa* be able to sustain 6 knots for hours on end? What happens if the turbulence created when the locks fill with water bashes us into the side of the canal and snaps our masts? What happens if I run out of Coke for the line-handlers? Will Dash be a good boy?

Time is ticking by, so I radio the control tower again.

'The pilot will be with you in ten minutes.' And she is right: exactly ten minutes later Christian is on board, ordering the anchor up, the motor started and full speed ahead to the entrance. He is very professional and calls Ross 'Captain'.

Space is at a premium so Dash and I squat on the cabintop. I am not going to cook my way through the canal, I will be on deck, thank you very much.

Te Ikaroa goes faster than she ever has before — 6 whole knots — and to avoid any embarrassing breakdowns Ross keeps her at 2300 revs. It's not fast enough. The barriers are coming down. We have missed the transit! If we don't make our transit time we have to pay another $US1000. I look back at Ross.

'There are cars driving over the lock! *Shit!*' I mouth, as I don't want to appear vulgar around the pilot. Ross shoots Christian a look of 'Seriously, have we missed it?' Christian keeps cool — I mean, this man does this every day, transiting the canal is how he makes a crust.

'You are OK. They will open it for us — there must be a backlog of traffic.'

Te Ikaroa squeezes into the first of the Gatun locks just in time. Another yacht, *Space,* is next to us.

'Raft up, Captain, quickly.' Emil leaps into action, lashing ropes and pulling lines, rafting us up to *Space*. This yacht looks much flashier than our old girl. In front of us is *Arctic Sea*, a middle-sized orange cargo ship which seems to take up the entire width of the lock, and behind that a three-storey passenger ferry. We are all to transit together.

'Monkey fist!' the on-shore line-handlers call out, throwing dangerous-looking knotted balls our way. Dash and I duck into the cockpit. Crack! One bounces on the stanchion and lands next to Gatto's big, wide, flat foot. He hauls it in and we are in business.

Emil and Gatto hold the lines on the boat, four officials hold the lines on shore, and the hundred-year-old gates slowly close on the Caribbean as the water begins to fill the lock.

'Stand by your engine, Captain, increase to two and a half thousand revs.'

We are lifted by thousands and thousands of gallons of swirling, thrashing water. I watch as we rise higher, 25 metres, 40 metres, 90 metres. Pin-picks of light start appearing on electrical mules as the locks are illuminated for the night, the sky turns an inky blue and the rain holds off.

Three times we are raised up until we are level with the lake. *Arctic Sea* powers ahead, making easy work of the 24.2 kilometres to the next locks. *Space* and *Te Ikaroa* are ushered towards a bright red buoy and told to wait here for the night.

The ebony Adonis and his mates are hungry. Emil does chin-ups in the companionway as I start cooking up a feast on one gas burner with a toddler hanging on my hip. Rice and beans, sausages, watermelon, pineapple, corn fritters, fried cabbage, hard-boiled eggs, beer and rum. As we settle down for the night, the smell of four men farting in unison ekes into the cabin. What. Was. I. Thinking? I am gassed into unconsciousness. Thank. God.

I wake up feeling like I have been bashed by a forest of ugly sticks. My watch says 5.50 a.m., and out the stern window the Panama Canal Authority boat is charging towards us. Rats — I'm in a pair of panties with my boobs hanging out. I wrestle on my floral yellow dressing gown, collect Dash from his cabin and get the coffee brewing.

Our new pilot is a no-nonsense man. He downs the coffee in one, and has us motoring across the lake before I have time to crack the eggs.

On deck, Emil takes some 'time out' to wash his smalls in the fresh water. His muscles ripple as he launches the black rubber bucket over the side and he stands tall and proud as it drags, filling with water. (Usually at this point I am bracing myself on the toerail, screaming, 'I can't hold it!') Then, as if he were picking up a little lost lamb, he brings the bucket back on deck, produces washing powder out of his duffel bag and proceeds to scrub his undies as we cruise the Gatun Lake. As much as I love watching grown men do laundry I feel like a bit of a perv, so Dash and I retire to the cockpit to read *I'm So Handsome*. When I look up again, Emil's gruts are flapping on the lifelines.

The Gaillard Cut is being widened but we can still make out the century-old marks of the steam shovels on the rock. Many men died creating this monumental incision through the continental divide, but unlike the wall in Cartagena, the only kissing going on here is Dash smooching Emil.

The day turns grey and thunderclouds darken the sky, but Dash sits on deck spotting diggers, dredges, birds, boats and having the time of his short life. Ross is grinning from ear to ear.

The beautiful Centennial Bridge towers on the horizon. The cable-stayed design resembles two triangular sails. We crane our necks and have to get the binoculars to check out the bottom. At 80 metres we are dwarfed by it.

Te Ikaroa is holding up well — no over-heating or unexplained breakdowns. Ross and I raise our coffee mugs to Elvis.

Next come the Pedro Miguel locks. This time the water flows out. I imagine us hurtling down into the artificial Miraflores Lake like you do on a hydroslide but it is all very controlled and civilised.

Our descent into the Pacific Ocean has begun: only the two-stage Miraflores lock system to go. We hold our breath — we are so close. Come on, *Te Ikaroa*, don't fail us now!

The gates inch open. Dashkin, Ross and I stand together as the Pacific stretches before us. It's blowing 20 knots on the nose.

Tears well up in my eyes. We made it, we are in the Pacific! Now there's only about 4000 miles between us and the Marquesas . . .

36

Bogans of the World!

Hailing from a city where people name their children Levi, after the jeans, Kahlua after the drink and Harley after the motorbike, it is no wonder I have more than a passing interest in the bogan.

As a nineteen-year-old working at the Tui milk factory I had the opportunity to stand shoulder to mullet with many a Palmy bogan. Chat over the cottage-cheese tubs revolved around how much Jack Daniels had been consumed the night before, who was fucking whom, exactly what is was that Meatloaf wouldn't do for love, guarding your stash from your kids, how many dream-catchers you need in a flat and how fucken awesome Leanne's new tit tattoo was.

I loved it. They all thought I was a posh bitch 'cos I was at uni, and I thought they were slightly thick 'cos they worked in a milk-processing factory. Yet we got on surprisingly well, aside from the time they threw me in the vat of 'turned' cottage cheese. (That's another story.) So well that sometimes, after our twelve-hour shifts, Roxanne would give me a lift home in her Subaru Legacy. It had a killer spoiler and air-brushed flames licked the bonnet. Even before we had hit the Longburn turn-off, she'd have pulled a pack of Rothmans out of her purple crushed-velvet dress and sparked up the first of fifteen fags using her 'They don't make chicks this hot for nothing' lighter.

In the back seat was a spectacular example of bogan rug art. Against a polar-fleece background, a chunky-thighed goddess rode a flying unicorn across the night sky, while a panther with glitter for eyes stared out of the darkness. It was always covered in Alsatian dog hair. 'Dirty Deeds' blared out as we caned down the straights of the Manawatu.

One day I mentioned how much fun I was having 'mixing it up with heaps of bogans — you guys are great'. The room fell silent. 'What the fuck is a bogan?' they demanded. At first I thought they were winding me up, like when they told me to go and get some Kryptonite but I soon realised a true bogan never self-identifies.

It was awkward. A bogan who feels they are being mocked is the most dangerous of all bogans, much like a glitter-eyed panther would be in the wild.

I had to think clearly and quickly. 'Bogans . . . umm, well, they are the backbone of New Zealand, the salt of the earth. They're kinda stuck in a 1970s time warp but in a good way. They can be identified by their love of AC/DC, Metallica, leather waistcoats, greasy pony tails, peroxide two-toned hair, Kahlua and Harley-Davidsons. Peter Jackson — he's a cashed-up bogan! He'd love those gargoyles that you've got on the goblets at your place, Rox — he puts them in his movies! Bogans are cool.'

I failed to mention that they are usually poor and white and that there are many sub-species, like the rural bogan, the hippy bogan, the ironic bogan and the hard-core bogan.

So you can imagine, then, how over-excited I am to find the Panamanian bogan. Spying from the deck of *Te Ikaroa* while anchored in Las Brisas de Amador, I clock a take-your–breath-away sight: van art of the highest order. Like all true bogans, the Panamanics (I can't help it, calling them Panamanics makes me snort-laugh) *love* van art. Their commitment to the decorative aspect of bogan culture is so profound and absolute that the public transport system is covered in it. Covered in it.

Where do I begin? Think winged horses, bikini-clad Amazons, fork-tongued snakes, Jesus looking like he is on crack, guns, flaming crosses, skulls, dream-catchers, football insignia, all manner of horns, hawks, weird mythical landscapes, tits, arses, axes and, inexplicably, dead children, all air-brushed on to old American school buses!

Mental driving and nonexistent road rules make the streets of Panama a moving homage to bogan art. It beats the shit out of the Wellington city buses any day. And to make it even better, they are called Diablo Rojo or the red devils.

'OK, darling, I'm just off to catch the Red Devil — you got a spare twenty-five cents for the fare?' Imagine starting your day like that! Imagine. Go on.

There are two drawbacks:

1. They are god-awful polluters. Black smoke literally pours out of them. Get stuck behind one and you will be blowing grimy snot out of your snout for weeks.

2. They are death traps. A few years ago, nineteen people were incinerated when the Red Devil they were riding in caught fire. The emergency back door had been padlocked from the outside! No amount of van art will save you from that.

Cue the Panama authorities replacing them with cleaner, greener, downright boringly adorned buses. Each owner-driver is given some cash and the directions to the Diablo Rojo graveyard. The final drive takes them over the Bridge of the Americas towards Vera Cruz, turns them right into a huge paddock and leaves them to take their chances as the jungle engulfs them. At least they look good doing it.

37

Paramour

The sailing fraternity
are an interesting bunch:
American retirees whiling
away their sunset years,
rich Italians in 50-foot
Beneteaus laughing like
horses over expensive
bottles of Chianti, old salty
dogs with long ragged
beards who never leave
anchor, arrogant French
sailors who everyone hates,
young men who strip off
and sail into the sunset with
their nuts hanging out . . .

German couples who have been sailing for forty years and make it look easy, single old coots with bad teeth and yappy dogs, skinny super-tanned ladies with very wrinkly faces waiting for the melanoma to suck the life out of them, amazing adventurers who inspire the hell out of me, the very occasional family, and the guys in the throes of a full-blown middle-age crisis. The marinas are full of the latter, the ho-bags of the sea.

Take Chris, for example. We meet him the night before we are to leave Las Brisas de Amador. Chris is a forty-three-year-old American divorcée with his own 45-foot yacht (i.e. the ultimate knicker-dropping accessory). He enjoys walks on the beach, moonlit nights on velvety seas and shagging. Lots and lots of shagging, with as many different people as possible.

He invites himself over for a drink. As soon as he is on board Ross and I are 'treated' to the details of his 'all-embracing' love life. I am no prude and my chequered romantic history has, at times, been like watching a soap opera, but this guy's biography has to be titled *Around the World in Eighty Lays*! He is a machine! He starts us off easy: 'Karen, my two-timing bitch of an ex-wife, was shagging my best friend. Can you believe that? [I could.] And, get this, she belonged to *Mensa*!'

Then there was Maree in the Bahamas: 'I was shagging her

while her husband was away, but she got pregnant and had an abortion without telling me. And you know what? I really want more children.' Ross and I look at each other, thinking we are pretty sure a child would cramp his style.

Then we hear about 'Amanda Pander', a stripper from Vegas who he met online. 'There is this amazingly great website where you can post ads for crew. Amanda Pander came for a holiday, she stayed for a month and treated me like a king.' I decide not to press him for more details — suffice to say there are lots of poles on a boat.

By this stage he has been talking non-stop for forty-five minutes. He's not bragging — it's more like we have become his shrinks. 'The woman I am currently cyber-romancing is after adventure — she wants more than her dull life in Minnesota, and I can offer her that.' Oh, spare me — a real-life sexual Samaritan in my saloon. 'She was going to come across the Pacific with me, but she's got bronchitis.' A lucky escape, methinks.

And then we hear, in *way* too much detail, about Celeste, the twenty-three-year-old English backpacker he met three days ago at a bar in Panama and who is, currently, this very minute in fact, lying in his cabin waiting to be shagged when he gets back. 'I tell ya, being a captain is a pussy magnet.' I taste a little bit of sick in my mouth as I gag. He is gross.

I don't care that he is on a shagging rampage, I truly don't. You don't need a psychology degree to figure out he is looking for love in all the wrong places, searching for love in too many faces . . . *I* care about going to bed. This is our last chance for a good night's sleep for three weeks. I surreptitiously check the clock: 10.45 p.m. Come on, Chris . . . bugger off! Go home and shag your twenty-three-year-old bit of totty.

BOOOM! Suddenly there is an ear-splitting explosion. I hit the cabin floor. Chris slides down the couch, bleeding and covered in glass. What the fuck?

Ross and I frantically check the saloon . . . has the gas canister exploded? Has the porthole shattered? Is there someone on deck firing into the saloon?

'Chris! Chris, are you OK?' He looks up, razor-sharp shards of green glass embedded in his hair. BOOOM! There is another explosion.

'Shit!' I scream, covering my head with one of the cushions. Chris is on the floor covered in a sticky liquid. I crawl over to him.

I help him back onto the couch and start picking out bits of glass.

'What the fuck is happening?' he screams.

I look at Chris, Chris looks at Ross and Ross smiles.

'Look.' Right behind Chris' head are the remains of two bottles of cava. We are not being shot at, our $4.50 bottles of cava have burst. The entire cabin is coated in warm, sickly sweet-smelling booze and tiny shards of super-sharp glass.

'I'm outta here, guys! This is too freaky for me.' Chris is out the hatch, into his dinghy and en route to his root in seconds.

Ross and I begin the clean up. Cava has dripped into all of our provisions, all through the fresh fruit I have bought, and to top it off my newly laundered soft furnishings (in preparation for three weeks at sea) are sodden and stinking. This really rips my undies.

Already we both have nasty nicks on our hands and feet. Blood and booze mix together like the high point of a Catholic mass. I am tired and emotional and as is often the case in situations like these, I feel a hymn coming on. I can't stop it. I open my mouth, hit the highest octave I can manage without waking Dash and sing, 'Through your pain you will discover me . . . Strong and constant is my love . . .' Soon we are giggling and scrubbing.

'Well, that shut him up!' Ross laughs. 'Thank God it wasn't the Moët!' And with that we collapse into bed.

38

Viva South Central America!

Viva South Central America! Land of super pollo, crappy plastic shoes, far-too-tight denim, heat, sunshine and wolf whistles!

This is a Bitch's paradise. If Palmerston North is the Real Hot Bitches' spiritual home, then South Central America is its wardrobe. Everywhere I look there are women sporting outfits that would make any RHB squeal with delight.

Sequins, animal print, Lycra, mesh, neon lace, fake leather, feathers, glitter and spray-on denim casually walk the streets, unaware of the fact that in New Zealand, at the Island Bay Surf Club on a Saturday afternoon, they would be worshipped as Superstars of Trashion.

Going to the supermarket here is like stepping into a Bitch's wonderland: '80s music is pumped through a kick-arse PA system; the painted hues of purples, blues and neon highlight dark eyes as they flash in search of the best deal on beans; nails like talons reach for the pineapples; and tiny T-shirts do their best to encase unnaturally perky bosoms.

This is everyday bitchin'. Every single day! I love it.

For some, the fashion here may be considered vulgar, tasteless and highly inappropriate for most people's body type. It's true there is nothing nymph-like about these ladies but the women of SCA have had the bitchin' motto of 'more is more' tattooed onto their collective subconscious. They live it and breathe it and they don't give a rat's arse if anyone sees their arse!

In comparison, I have never felt so dowdy. My 'capsule wardrobe' of a few T-shirts, two pairs of shorts and a couple of dresses just doesn't cut it. Even when I put on my golden jandals I can't compete. Sure, I have my golden leotard but breastfeeding has meant 'the girls' are a shadow of their former, firmer glory.

Surrounded by so many examples of bitchingness, however, it was only a matter of time before my inner bitch shone through. After all, you can't fight your nature. As luck would have it, my respectable-length cut-offs were lost overboard, thus creating the perfect excuse to join the South Central American league of Real Hot Bitches.

I threw modesty to the wind and squeezed myself into the smallest pair of shorts I have ever owned. I can hardly breathe and I feel like I am walking around in my undies, but boy oh boy have they got me noticed! Even when I am pushing Dashkin down the street men are hanging out of car windows whistling at my butt. There is no supportive Lycra dance tight hugging my thighs into shape, there is just my unadorned, slightly tanned flesh — which seems to be a South Central American man's fantasy.

These shorts are like magic. A few days ago I packed up our laundry, hung it over the handles of the pushchair and headed off down the Amador causeway towards the *lavandería*. In twenty minutes I counted no less than seven wolf whistles — and that was before I passed the construction site!

Unlike my SCA sisters I got flustered and didn't really know where to look. With Dash in the pushchair it felt wrong to wave back. I crossed the road to avoid a 'situation' and at the same time the handles on our laundry bag broke, scattering dirty washing everywhere. I blushed scarlet. Of course it had to be a week's worth of frilly knickers blowing in the breeze. Soon the workers on the construction site had downed tools and were cheering and clapping as I bent over in my tiny shorts to pick up my 'smalls'.

But it wasn't over. I had yet to meet Raul.

We finally made it to the laundromat, and with the washing safely in the machine Dash and I sat outside and passed the time playing our favourite game, inspecting giant ants.

Suddenly a motorbike came roaring around the side of the building. There were two men on it, dressed in combat fatigues, one of them holding a pump-action shotgun to his chest. I stood up, ready to hand over our cash. Instead of robbing us, however, they both flashed wonderful white-toothed smiles and said '*Hola.*' These were the police.

While the driver went inside the laundromat to pick up his newly pressed uniform, Raul waited outside.

'*Buenos,*' he said in a sultry tone.

'*Buenos,*' I replied, acutely aware of the shotgun.

'I am Raul. You are?'

'I'm Angela.'

'You like dancing?'

If only he knew! 'Yes, I love dancing.'

'You like night clubs?'

'Ah yes I like them, but you know, it is difficult with a child to go out dancing,' I said as it dawned on me that he was trying to pick me up.

'You here for a short time or long time?'

'Just a short time, we are on our boat,' I smiled.

'You and your son?' he said, still in his smooth-operator tone.

'My husband and I and our son,' I said, gesticulating with my wedding-ring finger.

'You want to go dancing? You have nice eyes,' he said, looking at my legs.

Man, these magic shorts don't know when to stop! (Let me be clear, I am not blessed with a killer bod or long legs. So I can only put it down to the shorts.)

'Thank you, but I have a husband and I am happy with him.'

He raised his eyebrows and shrugged. 'OK.'

His mate came out, handed him his uniform and they sped off into the traffic.

'Very nice man, Mama,' Dash said, looking up from the ants.

'Yes, he was,' I said as I stood up a little bit straighter and thanked my lucky shorts. 'Son, this place is real, it's hot and it sure is bitchin'.'

39

Haul on the Bowline!

The dishes are done, the anchor is up and we are off! Even with all the butt-ogling glory of the last few days, a week in Las Brisas de Amador is quite enough for me.

After much gnashing of teeth and pleading before we had left Colón, Tito had finally came through with our *zarpe*.

'Don't show this to anyone in Panama, friend,' he had said. Ah, so that would be some sort of forgery then, Tito? 'Just you be careful.' I suppose getting it stamped by an 'official' who works out of a shed with thirty-four stray cats loitering around should have raised my suspicions.

A *zarpe* is like a letter of introduction. You let the custom authorities know which port you are heading to, give them your crew list, and say that you are not smuggling drugs, booze or people and they will issue you with a *zarpe*. Then when you arrive at the next port you show this to the customs officials there and so on. You are expected to arrive within the time limit at the designated port, and the only thing that can override this is force majeure. It is a good system that seems to work well.

But getting a *zarpe* for the Galapagos Islands is becoming increasingly expensive. Ecuadorian authorities demand US$800 — just to anchor! To get around this, most people get their *zarpe* to the Marquesas Islands. Tito assures us that ours has everything we need to avoid to paying the exorbitant rate.

We haul up the anchor and head out of the bay. In honour of the occasion I am sporting a new neon green and blue leopard-print bikini, purchased for maximum sun exposure, not for its supportive qualities. Ross is on the tiller and I am scrubbing nappies — just another day in paradise.

We motor past anchored boats and I notice the bikini attracting attention from the crew of the fishing boat *La Rosa Mystic*. It would be rude not to acknowledge these wolf whistles so I throw a queenly wave towards the starboard bow. A cheer goes up. Luckily they are far enough away not to see how much I am sucking in my stomach.

We head past the massive ships in the 'holding pen' for the south–north transit of the canal, past a Raratongan tanker with almost the same name as us — *Te Iku Roa* — and out towards the Las Perlas Islands.

We make good time and manage to stay on our 125 degree course. Dash has a long, three-hour sleep, allowing me to combine quality tiller time with quality tanning time. Ross sets the yankee and the mainsail and has a kip on the deck. So far so good — maybe it won't be as bad as I am expecting.

We cruise along, dreamily sailing closer to Saboga. Rickety old fishing boats chug past us, a catamaran sinks over the horizon, starboard tankers loom large and then disappear. The day has a lovely meditative quality.

I hear a little voice calling 'Dolphins!' Dash has woken up and is standing with his nose pressed up against the porthole. Twenty dolphins have surrounded the yacht and are making a spectacular display of showing off. I lift Dashkin up on deck as they leap over the bow and dive under the yacht. They're slick and agile and provide a wonderful distraction for a cranky, just-woken-up toddler. Dashkin waves and claps. I wave and clap. It is such a privilege to see them in their natural habitat, instead of gracing the ankle of some bogan as a tattoo.

Dash gets bored before they decide to leave and wanders off to draw ladybugs. Ross takes the tiller and guides us into the bay at Saboga. Day one done.

'So I am not allowed to put the camera case on the navigation table? I didn't realise it would be such a pain. I will remove it immediately, *Captain!*' I storm down below and make a big show of uplifting the camera case and putting it 10 centimetres to the right, in the galley. 'Happy?' I huff back upstairs, grab the tiller out of Ross' hand and fume.

'Ange, it needs to be clear so I can see the charts,' he explains through gritted teeth.

'You could move it yourself, you've got hands!'

Ross and I try very hard not to fight. We try to address issues immediately before they fester and turn nasty, but over the last few days I seem to be copping a *lot* of flack. Stress is mounting and Ross and I are feeling the pressure. There are so many unknowns. We have prepared as much as we can, our boat is strong and we are confident she will make it across. The engine is working well, we have lashed the broken stanchion securely . . . it is just us, getting snippy with nerves and anticipation.

Ross goes below to pour himself a rum, calm down and plot our position and I realise that I need to I come up with some strategies to ensure we don't end up as one of the 2011 divorce statistics. After some soul-searching I decide these two should cover all eventualities:

1. Attempt to be kind at all times.
2. Don the gold leotard at least once a day.

We are on course, so I tie off the tiller and pick up my book. I am reading *Moby Dick*. Yes, I am aware of the blindingly obvious perils of reading it while sailing. I'm at the part where Ishmael is

musing on the whiteness of Moby Dick — it's engrossing and I
know will provide great discussion points for Ross and I to debate
later. I am also on watch, which means I read a few sentences,
scan the horizon, check the compass rose, adjust the tiller and
then go back to my book. It is multi-tasking of the highest order
and, like all multi-tasking, it is a bit shit.

Things get mixed up. On the starboard bow I see a plume
of water. What is that? I put the book down, squint into the
sun and wait. Pfffffffff, I see it again. No, surely not? The
coincidence is too great. It's just dolphins jumping high. Then
again, pffffffffff and this time something breaks the surface. It
is a whale! It really is a whale. It is breathtaking and enormous
and dead ahead.

'Whales fine on the starboard bow!' I call. Ross races up on
deck and we watch the majestic animals swim right in front
of us. I turn the tiller to port to go behind them. Some sailors
are so afraid of running into them that they empty a diesel jug
overboard, which gets into their blowhole and chokes them.
I find this idea absolutely repulsive and the people who do
this criminals.

The whales swim near *Te Ikaroa* for half an hour. Every time
their fluted tails dive deep I get so excited I dance around the
deck. Dash thinks this is great fun and squeals and whoops with
delight. 'Kevin Costner, eat ya heart out . . . coming to a theatre
near you is *Dances with Whales* staring Mama and Dash!' This
is why we came sailing.

After an exciting, action-packed day we anchor in the bay of
Espiritu Santo. Frangipani scent is on the wind, crickets chirp
in the jungle, the ocean washes the shore, and in the distance is
the sound of German chit-chat. An older woman is jogging up
and down the beach in her bikini while her bearded husband
builds a fire out of driftwood.

As soon as we have stowed our sails, he waves, and like a
true sea bogan leaps into his dinghy, kicks the motor into life
and zooms up alongside us to say hello. His grimy top says
'Old Blue Eyes'. We chat and discover that he is Eric Bauhaus'

father. He is therefore sailing royalty, the dynastic leader of the Bauhaus clan. The man whose son charted these very shores, who sounded these very depths. We fawn all over him.

Dash screams, he shakes, he claws at my neck. 'Go away! Away! I don't like!' Our sweet-natured little boy has taken an instant dislike to Old Blue Eyes. I have never seen him react to anyone like this before.

I take him down below. 'What is wrong, darling? He is a very nice man.'

'Long beard, I don't like!' Dashkin is genuinely terrified. Mr Bauhaus gets the message and heads back to his boat, but before he leaves he spots the broken stanchion and says he will weld it for us tomorrow.

When you are about to embark on something that is so totally and utterly outside of your wildest imaginings, on something that sees you so far removed from the life you have led for thirty-six years, something that is way, way, way out of your comfort zone, you realise what is really important to you . . . I have finally lost that extra five kilos and have a golden tan.

I am aware of how intensely shallow that makes me. I would like to be a more noble, erudite person but the fact of the matter is my personal goal, for this entire journey, has been concerned with looking good in my togs.

OK, confession time: I have been tracking the thinification of Angela Meyer by obsessively taking arm's-length self-portraits. On the whole I have been pleased with the results. Granted, if I hold the camera above my head, look up and relax my jaw I do look thinner than if I snap one off directly in front of me. The bout of giardia has done wonders, seasickness keeps me in check, my tan is deepening nicely (and as everyone knows, a tan makes you look *heaps* thinner) and my spirits are high.

But after one comment by my crushingly honest husband, I am a mess. Ross told me that my bikini top and full skirt combo was making me look fat. I am all for honesty in a relationship but I do not need to hear that I am looking lardy. Believing I was losing weight was the thing that was making me feel OK about heading out for weeks into the middle of the ocean where there is *no one* else around and *hundreds* of things that could go wrong. At the risk of sounding like someone with a full-blown eating disorder, it's the one thing I can control!

I am embarrassed. It's pathetic that I care so much. I mean, we are standing on a pristine 100-metre long beach on a secluded island off the coast of Panama. Dash is playing with crabs in the rock pools, Ross is looking for fossils and me, I am wanting to end it all! All these months of mothering a small child in crazy heat, of living on a shitty old yacht are for naught. *I am fat*. I feel like Ross has deliberately decided to take side swipes at me, deliberately gone for my muffin top.

We get back to the yacht and I have it out with him. There are tears — mine, of course. I am defensive because I am embarrassed. Guys just don't get it.

It is moments like this that I wish I could click my fingers and be magically transported back to New Zealand, where I can hang out with my friends, have a laugh about how silly I am being and then catch a lift on a magic carpet back to the yacht, arriving happy and confident and ready to tackle the Pacific Ocean. That doesn't happen. Instead, Ross and I have a big heart to heart, about how challenging we are finding spending every waking and non-waking moment together, about how it is tricky to be a parent in such a small, confined space, about our expectations of each other, about our hopes and dreams. Two hours later the air is clear and we know there is nowhere else we would rather be.

We are as ready as we will ever be to take on the Pacific.

40
This Is It

—

On 4 July, at 8.45 p.m.,
we launch ourselves from
Punta Cocos in the Las
Perlas into what Mr Herman
Melville described as 'the
unshored, unharbored
immensity of the Pacific
Ocean'. We are ecstatic.

We are ready for the hard yards: we have food and water, we have playdough. Our engine has been overhauled, we are confident in it working, our boat is tight and, while no luxury cruiser, she's comfortable. Ross has spent the last two years researching weather patterns and ocean currents. He's read hundreds of blogs and most of the books ever published about sailing across the Pacific. We have talked at length with other cruisers who are making the same attempt this season. We're armed with Nigel Calder's books *Repairs at Sea* and *Fixing Your Boat's Essential Systems*. We are ready.

Our plan is to head south until we have crossed the equator, then motor through the Doldrums until we can pick up the westerly trade winds and sail on to the Galapagos Islands. All going well we hope to reach them in time for Dashkin's second birthday on 12 July.

'This is it, Angela. The Pacific Ocean. The biggest ocean on earth. Thank you for doing this with me,' Ross says as we look up at the stars. It seems fitting to offer a quick prayer to Tangaroa, god of the sea, and ask him to take care of us and send us fair winds.

All day I have had butterflies; I spent my time preparing food, knocking down seasickness pills, cleaning, stowing and transforming the stern cabin into a child's play area that at night will double as the family bed.

Dashkin is sleeping soundly as we fly south from Punta Cocos at 6.4 knots, past an obnoxious fishing cruiser with its extremely bright torch and crap music. Hanging low to starboard is an amber moon, the dark sky above full of stars, and to port the beginnings of an electrical storm illuminates the sky erratically.

It's beautiful. For the first time in five months the wind is tickling the back of my neck instead of blowing in my face. As far as omens go we are sitting pretty.

As the night deepens, the electrical storm grows closer. It's as if the heavens are short-circuiting. Then suddenly it's upon us. Massive forks of lightning explode all around us. I am terrified. The thunder is so loud it reverberates through our boat and makes my heart tremble. I have visions of us being hit and losing all our electrics.

Ross stays on deck all night; I strain my ears to hear him over the roar of the rain. Leaks start appearing in *Te Ikaroa*, one right above Dashkin's sleeping head. I drag him down the bed and try to stuff a tea towel into the drip. It sort of works.

As dawn breaks a very wet Ross sees a water spout in the distance. Despite the pills, my seasickness is in full flight and it is just a matter of time before the hallucinations kick in.

Finally the sun comes out.

'Let's hope we don't have too many nights like that,' Ross says as he comes off watch.

The wind is once again on the nose. I am feeling terrible; all I can think about is sleeping. But there is another fourteen hours to go before I can safely put my head down.

I put on Dashkin's harness and we head outside for some fresh air. I know the pattern — I know that for four or five days I will feel sick and then hopefully once I have got my sea legs an incredible transformation will take place and I will return to being my fun-loving, few-kilos-lighter self.

The winds are light and flick around the compass. It takes

me ages to master the tiller. I imagine the wind is a group of American cheerleaders with flicky ponytails and shake my fist at the sky. Dashkin has been very patient playing with his new cars in the cockpit, but now he wants a hug. His sidles his way over to the tiller, climbs up on my knee, snuggles into my neck and for the very first time ever says, 'I love you, Mama.' Unsurprisingly, I am overcome. This is big. This is a take-it-to-my-grave moment.

We get through the day and Ross comes on watch for the night shift. I give Dashkin some crackers, a sausage and a slice of cheese for tea and put him to bed, then I go and sit with Ross.

High in the sky is Scorpio. It is so dramatic and comforting to see it so clearly. I find the nights at sea with low cloud cover very claustrophobic. Strange but true.

The next day is stunning. A catamaran we have seen in the distance easily catches up to us. As it passes us we spot a man sitting on a deck chair reading a book. Ross and I both get pangs of jealousy. We will not be outdone and decide that it is family bucket-bath time. Kit off, buckets out!

Dashkin jumps in and out of the buckets, fills cups with water, pours them over our heads, giggles and hugs. Ross and I take turns sunbathing until a little body leaps on our backs and demands a horsie ride. We have managed to get *Te Ikaroa* to sail herself. We launch into a rousing chorus of Dashkin's favorite bedtime song, a variation of a song my sister Emily made up when we used to go on long car journeys.

Oh Dashkin, you're so beautiful
Oh Dashkin, the trade wind in your hair
You'll always know, how much we love you so
You'll always hear the words we long to sing
Oh Dashkin . . .

Despite having the occasional spit over the side, this afternoon is one of the best of my life.

For the next two days we battle to windward, cranking the motor to make any kind of headway. A mushroom-coloured booby (a type of gannet) with a lavender beak and pink feet hitches a lift. Dash and I go out and watch it as it clings to the bowsprit, and it shits all over the deck. Luckily we are plunging so much that sea water sluices it away.

I think to myself how fetching the booby's colour combination is, and that when we are back on dry land I will create an outfit in his honour. I grow incredibly fond of this bird. He keeps me company on the long watches. When he flies off to fish I get anxious that he won't come back.

My seasickness is not getting better; in fact it is getting worse. I spend the afternoon holed up in the stern cabin tripping out of my mind. We try to make some pasta but it is too dangerous to boil water in such heavy seas. Ross and I both have splitting headaches from exhaustion but we are feeling positive. We are still heading south!

Then Dash wees in the toy box. Ross explodes. I send him to bed and take Dash up on deck to stand watch with me. It is a disaster. Dashkin falls asleep on my knee, we are slap-bang in the middle of the shipping lane and my hallucinations are going crazy. We are heeled to port and as we crash and bash into the wind I keep whacking my back on a piece of metal. It is tricky to move with a sleeping child, I can't let go of the tiller in the shipping lane and Ross desperately needs to sleep. We inevitably go off course. On the plus side I spot a lone turtle, two sharks and a leaping dolphin in the distance.

'We are doing it, baby,' Ross says every time he plots our position. 'We are getting south, we are crossing the fourth parallel. Ten yachts have turned back this season because the weather has been so bad, but we're making our way south. *We are doing it!*'

41

Shattered Dreams

For the last seven hundred and sixty days, I have thought about sailing across the Pacific Ocean. In all these imaginings I never, ever thought we wouldn't make it. Not once.

Six days into our crossing from Punta Cocos, Panama, to the Galapagos Islands we have to turn back. We are at two and a half degrees north and have only 160 miles to go to the equator when things start to go wrong, very wrong.

On the evening of the fifth day we sat down for the first time together in the saloon. The boat was sailing herself and Dash was asleep.

'Five days at sea, darling. I think we are doing pretty good — not weather-wise, it's not as if we haven't had enough of beating to windward in metre and a half seas! But this is nice, darling. We are doing it!'

Two minutes later, everything changed. We opened the bilge and there was water — lots and lots of water.

'Oh shit, Ange, this is bad. Really bad.'

'Where is it coming from? Taste it. Is it salty?'

Ross dipped his finger into the greasy water. 'Yep, it is definitely salt.'

At this point the adrenaline kicked in. Somehow we had broken one of the cardinal rules: 'Keep the water out of the boat'. This was not good. We checked all our through-hulls, our sea cocks, our prop shaft and they all looked good.

In desperation we consulted Nigel Calder's *Repairs at Sea*. There was a possibility the water may be coming in through the exhaust pipe. We tacked and heeled her over to the other side, but still the water continued to come in. Our bilge pump blew a fuse so Ross was busy hand-pumping the water out. He was keeping on top of it . . . just . . .

I went on deck to check for ships and noticed that the engine was stinking. This was not just the usual diesel fumes but the kind that choke in your throat and cover everything in a dark, sooty film. The oil-pressure gauge, which had never moved before, suddenly started fluctuating. Ross immediately turned off the engine and we hove to. We sat there looking at each other with that wide-eyed look you get when you are in the middle of the ocean and your boat is leaking and your engine is a bit farked. We spent the rest of the night being bashed around, slowly drifting towards the South American coast which was 150 miles away. Things were not looking good.

But they got worse. Our headsail blew out. We hauled it down and looked at the ragged edge. It was repairable, but in heavy seas that was not going to happen.

I tried to get some sleep knowing that an almost-two-year-old would be awake in about four hours and would want to be entertained. I crashed, but soon Ross came in and lay down next to Dash and me in our stinky cabin.

'I am going to turn her around. There is no way we will clear the South American coast in these winds and current — or even make a landfall. We don't have any charts of this coast, and, because we had to motor so much, we won't have enough fuel. We are leaking and I have no idea where it is coming from.'

I breathed in a huge gulp of the diesel-reeking air.

'Are you sure? This means giving up on our dream. Are you sure we can't make it into Ecuador?' I whispered.

'It is not safe, Ange — we could start taking on more water at any time. We will turn back and when we get into the shipping lanes we will call for help.'

'This means giving up on everything you have planned for. We won't be able to make another attempt this season. Are you really sure?' I asked.

'Yes.'

'OK,' I said, stifling a sob. Ross went back on deck and I lay there, desperately sad that my husband had been forced to make this decision, as Dash snuggled into me and mumbled something about a tractor.

The next morning at dawn we started sailing back. We were going to try to make it to the Las Perlas Islands, regroup and come up with another plan. The weather was terrible, with howling rain, and the tiller was hard work. We did four-hour watches and kept trying our radio.

'All ships, all ships, this is the sailing vessel *Te Ikaroa*. We are taking on water and have limited power. We are a danger to shipping . . . copy.'

We had seen lots of ships in the previous days but now, when we desperately wanted to make contact with someone, there were none to be seen. We were all alone.

When we left New Zealand, my dear friend Rebekah (aka Pearl Lusta) had given us a card which read 'Keep Calm and Carry On'. More than once I have squared my shoulders, taken yet another deep breath and repeated this mantra to myself.

We were getting tired. The thing with sailing with a child is that you can't come off watch and go to sleep or chill out. You come off watch and you are right into parenting. If you are the mama, often you are on the tiller with a small child sitting on your knee. It is hard work. Really hard work.

Despite this, Dash is a darling. He keeps busy drawing ladybugs and singing 'Old MacDonald Had a Farm'. Sometimes he picks up the egg timer. '*Te Ikaroa, Te Ikaroa*, Galapagos Island,' he says, imitating us on the radio.

Soon we cut down to two-hour watches. I struggled to keep all 16 tons of yacht on course. The seas were erratic and the winds strong. The irony was that this was the best sailing we had had in the whole time we had been afloat. It would have been exhilarating if we hadn't been so stressed out — and if we had been going in the right direction.

On 12 July, Dashkin turned two and he got a tractor. We had hoped to be in the Galapagos Islands looking at giant turtles.

During my night watch I thought about where I had been two years earlier: in Wellington Hospital, becoming a mother. I thought about how scared and worried I had been then, but how wonderfully it had all turned out. It was strange to have such similar feelings again now, and I prayed that things would turn out OK this time too . . .

We tried the engine again, but nothing. Again Ross went through all the things that could have gone wrong, and again everything appeared to be OK. We tried a few more times but as one of our wind turbines had broken and the days had been too full of rain to charge the solar panel, we needed to keep the power for our GPS and radio.

Day after day we drifted. First we were becalmed, then the wind blew up. Gone were all the birds and whales and dolphins. We kept trying our radio, but nothing. We were so tired we were starting to make silly mistakes. Our dream was shattered, and we started talking about setting off our EPIRB (Emergency Positioning Indicating Radio Beacons).

We are Kiwis — we don't give up, we don't ask for help, there are always people far worse off than us. But we are in the middle of nowhere, with no power, no engine, no headsail, and we are taking on water. We can't make a landfall . . . We have a two-year-old son . . . Around and around these thoughts went in my head. Finally, after five days we pushed the button marked 'only in emergency'.

For some reason I expected help to magically appear over the horizon in two hours. I ran around getting our grab bag together.

Then, I just lost it. I was looking around our boat, looking at what I would leave and what I would take, and I just freaked out. I braced myself against the bench in the tiny galley and cried.

How had it come to this? What were we thinking? What kind of mother was I? I was so tired. I just wanted this whole ordeal to be over and for us to be safe.

Ross held me and we both had a bit of moment until Dash asked for a family hug. I wiped my snotty nose and we all had a salty, tear-stained hug. 'Draw tractor, Mama?' he asked, so once again I kept calm and drew a tractor.

I must have still had my wits about me as one of the first things I put into the grab bag was the bottle of Moët. This boat might be sinking but I was going to drink the champagne, come hell or high water.

We waited and waited and nothing happened. This was the worst day of my life. I was humiliated and really defeated.

42

Rescued by Hotties

— ◆ —

**Twenty-four hours later
we realised that we were
going to have to get
ourselves out of this.**

'OK, there is no one coming. We have to try to sail somewhere,' said Ross. It was back to attempting to get to the Las Perlas.

'I totally agree,' I said.

We planned to just try to get closer to Panama. The winds were kind of in our favour so we kept sailing north.

I had just come down below and was about to put Dash down for his nap when suddenly, 'Ange — oh my God, it's an aeroplane!' Our VHF crackled into life.

'Are you the vessel experiencing difficulties?' an American voice asked.

I lunged at the handset.

'Yes, yes we are.'

'OK, ma'am, what is your situation?'

I relayed all of our problems.

'Copy that, ma'am. A chopper will be overhead in zero five minutes.'

Then he went on to relay everything to the US Coast Guard.

We had thought maybe that the Ecuadorian or Colombian Coast Guard might respond; we certainly didn't expect the American Coast Guard.

'Oh my God, Ross, they are on their way . . . Oh my God, we are going to be OK!' I yelled.

Ross came downstairs and continued speaking with the aeroplane while I got Dash into his harness and life jacket.

As promised, a red helicopter was overhead and on the VHF within zero five minutes. I was sitting on deck with Dash, who was beside himself with joy at seeing a helicopter hovering so low overhead.

'Helicopter, Mama, waving at nice man,' Dash said. In Dashkin's world, there are two types of men: nice men and not-nice men.

'*Te Ikaroa*, the coast guard *Active 3* will be with you in three zero minutes. Copy? We will continue to be overhead until they arrive.'

'Copy that, thank you so much,' I almost cried down the handset.

Now we had one Andover and one helicopter circling our boat. The Kiwi in me was deeply embarrassed.

By this stage Dash had fallen asleep in my arms. I daren't move as he was exhausted and I couldn't bear to wake him.

I looked behind me and there, bouncing across the waves at 40 knots, was the *Active 3*. The closer it came, the more I felt sick. 'Oh God, Ross, what if they think we are dicks, what if they think we are being drama queens? Everything is going to change. Oh God, what if they charge us for the plane and the helicopter?'

'I know, darling, but as soon as we turned that EPIRB on we had to give ourselves up to whatever is in store.'

Active 3 drew closer and suddenly there was a boat full of movie stars pulled up on the port side. I couldn't believe my eyes. Rescued by hotties!

'Ma'am, I am going to need for you to put on this life jacket,' one called Ryan said, not realising I was wearing a jazzy neon orange one. (Dash was covering most of it). 'I have engineers on board and a bilge pump, may we board your vessel?'

'Yes, yes, please do,' Ross and I chorused.

Then, from it just being us, there were now four huge men

in blue uniforms on our boat. They were so competent and in control and so kind.

'Ma'am, I am going to need for you to write down the name of your vessel, your name, your dates of birth and your home address,' said another Mr Handsome.

'Sure, of course. Can I pass you Dashkin while I go below and get a pen?'

Now one of the men in blue was sitting on the pile of shredded headsail cradling a sleeping two-year-old. I squeezed past the other men to get a pen and paper.

Soon they were pumping the bilge and had the engine open and were trying to find the source of the problem. Radios were whirring as information was being passed overhead and back to the 'big boat' as they called it.

It was decided that the engine was really broken. It was the injector pump, which is something that cannot be repaired at sea. The leak was searched for but not found but the bilge was sort of dry.

'Ma'am, I sailed around the world with my parents as a kid. Looking at your little boy is like looking at myself,' Ryan said.

All I could manage was, 'Oh really, that's great.'

They worked on the engine for a couple of hours. By this time one guard had started getting seasick and had to come up for air, and another was ready to leave.

'Ma'am, these are really hard conditions.'

I don't know why, but having these grown men say that made it OK. It made all of the anxiety and fear I had been feeling seem legitimate.

'We are going back to the big boat to get another mechanic and we will be back in thirty minutes. If you need anything, wave your arms. An officer will be trained on your boat at all times.'

'Thank you, thank you, OK, thank you.' And then they were gone.

It had been decided that we would try to sail her as far as we could. The coast guards were going to be right behind us and if we needed anything they would be with us in ten minutes. We both felt so much better.

Ten minutes later we heard, '*Te Ikaroa,* this is the captain of the coast guard cutter *Active 3*, we are going to put four men on your boat and take your wife and child off so that you can get some sleep, is that OK with you? We will be back at five p.m.'

By this stage I was a wreck. Tears started welling in my eyes. I desperately wanted to get off the boat but was so shattered I couldn't imagine being with lots of people I didn't know.

'Yes, that is great,' Ross replied.

At 5 p.m. Dash and I were sitting on huge shock-absorbing seats making our way to the big ship. Four young, non-sleep-deprived sailors (including the handsome Ryan) were on board *Te Ikaroa*. I expected Dash to be totally overwhelmed by so many new faces but he loved it.

I got off onto the larger coast guard boat and looked up. There were lots and lots of young men with huge biceps and tattoos all looking at me. I hugged Dash tightly and as I walked towards the flight deck, around the corner came a female officer.

'Hello, I am Jane. Welcome aboard.'

As we went into the officers' mess, I was acutely aware of how much I smelt, how shabby I looked and how incredibly strung out I was. The captain's first words were, weirdly, 'Hello, does your son have any allergies?'

'No, he eats everything,' I replied.

'Have a seat, ma'am,' he said.

As we sat down in cool black leather seats, the door opened behind us and in walked a man with a huge cake in honour of Dashkin's second birthday. 'Happy Birthday' was being sung — quietly, so as not to scare Dash. As the cake was deposited in front of us, Dash clapped his hands and said, to my utter pride,

'*Muchas gracias.*' I started to thank everyone but again the old Meyer genes got the better of me and I stuttered a 'Thank you so much' through a flood of tears.

'Let's go down to your cabin,' said Jane.

We went down four flights of very steep stairs until we came to the student engineer's cabin. Jane turned the handle and there in front of us was a bunk. Grey blankets that didn't smell like sour milk or wee, a bathroom with a flushing toilet and, wait for it, a *hot shower*. Jane had put a computer loaded with kids' movies in the room and had arranged for me to send a message to Mum and Dad letting them know we were OK.

Dash and I hugged until he fell asleep and then I washed. I was filthy and not in a bitchin' way. This was my first hot shower in five months. Sixteen days of no showers at all meant my hair was a matted mess, I reeked and my armpits were becoming forests.

I looked at myself in the mirror, and a frazzled old lady with hollow eyes looked back. I turned off the lights, plunging us into pitch blackness, climbed into the top bunk and, shaking with fatigue, shut my eyes and tried to sleep.

It didn't come. I lay there freezing as the air conditioning was so cold. The strangeness of being on board a US Coast Guard vessel and away from Ross, the unfamiliar sounds and the craziness of the last sixteen days were too much. I remembered my mother saying, 'Just rest your eyes.' Eventually I went to sleep.

Breakfast was between 7 and 8 a.m. Dash and I found our way to the mess hall and stood in line. It was like being in a movie: the accent, the clothes, the bodies . . .

I held out our plate and scrambled eggs, hash browns and bacon were heaped on. I have been a committed vegetarian for twenty-five years but on this morning I found myself gobbling up bacon. (I have often been asked what would it take for me to eat meat again; well people, this is it . . .)

We were invited on to the flight deck, where Dash was able to sit in the helicopter. Two young officers arrived and gave him a necklace they had made out of a medal, another man pinned a petty officer third class brooch on him (later in the day he was promoted to second class), lollypops were offered, hugs given, photos taken. We went into the officers' mess again and Dashkin was the guest of honour, *Shrek* was put on a massive widescreen TV for his viewing pleasure. Dash had never watched TV and was mesmerised.

I spent my time finding out about the high divorce rate in the coast guard, how the boat is dry (not a drop of booze at all), the intricacies of the narcotics trade in the Central American region, and how many children all the men had.

'It is great to have a child on board,' I overheard one man saying.

One of the young sailors had requested to come back from *Te Ikaroa* to the big ship. I met him as he came off the dinghy.

'Ma'am, that is hard work. I have no idea how you have coped, and with a young son. I have total respect for you.'

Again, it was very nice to hear.

At 5 p.m. it was time for Dash and I to go back to *Te Ikaroa*. We waved goodbye and Dash, now sitting on the knee of the driver, steered us back. In the distance I saw a whale spout and its beautiful fluted tail as it dove deep.

We had only just got on board when the Panamanian Coast Guard came roaring around the headland of Isla San Jose, belching huge black clouds of smoke. It pulled up alongside us and, with no communication, started to try to get close enough to raft up.

A far cry from the Americans, these guys bashed into our boat and only after Ross and I screamed at them not to come alongside did they relent as they realised that we were inches away from smashing into their radar and comms gear with our mast. Finally a rope as thick as my arm was thrown over and we were towed in, all the way to Panama. It was 65 miles away.

They towed us slowly at 7 knots so that we wouldn't fishtail. We arrived back at Las Brisas de Amador at 3.30 a.m. I can honestly say I have never been so thankful and so tired. However, instead of the quiet anchorage we had left three weeks earlier, a massive techno rave was in full swing.

As we were anchoring, four smaller boats started zooming around us, clicking off pictures. A video camera was produced and the next thing we knew we were being interviewed in Spanish about our ordeal.

I was aghast, thinking this was for the newspapers, imagining my frizzy hair and haggard face splashed across the Panamanian dailies, but it turned out it was for the coast guard records.

Ross and I shared a cup of tea and collapsed into the stern cabin where Dash was sprawled. The terrible beat of shit '90s dance music blared in our ears and we finally drifted off to sleep for two hours before Dashkin woke ready for 'Playtime, Mama and Papa?'

43

Bad Luck, Good Luck

Our dream of sailing across the Pacific is dead, and we are in a bad way. We don't have enough cash to mount a new attempt at the start of the next season in March 2012. There are no sailmakers in Panama City so we can't fix our headsail.

We are having trouble finding a mechanic to come on board and look at our engine; the anchorage has no power, no shower and no water — apparently the guy who owns it hasn't paid his taxes so everything has been cut off. There are daily squalls which have boats dragging their anchors all over the place. They can come from any direction and usually blow 40 knots for about twenty minutes — not long, admittedly, but like all the other sailors we are out on deck watching carefully for any sign of trouble. Raw sewage floats past us most mornings, and a couple of days ago we watched in horror as a three-storey ferry dragged its anchor and came very, very close to us. We have no engine so there was no way we could get out of the way.

To be honest, we've had a gut's full.

We stumble through our first day back in Panama, our eyes watering with tiredness. Immigration and customs need to be sorted and with adrenaline still giving us that horrible shaky feeling, we walk along the causeway to Flamenco Marina.

Out the back, past the duty-free shops emblazoned with advertisements showing white horses galloping along a beach, are three little rooms. In the middle one are five government agencies jostling for space and, wait for it, a TV playing '80s music videos! To the soundtrack of 'That's What Friends Are

For' we handed over our passports.

It seems everything 'costs' twenty bucks here. Immigration stamp, twenty bucks, customs clearance, twenty bucks and a new one, 'Agricultural Tax' — you guessed it, twenty bucks. While Ross pays the backhanders Dash decides he has had enough and lets out the most ear-piercing scream known to humankind. Embarrassed, we slip into the nearest café and attempt to order coffee. After days at sea the air conditioning is chilly and despite having put on my 'good' golden jandals and a sun-bleached frock we looked like beggars.

'*Dos espressos, per favor,*' I ask the lady behind the counter.

'Uh?' She stares at me blankly.

'*Dos espressos, per favor,*' I repeat as I point to the coffee machine. Still a blank stare. At this point my eyes are rimmed with red. Again I ask and point and, in desperation, mime drinking a cup of coffee. Surely she just has to look at me to see how desperate I am for a coffee!

'Oh, *dos espressos,*' she finally says and turns to make them.

'That is what I said,' I mutter to myself.

In less shattered circumstances I enjoy chatting and practise my Spanish. Not today.

Ross and I sit looking at each other.

'It's OK darling, we will sort something out. Let's just get through today,' I say. He nods and slugs down the coffee. Dashkin sits licking his ice-cream; despite the air-conditioned loveliness it is melting faster than he can eat it. Soon he is covered in chocolate. The rust on the pushchair, a victim of many days and nights in the salt air and torrential rain, gives us an air of poverty that is not entirely without basis.

'Come on, let's go and look at some tractors,' Ross says, and we slowly haul ourselves out of the chairs and into the ever present, energy-sapping, blowtorch-like heat. Even Dashkin, who is a tractor/grader/bulldozer aficionado, is subdued.

The next day we brave the mall. And there, in the Cyber Space café, our luck changes.

'OK, I'll see you in twenty minutes,' I say to Ross.

'Yeah, OK,' he replies.

'Australian or New Zealander?' a grey-haired women asks me as she looks up from her computer.

'New Zealander.'

'Same — which part are you from?'

'Oh, the thriving metropolis of Palmerston North — but I lived in Wellington,' I quickly add, trying to make myself seem cooler.

'I'm originally from Timaru, so I can't talk, but I lived all over.'

'Are you on holiday here?' I ask.

'We retired here ten years ago.'

She sounds so worldly; I knew Americans retired in Panama, but a Kiwi? Never!

'And you? Are you living here?' she asks.

I have been setting up my ancient computer and talking to her at the same time. Now I sit myself down on an annoyingly high barstool-style chair and look at her.

'No no, we don't live here, we are on a boat.' And once I start I can't stop. I blurt out our whole sorry tale to this poor unsuspecting stranger. I don't know what I am expecting her to do; I just desperately need to talk to someone about it.

'Thank God you are alive. I will let you get on and email your mum,' she says quietly.

I look down at the keypad. Oh my God, Ange, what were you thinking? This poor woman thinks you are nuts. Why didn't you just shut up and let her do her internetting? Now you look like a total loser and have absolutely no dignity left, I chastise myself as I try to get the bloody computer to connect.

At this point Ross and Dash come back from walking around the mall. We tag-team taking Dashkin for 'walks' while the other one checks their emails. With me, Dash ends up in the Zara changing room while I try on fabulous outfits and he says things like, 'Nice undies, Mama' in a loud voice. With Ross, it's throwing a ball around in a long-forgotten corner of the megamall.

Anyway, Dash and I head off while Ross has his turn online.

'See ya,' I call to the woman.

'Good luck, love,' she calls back.

I do what anyone with a heavy heart and a restless toddler does: I buy more ice-cream. We sit in a huge neon-lit food hall looking at happy shoppers as they stuff their faces with chicken and rice. Central America rivals South America for chook consumption and I dread to think how many of my feathered friends are slaughtered each day.

After about forty minutes, we slowly make our way back to the internet café, and there is the same woman talking earnestly to Ross.

'Hi again,' I smile, hoping she doesn't think I am a nut job.

'Hi. I have just been talking with your husband and I want you to know that if you want to come and stay for a few days while you get yourselves sorted, we would love to have you. I mean it. Truly,' she says.

I look at Ross, whose eyes are filling with tears. I look at Dash, who has spied the jellybean machine and is about to start demanding them. Then I look at the extraordinarily kind woman.

This is no time for false modesty.

'We would love to. Thank you. How do we get there?' I ask.

'How about we meet you here tomorrow at three and we can take you home. We live a little way out of town, but we have lots of room and after all, you are Kiwis,' she laughs.

'OK!' I beam. 'We'll bring the Moët — we had hoped to drink it when we crossed the line but this seems like a great time.'

'Great.' She hands over her card, which says 'Jan (retired)'. 'Give me a call if anything changes.'

And then she is gone.

'What just happened, Ange?' Ross asks.

'This is amazing. I am pretty sure a woman just asked us to stay with her for a few days. She doesn't look like a serial killer or a recruiter for a weird religious cult, and I think she is actually going to show up tomorrow and we are going to have a few days away from our boat!' I say, my voice getting more excited with every word.

'Oh my God — the kindness of strangers, the universe provides, good things happen to good people, ask and you shall receive, trust that you are right where you should be, *destiny* . . . I will never mock these things again. Ever since we turned the beacon on we have been helped by amazing, kind, generous people,' I gabble.

At 3.05 p.m. the next day Jan and her husband David turn up. We have been waiting since 2.30 p.m., obsessively checking the clock.

'We came! I bet you thought we wouldn't!' Jan is obviously also a mind reader. 'Right you lot, let's go.'

David takes our bag and Jan pushes Dash as Ross and I lug some shopping and toys.

'Car, car. Dash go ride car!' our delighted son squeals as we come closer to their four-wheel-drive.

'Yes, darling, we are going for a ride in the car. We are going to Jan and David's house,' I explain.

'Very exciting!' Dash pipes up.

'Let's stop at El Rey for a few supplies,' Jan says as we swing into the car park of Panama's snazziest supermarket. 'You can get some things for Dash and I have a few things to pick up.'

'Great, we will get the beers,' Ross says.

Once back in the car we crack open a cold beer and start to get to know these amazing people. Twenty minutes later we arrive at their home. It is like something out of a *House & Garden* magazine.

Wide, polished wooden steps lead into a tiled entrance hall. To the left are bedrooms, to the right a kitchen, lounge and TV room. Downstairs is a big covered patio, a 25-metre swimming pool and a self-contained flat! It is all beautifully decorated with a mix of South American and Maori artwork. It feels warm and inviting.

Over the course of a fair few more beers, a swim in their beautiful pool, a delicious three-course meal and wonderful conversations, a new plan is formed. Jan and David are heading to the United States for six weeks and we are going to house-sit their amazing home in Majagual for two months.

'Very good luck indeed,' I whisper to Ross as we fall asleep on dry land for the first time in six months.

44

Huffer

We stay for four days with these huge-hearted, generous people. I have never felt so grateful for anyone's kindness. We spend our time in the pool, watching hummingbirds feed on the nectar of the tropical blooms. Brilliant blue morpho butterflies flutter across the garden, and someone tells me how they live for only one day. I get completely lost in the melancholic tragedy of this.

I later find out it's not true — they live about the same amount of time as any other butterfly.

Frogs croak all night long, bats whip up the night air, moths the size of my palm wake us as they bat against the windows. Dash spends his day pushing around his pushchair and chasing the dogs (three-legged Midgkin and Lucy the Doberman). Ross and I remark on how there is a three-legged-dog theme running through our lives: Reinhardt had a three-legged dog, the man from whom Ross bought *Astra* had a three-legged dog and now Jan and David have a three-legged dog. Spooky. Ratbag, the cat, stays well away. We eat and drink and swap stories about our lives. We are all pleased to have other people to talk to. But then we go back to our boat.

It feels like a prison cell. I feel claustrophobic and nervous about dragging our anchors. It smells of hard work and defeat and humiliation. The pains in my stomach have returned. I am trying to stay positive and strong but getting back makes me feel as if I am trapped in an airless hell hole.

Dashkin immediately starts playing up — he wants to be on dry land and running around. Ross hits the rum bottle and I just feel stink. Really stink. I feel like a total loser, a failure, a dickhead. We didn't make it. We had to get help. What kind of people are we? Losers is what. We have twenty-three days on board this boat of doom before we can go back to Jan and David's palace of tranquillity.

I decide to jog. It is either that or get divorced, abandon my son or leap overboard. I am desperate. I need endorphins like I have never needed them before. I need that heady, out-of-body feeling that you get after a run.

I put my gears on, jump in the dinghy, scramble up some rocks and hit the Amador causeway. Five kilometres of straight road. It looks like a lifeline. I stare down to where a new Frank Gehry-designed Museum of Biodiversity is being erected. It doesn't look that far away.

Dashkin and Ross will walk the causeway, checking out bugs and neon caterpillars and trying to spy sloths. I am going to run. I am not going to walk. To walk would reinforce my loserdom and the whole point of this run is to make me feel better.

I trot off optimistically. I can feel my hips creaking, my ankles realigning themselves. 'Shoulders over hips, stomach in, breathing, easy and relaxed,' I chant to myself as the sweat starts to pour off me. It is 32 degrees and it's only 8 a.m. The cap the US Coast Guard gave Dashkin feels like a roasting oven on my head. I had put it on to ensure anonymity. I am clearly going nuts. We don't know anyone in Panama. There is no one who can recognise me, no one who will judge me, because no one I am going to meet while jogging along the frickin Amador causeway has a clue who I am and that I had to get rescued by the US Coast Guard!

It may be delusional but it is certainly motivational. I am at the museum in fifteen minutes. My breathing has settled down and I am displaying a relaxed gait. I decide to continue on to the Balboa Yacht Club. It is actually quite nice along this stretch: there are no cars, parkland to my right, the ocean to my left. Other people are out recreating, families trundle past on crocodile bikes, nannies push fat babies in prams. I huff out the occasional '*Buenos*' to be friendly.

The yacht club is a bit further away than I thought. But I *cannot* give up. I *must* continue.

The sweat is trickling into my eyes. I wish I had one of my 1980s comedy headbands.

An insanely gorgeous woman with a perfect hourglass figure rollerblades past me. She looks like she has liposuctioned her way to that figure; no amount of rollerblading would produce those results.

Ten more metres to the yacht club, where I can stop. I sprint towards it then flop forwards, hands on knees, and suck in great lungfuls of steamy air. I check the watch: forty minutes. Great. That's good. I am light-headed. That's good too.

Now I have to get back. That is not so good. I am shattered. I think of Dashkin in his pushchair and wish I was 92 centimetres tall and weighed 12 kilograms.

A loser would give up and walk back but I refuse to be a loser so I shuffle off. My legs hurt. I am suffering in my jocks, literally. I wore the wrong undies and over the course of the jog they have got lost in my butt cheeks. My speed has dropped right back so I am barely moving faster than a quick walk. But I am still jogging.

I have a long way to go. I start making deals with myself. If I jog quickly to the next palm tree I can go slow to the one after that. This seems to work. In the distance Ross and Dash are walking towards me. Seven minutes, six minutes, five minutes . . . I am almost there. Dash is calling out to me. I must keep going; I can't let him see his mother give up.

Everything is screaming *stop!* — my legs, my lungs, my so-hot-it-is-about-to-explode head. One minute. *Finally* I pull up.

'Good run?' Ross asks. I can't speak. I collapse on the ground and fumble in the back of the pushchair for some water. My hands are shaking as I try to undo the lid. I don't care who sees me. I did it. I jogged the causeway — and then some.

I am flooded with endorphins. The world is a better place. I am a winner. Dash and I fist-punch the air. 'Good job, Mama!'

I am also covered in sweat. The sea around these parts is full of used condoms and other detritus of modern living — I don't fancy a dip in that. At the flash marina, I ask if I can use the showers. I even offer to pay five bucks but the sour-faced man looks me up and down, sniffs the air and tells me politely to bugger off. I end up having a bucket bath on deck, then passing out with heat exhaustion on the sofa.

The next day I feel better. We have twenty-three days to try to get the boat fixed. Hernan, a twenty-eight-year-old Argentinean sailor, has also had to turn back, after his boat was pounded by the unseasonable weather. He comes over for a commisoratory drink. Eric and Simone, a couple with twelve years' experience of living at sea, are about to make their passage. Eric has bought another engine and taken it apart to use as spares. Ross and I nod. Why didn't we think of that? Oh that's right . . . we have bugger-all cash!

Our plan now is to try to get the engine and the headsail fixed and sell *Te Ikaroa*. It seems drastic because it is. We just don't have the cash to spend six months in Panama waiting for the next season. We are living on about US$5 a day, and we have budgeted $2000 to fix the engine. We will try to sell *Te Ikaroa* for $20,000 and from that we can buy our tickets home.

We list her with the broker we bought her off and hope for the best. Finding a diesel mechanic in Panama City is much, much more difficult. Despite being adjacent to one of the busiest waterways in the world and the launching point for sailing across the Pacific, getting any repairs done here is nigh on impossible. There are no sailmakers; one guy we meet on the wharf is on his way to Miami to get his mainsail fixed.

After much ringing around and with the promise of beers we finally manage to entice Dave out to the yacht. He has a deep tan, deep voice and it turns out he is from the deep south of the United States. He is proud of the fact that at fifty-five he looks forty, he skites about marrying a woman half his age, and he tells us in great detail about the trouble they are having conceiving children. I nod and um and ah but all I want him to do is go into the engine room and tell us what is wrong, how we can fix it, how much it will cost and how long it will take.

'I cost a lot, but you guys seem nice so I will do you a deal. If you get the parts and install the electric lift pump, I'll come back and have a look — but to be honest, an old Peugeot motor and dirty fuel doesn't bode well.'

I am failing to see how this is a deal, but given that we are desperate we take it. I can see Ross is less than enthusiastic about spending more time in the engine room.

We dutifully get the parts and attempt to install them but it turns out Dave has given us the wrong measurements and it's all a bit of a disaster. We never see him again.

The only other mechanic who works on yachts in the whole of Panama is named Kenny. He is also American and knows Jan and David, and as a favour he takes off the fuel injection pump. Ross takes it to a specialist workshop and they tell us it is not worth repairing, and that to source another one would cost $4000 and take months.

Right now there is nothing very positive about our poverty. Thank God we can go and housesit.

45

Casa
Pacifica

—

We are two and a half
weeks into house-sitting
Casa Pacifica.

I t is glorious — a total change of pace from the last three years. Instead of planning, painting, sailing, scrubbing and squinting into the vast blue ocean we languidly sit on the balcony and gaze out on to a sea of tropical green vegetation.

We examine bugs that look like they could be extras in a sci-fi film, collect rotting tarantulas for Dash to inspect, float on our backs in the pool and observe the kettle of vultures circling high above us. At night, fireflies zoom around the huge mango tree in the middle of the garden. Our mammalian charges require petting and medicating and Guacamole the parrot likes fresh nuts each day.

And the whole family runs. 'Exercise hour' we call it. Ross and I take turns on the treadmill, while Dashkin does circuits around the property. Unlike the stifling air of my jaunt along the causeway we have set up a fan next to the treadmill so every time I get on I feel like I am in an '80s music video. This hour is keeping us together.

Ross is also busying himself learning Spanish. While we were sailing and repairing the yacht we used *Spanish for Cruisers* to make ourselves understood, but as we have found ourselves on extended leave in Panama it seems churlish not to try to brush up the Español.

The first thing he translated from the newspaper was an

article about the discovery of a cadaver under a stone altar dedicated to the Devil in La Paz — it turns out Satanic worship is big in Bolivia. My inner Catholic sees me poring over the article in a ghoulish fashion. I am tempted to suggest an overland adventure to check it out.

But it is not all papaya and rum in paradise. Every night the neighbourhood dogs howl and howl and fucken *howl*! The mangy golden Labrador next door makes a sound like it is being slowly tortured to death — which is exactly what I would do to it if I could get my hands around its neck. There is no way you can sleep through it. I've tried. We have less sleep now than when Dashkin was a tiny baby.

We are both coming to terms with the fact that we are not sailing across the Pacific; that our boat doesn't have a working engine; that we are, in lots of ways, stuck in Panama. Ross and I snip and snipe at each other. I find myself thinking that when we get home we can get divorced and pretend this never happened.

One night I finally say this out loud. Ross looks at me. He has more faith than I do in our ability to get through this.

'Darling, it will get better, we can do this.' I go to bed and think about it.

We seem to take turns feeling positive. The next day I wake up and feel much more enthusiastic about our marriage, but today it is Ross' turn to have doubts. For the next few weeks we have a rough time. I try to remember to be kind. That's all — just be kind.

We get a nibble. A guy from Maine is interested in *Te Ikaroa*. He knows she is a bargain — a once-in-a-lifetime bargain — and as a mechanic he can do the repairs himself. For three weeks emails fly back and forward. We research places that he could haul her out; he researches moorings. And then, when we have lowered the price to US$12,000, he agrees to buy her.

He has secured a mooring in Taboga, the island we gaze at in the distance from Jan and David's balcony, and arranged for the people who own the moorings to come over to Las Brisas and tow us back. We polish *Te Ikaroa*'s wooden interior one last time, sweep out her cabins, and scrub the deck. I, of course, start to cry. It feels so sad, despite the love-hate relationship I have with life on the ocean. She is still the first home I have ever owned and we had some great times in her.

Ross is just relieved: pleased that we have sold her, that we don't have a liability in Panama, that she is now someone else's problem. We board the ferry back to the mainland and stand in the doorway, waving goodbye to *Te Ikaroa*. It starts to rain and my tears mix with big fat tropical drops of water.

Three days later we leave. Jan takes us to the airport. I honestly can't think of the right words to thank her, so I just hug her. 'Bye-bye Jan-Jan, thank you,' Dash says as he waves goodbye.

We fly to LA via Atlanta, then on to Fiji. As Ross and Dash sleep curled up under the cheap blankets of Air Pacific, I sit awake. Breathing in the stale air I think about all the things that have happened this year. I think about whether it was foolish and naive to expect that we would make it to Brisbane. Maybe in retrospect it was.

Different people chuck in their day jobs for different reasons — I did it for love. I did it because ever since that day my grandfather showed me the photos in the tin I have wanted to live a life that I can look back on and say 'Yep, I gave it a go.' If I had a dollar for all the times people had said 'You are such a dick — that will never work', I would have a mountain of money up to my chin and I'd still be living in Palmerston North.

I wouldn't have run a dating agency, attempted to break a world record, blushed like crazy when Ryan from the US Coast Guard cutter asked me to put on a life jacket, been in the middle of a spectacular electrical storm, run aground or met Jan and

David. And I wouldn't have married that sailing fox and had a beautiful little boy.

We start our descent. Dash clambers over Ross and me and looks out the window. The green of the North Island stretches out below us.

'What's that, Mama?'

'Home, darling.'

'Exciting!' he says, and I nod.

'It sure is, Dash.'

ACKNOWLEDGEMENTS

It takes a lot of people to attempt to sail from Aruba to Brisbane. There are people whose names I don't know who helped us as we struggled through airports with bags and a baby, so thank you! Then there are people whose names I do know. These are people who listened to our crazy plan and encouraged us, cautioned us, and who made the leaving hard and the returning easy.

First, I want to thank Stephanie. Without you we wouldn't have had the money to go anywhere. Your generosity is something I will always be grateful for. Thanks also to Holly and Nina for understanding that I wasn't taking their Papa away — he was taking me! To Rosie for being the best bitchin' dance partner ever, Jane for all the hours organising dates and dance, Rebekah for reminding me to Keep Calm and Carry On, Gabe for her humour and friendship, and Bibby for not batting an eyelid when we said we were off with a one-year-old to sail the seas.

To Clare for cooking us dinners as we cooked up the plan, Jess for sharing the story of Good Luck, Bad Luck, Who Knows?, and Toby for the kind review, which landed me a book deal. To the ladies of Preggotastic for being so supportive, wise and funny. To Rick and Sherrie for all their kindness, Rudi and Leendrick for making us feel like part of the family, to all the people who read the blog. To Sean for all the adventures. To Jan and David for *everything*! To all the Real Hot Bitches for making my dreams of dance fame come true, over and over again!

To my sisters — Emily and Alice for believing in me, and most especially my big little sister Charlotte. You're right, 'All the freaky people do make the beauty of the world'. To Mum and Dad, who always open their hearts and home no matter how many times I arrive back a bit worse for wear. And to Ross and Dashkin. I couldn't have done it without you.

Muchas gracias.

ABOUT THE AUTHOR

Angela Meyer has turned her hand to many things in her lifetime including acting, EFL teaching, yoghurt packing, wannabe truck driver, comedian and pornographic cross-stitcher, but never, ever sailor. Suffice to say, she has never been shy of adventure. Otherwise she would never have hitchhiked to Alice Springs, travelled through Burma, moved to London with 200 bucks in her pocket, cycled around Great Barrier Island four months pregnant, started a dating agency, attempted to marry a vegan in Barcelona for a visa, been banned from exhibiting pornographic cross-stitch in Upper Hutt or been the proud owner of a 40-foot yacht in Aruba.

For more information about our titles please go to
www.randomhouse.co.nz